BIG DATA MINING AND COMPLEXITY

THE SAGE QUANTITATIVE RESEARCH KIT

Big Data Mining and Complexity by *Brian Castellani* and *Rajeev Rajaram* is the 11th volume in *The SAGE Quantitative Research Kit*. This book can be used together with the other titles in the *Kit* as a comprehensive guide to the process of doing quantitative research, but is equally valuable on its own as a practical introduction to Data Mining and 'Big Data'.

Editors of The SAGE Quantitative Research Kit:

Malcolm Williams – *Cardiff University, UK*

Richard D. Wiggins – *UCL Social Research Institute, UK*

D. Betsy McCoach – *University of Connecticut, USA*

Founding editor:

The late W. Paul Vogt – *Illinois State University, USA*

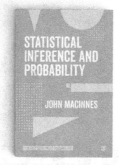

BIG DATA MINING AND COMPLEXITY

BRIAN C. CASTELLANI
RAJEEV RAJARAM

Los Angeles | London | New Delhi
Singapore | Washington DC | Melbourne

THE SAGE QUANTITATIVE RESEARCH KIT

Los Angeles | London | New Delhi
Singapore | Washington DC | Melbourne

SAGE Publications Ltd
1 Oliver's Yard
55 City Road
London EC1Y 1SP

SAGE Publications Inc.
2455 Teller Road
Thousand Oaks, California 91320

SAGE Publications India Pvt Ltd
B 1/I 1 Mohan Cooperative Industrial Area
Mathura Road

New Delhi 110 044
SAGE Publications Asia-Pacific Pte Ltd
3 Church Street
#10-04 Samsung Hub
Singapore 049483

This volume published as part of *The SAGE Quantitative Research Kit* (2021), edited by Malcolm Williams, Richard D. Wiggins and D. Betsy McCoach.

Editor: Jai Seaman
Assistant editor: Charlotte Bush
Production editor: Manmeet Kaur Tura
Copyeditor: QuADS Prepress Pvt Ltd
Proofreader: Elaine Leek
Indexer: Cathryn Pritchard
Marketing manager: Susheel Gokarakonda
Cover design: Shaun Mercier
Typeset by: C&M Digitals (P) Ltd, Chennai, India

Library of Congress Control Number: 2020943076

British Library Cataloguing in Publication data

A catalogue record for this book is available from the British Library

ISBN 978-1-5264-2381-8

Dedicated to Maggie, Ruby and Swathi

CONTENTS

LIST OF FIGURES

ABOUT THE AUTHORS

Brian C. Castellani is presently a Professor of Sociology at Durham University, adjunct professor of psychiatry at Northeast Ohio Medical University, Fellow of the Durham University Research Methods Centre. He is also co-editor of the *Routledge Complexity in Social Science* series and co-editor of *International Journal of Social Research Methodology*. Trained as a sociologist, clinical psychologist and methodologist (statistics and computational social science), he has spent the past 10 years developing a new case-based, data mining approach to modelling complex social systems – called the SACS Toolkit – which he and his colleagues used to help researchers, policymakers and service providers address and improve complex public health issues such as community health and well-being, infrastructure and grid reliability, mental health and inequality, big data and data mining, and globalisation and global civil society. They have also recently developed the COMPLEX-IT RStudio software app, which allows everyday users seamless access to high-powered techniques such as machine intelligence, neural nets and agent-based modelling to make better sense of the complex world(s) in which they live and work.

Rajeev Rajaram is a Professor of Mathematics at Kent State University. Rajeev's primary training is in control theory of partial differential equations and he is currently interested in applications of differential equations and ideas from statistical mechanics and thermodynamics to model and measure complexity. He and Castellani have worked together to create a new case-based method for modeling complex systems, called the SACS Toolkit, which has been used to study topics in health, health care, societal infrastructures, power-grid reliability, restaurant mobility, and depression trajectories. More recently, he is interested in mathematical properties of entropy-based diversity measures for probability distributions.

1

INTRODUCTION

Chapter Overview

The joys of travel

For those who know us, it goes without saying that one of the things we (and our families) enjoy most in life is travel. And the more often we get to do so, the better. There is little in life like travelling somewhere to catch a glimpse, albeit briefly, of how other people live. As Rick Steves, the travel guru, says, 'Travel is freedom . . . one of the last great sources of legal adventure'.[1]

Travelling, however, is not the same as taking a vacation. For Steves – and for many of the travel bloggers we follow[2] – while vacations are great, travelling is different. As a photojournalist recently put it, if your trip photos are mostly selfies, you took a vacation; if your photos are of the places you had visited, then you travelled. Vacations are about relaxing, which we all regularly need. But travel is about taking an adventure, which we also need. And we need travel because it pushes us to see the world and our lives in new and different ways. As Steves says, 'Travel destroys ethnocentricity. It helps you understand and appreciate different cultures. Travel changes people.'[3]

Data mining and big data travel

Steves's philosophy of travel is also true of the current book, insomuch as it is a travelogue of our adventures into the fields of data mining and big data, which we seek to share with readers. – all in an effort to see if we, together, can weave a new way of understanding the planet and ourselves vis-à-vis the global complexities of the data-saturated world(s) in which we live.

The challenge, however, is getting to our destination. A few years back, after some 18 hours of travel from the USA – including two plane delays, a several-hour layover in New York City, a cramped international flight, several tube connections, two UK trains and a taxi ride – we arrived exhausted in Northern England for a research seminar. Fortunate for us, we had several of our British friends awaiting us with dinner and drinks. At one point, one of them asked, 'Why on earth do you do it?' After a bit of a pause, one of us (Rajeev) replied, 'We like travelling, we just don't like getting there.'

We think it fair to say that, while people enjoy travelling to new places – be it to learn new methods, new ideas or experience new frontiers in research – the biggest hurdle is getting there. Hence our book's more technical purpose: we seek to make

---

[1]See www.ricksteves.com/press-room/ricks-travel-philosophy.

[2]Here is a list of some of our favourite blogs: https://thepointsguy.com and https://million milesecrets.com.

[3]See www.ricksteves.com/press-room/ricks-travel-philosophy.

the journey into the new world of big data and data mining as painless as possible, knowing that the journey, while worth it, presents a series of challenges. We have organised these challenges into two major journeys – that is, Parts I and II of the current book.

Part I: Thinking critically and complex

As the title of our book suggests – which our literary colleagues Tim and Mary Fowler suggested to us – the first theme concerns thinking about big data and data mining from a complexity science and critical perspective. The worlds of data and method have changed, expanding far beyond the confines of conventional research (Burrows & Savage, 2014; Veltri, 2017). But, because of this expansion, data and method have also broadened in their usage, becoming part and parcel of the daily life of most companies and public-sector organisations (Raghavan, 2014). In other words, data and method are no longer under the strict purview of academia. In fact, one is more likely to read about the cutting-edge of big data in *Wired* than most journals in the social sciences (Cukier & Mayer-Schoenberger, 2013). As a result, knowledge of big data and data mining within academia varies considerably (Castellani, 2014). For example, while the social sciences continue to study relatively static data sets using conventional linear statistics, other fields, such as physics, regularly study highly dynamic temporal/spatial data sets using the latest advances in data mining (Castellani et al., 2016).

And, it is here, with this imbalance in awareness, particularly amongst the social sciences, that we arrive at our first major challenge. In fact, some go so far as to call it a crisis (Burrows & Savage, 2014; Savage & Burrows, 2007), which they articulate as follows: the significant variance in knowledge of the tools of data mining and computational modelling and big data leaves many within the social sciences disadvantaged and discredited when it comes to the complex and critical discussions surrounding our currently data-saturated globalised world(s) – which is a problem for all involved, as social science is critical to such discussions (Burrows & Savage, 2014).

For example, many experts in data mining and big data see their respective fields as more than a simple advance on method, treating data science instead as an epistemological transformation, constituting an entirely new approach for data acquisition, management, modelling, analysis, output, results and decision-making – a paradigm shift, if you will, in social scientific thinking (Kitchin, 2014). Some critics, however, push back, arguing that data mining and big data are empty buzzwords for little more than the latest trend in data management or methodological technique – for a review of these critiques, see Kitchin (2014). Other critics, however, take this 'paradigm shift' claim seriously, arguing that while data mining and big data are touted as intellectual revolutions, they are at best only useful (albeit limited) attempts to deal more effectively with the data-saturated global world in which we now live. And, while some of these new attempts are innovative and thoughtful, others are not; this is key to why social scientists need to be involved in such discussions (Byrne & Callaghan, 2013). In fact, some of the latest advances in data mining and big data are seen as downright dangerous and foolhardy, potentially leading to terrible outcomes and decision-making (Mahnke & Uprichard, 2014). However, to be fair, many of the current conventions for data acquisition, management, analysis and modelling – in particular statistics – are often equally foolhardy and dangerous; hence, part of the reason data mining and big data emerged in the first place. Put simply, on both sides of the debate we need better scientific tools (Castellani, 2014).

Organisation of Part I

So, we are left with a challenge, which Part I of our book was written to address. For this section, our goal is to determine critically what it is about data mining and big data that is useful, and to what extent, and in what ways and in what contexts? Part I is therefore organised as follows:

- Chapter 2 begins with a critique of conventional method in the social sciences, specifically statistics. The goal is to explain how and why data mining and big data are presently overwhelming the social sciences, as well as exploring the consequences of the social sciences not overcoming this problem – from policy and polity to economy and scientific practice.
- Chapter 3 provides a quick but similarly critical overview of the field of big data and the conflicted arguments surrounding its development.
- Chapter 4 does the same with data mining.
- Chapter 5, finally, provides a fast survey of the complexity sciences, mainly to demonstrate (albeit, again, critically) the utility of this field for providing – at least to us – the best methodological framework for advancing the data mining of big data.

The purpose of Chapter 5 takes us to our next point. For us, while the term *big data* has proven, on some levels, to be useful, in the end it is too simplistic, as it suggests that the only real difference in the world of data in 2021 is more of it. But, as Uprichard (2013) points out, the data-saturated world(s) in which we all presently live are not just big, they are also complex. In other words, big data today is comprised of a multitude of different factors (e.g. ecological, geographical, social, economic, political, psychological, medical), which are distributed, interdependent, multilevel (macroscopic to microscopic), dynamic and evolving, often in real time, and spatial, self-organising, emergent, non-linear and network-like in their organisation. In short, data are complex.

Equally important, the globalised world(s) this data 'represents' are likewise complex (Capra & Luisi, 2014). Case in point: there are few social science topics that do not sit at the intersection of multiple data sets, governmental agencies or areas of concern. For example, food safety in a metropolitan area links to poverty, which connects with the region's ecology and infrastructure, which connects to its economy and political stability, which, in turn, links to other issues such as inequality and racism and access to education and women's rights and so forth.

In order to understand such complex issues, what we need, then, is an epistemological and ontological shift in thinking. As Stephen Hawking famously quipped, science in the 21st century is all about complexity. More specifically, science needs to embrace a complex systems view of the world (Byrne & Callaghan, 2013; Capra, 1996; Mitchell, 2009). Capra and Luisi (2014) state,

> As the twenty-first century unfolds, it is becoming more and more evident that the major problems of our time - energy, the environment, climate change, food security, financial security - cannot be understood in isolation. They are systemic problems, which means that they are all interconnected and interdependent. (p. xi)

Hence the need for the complexity sciences, which are fast becoming the guiding framework and critical carrier for the journey of many scholars into the worlds of data mining and big data. All of this takes us to the second part of our book.

Part II: The tools and techniques of data mining

In terms of the challenges and hurdles associated with our journey, the second theme revolves around learning new tools and techniques. No matter one's background, including mathematics, learning new methods is always hard going, particularly when it comes to data mining and big data – which have, over the last few decades, amassed into a rather significant number of new approaches. As shown in our book's index, this list ranges from machine intelligence and textual analysis to geospatial modelling and network analysis. Still, even with such a long list, learning about these methods need not be any more difficult than necessary.

Hence our rationale for Part II of our book, which seeks to provide readers two things. First, we seek to provide an ontological view of complexity, as seen through the lens of data mining and big data. And, second, we seek to provide a set of user-friendly mathematical formalisms that, once reviewed, should prove helpful in making sense of the wider fields of data mining and computational modelling. To accomplish these two tasks, we will ground the whole of our review within the framework of *case-based complexity* and its methodological ontology (Byrne & Ragin, 2013; Castellani et al., 2016).

By way of a brief introduction, case-based complexity represents one of the main avenues of research – as well as one of the most developed views on social complexity – within the complexity sciences. As Byrne and Callaghan (2013) note, case-based complexity is based on the key insight that, as pertains to social life, the cases we study are best viewed in complex systems terms; and, in turn, the complex social topics (a.k.a. social systems) we study are best modelled as cases or sets of cases. Let us explain.

Regardless of the technique used, data mining and big data analytics are ultimately about modelling, exploring, clustering or cataloguing cases, based on key characteristics or aetiological differences. For example, smart machines can be used to identify tumour or disease types; predictive analytics can explore public policies and their multiple outcomes; artificial intelligence can identify reliable investment opportunities; genetic algorithms can detect subtle changes in weather or traffic patterns; and network analyses can find the fastest route from a search question to its answer. And all of them (albeit to varying degrees) can be counted as an improvement on conventional statistics, mainly because they avoid aggregate-based one-size-fits-all solutions, focusing, instead, on identifying multiple case-based trends, which, in turn, they catalogue and examine based on differences in their respective profile of key factors. In short, all of these techniques treat the topics they study as evolving sets of complex cases.

The problem, however – which brings us to the heart of the challenge in Part II – is that few of the authors of these tools and techniques identify their work as such. Nor do they note their technique's similarity with other data mining and computational modelling techniques. For example, if you go to the SAS website[4] – a leading software package for statistical and computational analysis – it defines predictive analytics as 'the use of data, statistical algorithms and machine learning techniques to identify the likelihood of future outcomes based on historical data'. In turn, it defines data mining as 'the process of finding anomalies, patterns and correlations within large data sets to predict outcomes' – again, based on a broad range of techniques. As the reader can see, these two definitions, minus a few words of emphasis, are otherwise identical, as the goal in both instances is to group cases, based on profile differences, for the purposes of prediction. More important, they basically use almost the same set of techniques: machine intelligence, artificial neural nets and so on.

A similar argument can be made of machine learning and artificial intelligence. For example, according to Wikipedia, 'artificial intelligence (AI, also machine intelligence, MI) is intelligence exhibited by machines, rather than humans or other animals'. In other words, machine learning is really artificial intelligence, which is really part of predictive analytics, which is really part of data mining.

---

[4]See www.sas.com.

In short, and as these examples hopefully illustrate, while the techniques and tools of data mining and computational modelling are numerous, they are also highly similar in focus and design. And that is a good thing, as readers will see, as it allows us to create, based on the framework of case-based complexity, a mathematical and methodological shortcut. Hence, again, the purpose of Part II, which is organised as follows:

- Chapter 6 provides readers with an ontology and set of mathematical formalisms for thinking about data mining and big data, based on the theoretical framework of case-based complexity.
- Chapter 7 overviews the techniques of classification, including cluster analysis.
- Chapter 8 reviews machine intelligence and machine learning, with specific emphasis on neural nets, including the famous Kohonen topographical self-organising map.
- Chapter 9 examines the tools of predictive analytics, including Bayesian statistics, decision trees and regression.
- Chapter 10 deals with longitudinal and temporal data analysis, with specific emphasis on differential equations, dynamical systems theory and growth mixture modelling.
- Chapter 11, in turn, deals with geospatial data, exploring the techniques used to collect such data and, in turn, analyse them.
- Chapter 12 addresses the topic of complex networks.
- Chapter 13 deals with text and video mining, including techniques such as sentiment analysis, issue mapping and fitness landscapes.

Before proceeding, however, two caveats are necessary.

SAGE *Quantitative Research Kit*

While the number of techniques reviewed in Part II is somewhat exhaustive, our summary of these methods is by no means in-depth. In other words, our primary goal in this book is to use our mathematical/methodological shortcut to demonstrate the continuity and interlinkage of these data mining techniques vis-à-vis the challenges of modelling and studying complex data sets. Also, given the breadth of our review involved in Part II of our book, we will not have time to delve into important big data details such as how to best build a big data database or run a specific technique. Such concerns (along with a more in-depth analysis of specific techniques) is, however, a major goal of the *SAGE Quantitative Research Kit*. As such, we recommend readers explore these books as well. All of this takes us to our next caveat.

COMPLEX-IT and the SACS Toolkit

In addition to reading the other books in the *SAGE Quantitative Research Kit*, for those interested in taking the next step towards actually data mining their own big data, in Chapter 6 we provide a brief introduction to the SACS Toolkit and COMPLEX-IT. The utility of this combined methodological platform is that, while the SACS Toolkit provides the methodological framework for employing most of the tools and techniques we review in Part II, COMPLEX-IT provides a free RStudio software package for running and integrating several of them. As such, the SACS Toolkit and COMPLEX-IT function as a methodological/software companion to the current book. (For more on COMPLEX-IT, see www.art-sciencefactory.com/complexit.html; and for more on the SACS Toolkit, see www.art-sciencefactory.com/cases.html.)

The airline industry: a case study

In addition to the mathematical formalisms of case-based complexity – and their corresponding software – we thought another way to tie the book together is to pick a case study that would have wide appeal. And, given our focus on travelling, what better example than one with which most are familiar – the airline industry! In terms of a complex system of study that globally exemplifies the challenges of data mining and big data, one could hardly pick a better topic than the airline industry. Or, at least, that is the conclusion that we (Brian and Rajeev) reached one day while sitting in our favourite tea shop in Oxford, UK. The name of the place is *Cafe Loco*, themed on the famous Mad Hatter's tea party. Turns out that Brian's brother was with us that day, as Warren was part of our long-delayed trip to Northern England, which we mentioned above, and was equally perplexed by the complexities of international travel, which got us thinking: How does such a complex global system work, and with all that complex big data?

Consider, for example, Figure 1.1, which was created by Martin Grandjean.[5] It is a visualisation of the world's air-traffic network, based on airports located worldwide. How is such a complex network of data and activity managed, we wondered, as there is obviously no one command centre or central database?

And, that is just one aspect of the airline industry's complexity, vis-à-vis the issues of data acquisition, management, modelling, analysis, output, results and decision-making. Think also about the number of planes in the air at any given moment and their complex traffic patterns and schedules. Or how about the massive number of people travelling worldwide – let alone all of their baggage. How does it all reach its destination? And how about all of the discount travel websites and blogs and Face-book pages, and travel agents and related industries, such as tourism and hotels and restaurants? Or how about the credit card world and their point systems and travel

---

[5]See www.martingrandjean.ch/connected-world-air-traffic-network.

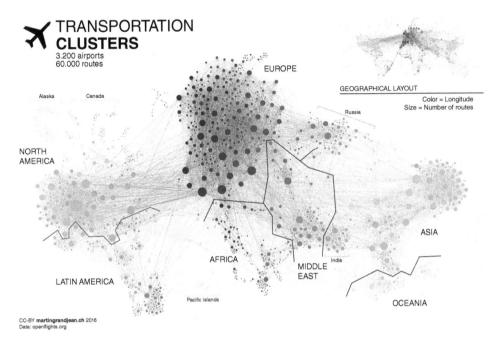

Figure 1.1 Global air-traffic network

discounts and all those databases that need to link up to one another? And then there is security and policing and safety data, as well as airport surveillance cameras and so forth, not to mention all of the data for each plane that is being compiled, managed, analysed and used to make sure it arrives safely at each destination? Or how about the other 50 things we forgot to mention?

Sipping his tea, Warren looked at us both and said, 'So, along with various other examples, why not make the airline industry the case study for your book?' Great idea we thought. Sometimes the challenges of life just seem to work out. Or, should we say, travel is worth it. Or that is the hope, at least, for our journey through the current book.

Chapter Summary

- We live in a global world saturated in complex big data.
- All of this data challenges conventional methods, including statistics.
- Data mining and the computational sciences offer the tools needed for today's complex data world(s).
- Using these tools, however, requires a critical approach, as they create their own set of challenges.

(Continued)

- This book uses a complexity science framework to engage in a critical review of data mining and computational science.
- The chapter ends with a summary of the book chapters and the approach the authors will use to guide readers on a tour of these new methods.

Further Reading

Byrne, D., & Ragin, C. C. (Eds.). (2013). *The SAGE handbook of case-based methods.* Sage.
This book is helpful for a review of case-based complexity and its methodological ontology.

Kitchin, R. (2014). *The data revolution: Big data, open data, data infrastructures and their consequences.* Sage. https://doi.org/10.4135/9781473909472
This book is helpful for a review of critiques of data mining.

PART I

THINKING CRITICALLY AND COMPLEX

2

THE FAILURE OF QUANTITATIVE SOCIAL SCIENCE

Chapter Overview

Suppose you are hired as a methodologist for a new airline company. Statistical software ready and running, on the first day of your job you are confronted with a dozen different questions, some of which require answers in real time. For example, your bosses ask, based on changing weather patterns and the delays they cause, how can you manage flight routes well in advance in order to reduce costs and delays? Or how about optimising your flight routes based on air traffic congestion? Also, in order to improve customer satisfaction, can you provide travellers some of this information in real time, as pertains to possible interruptions to their schedules, so they can likewise optimise their own travel? And, can you comb through terabytes of textual data on Twitter, Facebook, Google and other social media to recognise changes in this year's travelling trends?

In short, can you take the next methodological step to deal with all of the above unpredictables? And, in turn, can you move toward providing case-specific answers, which group your populations into multiple and different groups/clusters and outcomes, based on differences in their respective variable-based profiles, as they evolve across time and place?

Suddenly you realise, in the face of these different questions, your training in conventional statistics is not going to be enough. You need more methods. Actually, to be more specific, you need different methods: you need the data mining tools of the computational and complexity sciences. And, you would not be alone in your need for methodological advance, as most of the airline industry, the world over, struggles to similarly answer such questions. For example, in their 16 June 2017 article, 'The Data Science Revolution That's Transforming Aviation', Maire and Spafford put the challenge this way:

> Where artificial intelligence and advanced analytics can play the biggest role is dealing with the unpredictables the [airline] industry faces daily. With hundreds of planes, thousands of flights, and millions of employees and passengers, there is now too much data and too many variables for humans to sort through fast enough to fix problems or even prioritise potential threats. From big events like hurricanes and snowstorms to smaller disruptions like air traffic control delays, mechanical failures, or even lines of thunderstorms, computers and analytics are necessary for. While much of this activity today is mostly reactive, the next step will be for aviation to proactively avoid some of the delays, congestion, and inefficiencies that annoy passengers and keep the global industry at single-digit profit margins.[1]

In other words, like the social sciences, the airline industry today requires significant methodological advance. All of this takes us to the focus of the current chapter: the brilliant failure of quantitative social science.

---

[1]See www.forbes.com/sites/oliverwyman/2017/06/16/the-data-science-revolution-transforming-aviation/#411384ae7f.

Quantitative social science, then and now

Back in the 1980s, when the first author of this book attended university in the USA, the pathway to scientific literacy in the social sciences was straightforward: one took a research methods course, followed by a statistics course or two, and that was it – one was prepared to do science. Okay, if one was lucky, one might also receive a qualitative or historical methods course. But, overall, social science professors in the USA were pretty clear: the real science was quantitative methods and statistics.

Later, when the first author moved on to graduate school, little changed. Certainly the statistics got more interesting, which is one of the reasons that we (the two authors of this book) started doing research together. But the same old distinctions remained dominant, with quantitative methods and statistics holding the upper hand: hard science over soft science, quantitative method over qualitative method, math over metaphor, representation over interpretation, and variables over cases. And why? Because for many social scientists, statistics make the 'best sense' of the complexity of social reality – what Warren Weaver, in his brilliant 1948 article, 'Science and Complexity', called the disorganised complexity problem.

The three phases of science

According to Weaver, nuances aside, the problems of science can be organised, historically speaking, into three main phases. The first phase focused on simple systems, comprised of a few variables and amenable to near-complete mathematical descriptions: clocks, pendulums and basic machines. The second phase focused on disorganised complex systems, where the unpredictable microscopic behaviour of a very large number of variables – gases, crowds, atoms and so on – make them highly resistant to simple formulas. Hence, this phase was the golden age of statistics across the physical, natural and social sciences.

Finally, there is the third phase, which deals with organised complex systems. Here, the focus is on how the qualitative interactions amongst a profile of variables, and the emergent gestalt they create, determine their complexity: human bodies, immune systems, formal organisation, social institutions, networks, cities, global economies and so on. The challenge in the third phase, methodologically speaking, is that such systems, given their emergent, idiographic and qualitative complexity, are not understood well using the tools of the first two phases: simple formulas or statistics. Needed, instead, are entirely new methods, grounded in the forthcoming age of the computer, which Weaver, in 1948, saw on the horizon. Also necessary is a more open and democratic science, grounded in interdisciplinary teamwork and exchange – both critical to understanding and managing organised complexity. Weaver (1948) puts it this way:

These new problems, and the future of the world [that] depends on many of them, requires science to make a third great advance, an advance that must be even greater than the nineteenth-century conquest of problems of simplicity or the twentieth-century victory over problems of disorganised complexity. Science must, over the next 50 years, learn to deal with these problems of organised complexity. (p. 540)

That was 1948. It is now 2021. So, what happened? Did Weaver's prognosis about the third phase of science come true? Well, it all depends upon which area of science you are looking at. In the social sciences, despite living today in a world of big data, the answer is definitely no – we have yet to fully transition into the third phase, despite living in it. For example, a quick review of the current methods courses taught to undergraduates in the social sciences makes it rather clear that, over the last seven decades, little has changed: from Oxford and Harvard to Stanford and Cambridge to, in fact, just about most universities and colleges, the pathway to scientific literacy in the social sciences remains pretty much the same: conventional quantitative methods and statistics, grounded in mechanistic and reductionist experimental or quasi-experimental design, and with little if any mention of computational modelling, data mining or big data.

Now do not get us wrong, as there are social science departments that teach courses in computational modelling, data mining, mixed methods and interdisciplinary thinking. Nonetheless, even at the University of Michigan in the USA, which boasts of one of the most advanced methodological centres in the world – the Center for the Study of Complex Systems – the undergraduate social science curriculum is pretty standard fare, with heavy emphasis on the old distinction and statistics.

Still, we need to be clear. We are not uncritically saying that data mining and computational method are 'all good' for social inquiry. Neither are we saying that conventional statistics are benign or useless or wrong-headed. We are after all (in order of authorship) a quantitative methodologist and an applied mathematician. As such, we firmly believe that when used correctly, conventional statistics are very powerful. In fact, that is part of the problem with statistics: their usage throughout the social and human sciences has accomplished so much and helped humans understand so many different things that it is hard to believe they cannot, on their own, continue doing so. But unfortunately, they cannot (Capra & Luisi, 2014). In short, what we are saying is that if you received a social science education in conventional statistics alone, your professors most likely failed you. And, they failed you because they should have taught you five additional things vis-à-vis the issues of big data, data mining and complexity.

What you should have learned in statistics class

First, they should have taught you that conventional statistics limits their view of social life to disorganised complexity (Weaver, 1948). In a nutshell, and without nuance, the history of statistics in the social sciences, given their focus on disorganised complexity, is one of great achievement as well as error. Think, for example, of trying to predict the big data voting behaviour of all 1.32 billion people living in India. Your model's predictive accuracy at the microscopic level – that is, the level of any individual voter – would be, to put it mildly, very low indeed. If, however, you turned to the tools of statistics, with its laws of central tendency and its theories of probability, you might have a chance. Because now you would be focusing on calculating aggregate, average behaviour.

Remember the bell curve – shown in Figure 2.1? Based on your chosen degree of accuracy, you would seek to predict, in probabilistic terms, how the average person in India is likely to vote – the majority area of the two distributions in the Figure. And, being a good quantitative social scientist, you also would develop as simplistic a causal model of voting as possible, what Capra and Luisi (2014) call mechanistic or reductionist social science. Then, treating voting as your dependent variable, you would build a linear model of causal influence, hoping to determine the smallest possible set of independent variable(s) – for example, political views, gender, religious affiliation, age, geographical location and so on – that best explain the greatest percentage of voting behaviour.

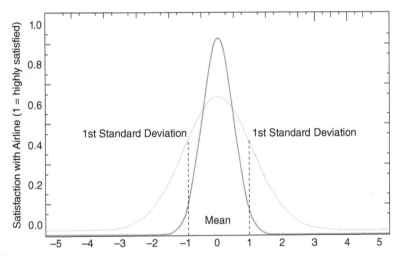

Figure 2.1   Gaussian bell-shaped curve

And that is it. That is the brilliance of the conventional quantitative programme in the social sciences: (a) social reality is a form of disorganised complexity that is best handled using the tools of statistics; (b) in terms of studying disorganised complexity (particularly in big data), the goal is to explain majority (aggregate) behaviour in terms of probability theory and the macroscopic laws of averages; (c) to do so, one seeks to develop simple, variable-based linear models, in which variables are treated as 'rigorously real' measures of social reality; (d) model-in-hand, the goal is to identify, measure, describe and (hopefully) control or manage how certain independent variables impact one or more dependent variables of concern; (e) and, if done right, these models lead to reasonably generalisable explanations of why things happen the way they do; (f) which, in turn, leads to relatively straightforward policy recommendations for what to do about them (Byrne, 2012). All of the old distinctions are upheld and social reality is represented. What else is there? Well, actually, a lot. All of which takes us to our next point.

Second, they should have taught you that – from feminist methodology and social constructionism to post-structuralism and qualitative method to ethnography and deconstructionism – there exists a long list of methodologists, philosophers and social scientists who do not think that the complexity of social reality is best viewed as disorganised and, therefore, as only statistical or probabilistic. Still, despite the overwhelming power of this list, it remains the case that quantitative methods education in the social sciences, with its emphasis on disorganised complexity and its continuation of the old distinctions, remains the dominant methodological focus, with little signs of changing.

In fact, building on our earlier point about social science education, the most common curricular response to the failures of statistics seems to be a push for even more statistics; as Byrne (2012), for example, points out in his critical assessment of the UK's new Q-Step movement, which, like the USA, seeks to address the quantitative deficit in the social sciences by teaching undergraduates and graduates more conventional statistics.

Again, do not get us wrong. There are times when viewing the big data complexity of social reality as disorganised is useful. In fact, there are even times when viewing systems as simple remains crucial (Andersson et al., 2014). The problem, however, is that, increasingly the big data global social problems we currently face suggest otherwise. All of this takes us to our next point.

Third, they should have taught you that, as Weaver predicted in 1948, the world got a lot more complex. And, it is not just social reality that got a lot more complex, but also the data we use to make sense of it. As we will explore later, the scholars involved in data mining and big data make the same point: from ecological collapse and data warehouses filled with terabytes of information to global warming and an endless streaming of digital data to the instability of global financial markets and the threat of pandemics, we contend, now, with a data-saturated world of social problems and organised complexity far beyond the pale of conventional quantitative social science.

Fourth, they should have taught you that, over the last three decades, a revolution in methods, as Weaver also predicted, has taken place – thanks, in large measure, to the computer, computational algorithms, cyber-infrastructure and big data. The result is a revolution in computational modelling methods. And, what is more, many of these new methods do not hold true to the old dualisms of quantitative social science. For example, given their focus on clustering cases and looking for trend differences, most data mining techniques are qualitative tools for modelling complex quantitative databases (Castellani et al., 2016; Castellani & Rajaram, 2012).

Finally, despite these limits, they should have taught you that Weaver's projected great advance in science did nonetheless take place, which scholars generally refer to as the emergence of the complexity sciences (Byrne & Callaghan, 2013; Capra & Luisi, 2014; Castellani & Hafferty, 2009; Mitchell, 2009). Despite minor differences in theory or method, the common view amongst complexity scholars is that social reality and the data used to examine it are best understood in complex systems terms. In other words, social reality and data are best seen as self-organising, emergent, non-linear, evolving, dynamic, network-based, interdependent, qualitative and non-reductive. They also agree that, when it comes to modelling complexity, conventional statistics are insufficient. Instead, a multiplicity of newer and more mixed methods and perspectives are needed, along with an increased focus on critical and reflexive thinking, grounded in interdisciplinary, application-oriented teams.

So, why didn't you learn these things?

So, you are probably wondering, why were you not taught these things? There are a handful of interconnected reasons, which a number of scholars have identified (Byrne & Callaghan, 2013; Harvey & Reed, 1996; Savage & Burrows, 2007; Wallerstein et al., 1997). Here is a quick list: (a) most social scientists do not receive training in computational modelling or data mining; (b) to do so, they would have to cross the campus to the mathematics, physics and computer science departments; (c) doing so would mean learning how to work in mixed-methods and interdisciplinary teams, talking across intellectual boundaries, being comfortable in what one does not know, overcoming the humanities-versus-math divide and so on; (d) in turn, social science departments would need to hire and promote scholars working at the intersection of data mining, big data, computational modelling and the complexity sciences; (e) as well as loosen their entrenched and outdated frameworks of research excellence; (f) and, in turn, a similar advance would be required of social science journals, which remain largely unsympathetic and even antagonistic to this work; (g) and, finally, these advances would need to result in major curricular revision.

However, as concerns these curricular revisions, it is not so much that the social sciences would need to be proficient in all the latest methods. That is the purpose of interdisciplinary teams. Instead, what is needed is an open learning environment where students can be introduced to the fields of data mining, complexity theory, critical thinking, data visualisation and modelling, as well as the challenges of mixed-methods, interdisciplinary teamwork, global complexity and big data. In short, the social sciences need to be opened up, as Weaver called for in 1948. All of this takes us to the crux of the problem that big data and data mining present to the social sciences.

While Weaver's call to open up the social sciences was incredibly prescient, it was not the last. In fact, as we will discuss in Chapter 5, many of the scholars involved in the complexity sciences have echoed similar opinion. Perhaps the most famous is the Gulbenkian Commission on the future of the social sciences, chaired by Immanuel Wallerstein (Wallerstein et al., 1997). Given the task of reviewing 'the present state of the social sciences' in relation to contemporary knowledge and need, the Commission began its report with a historical review, focusing (pointedly enough) on the same 50-year time period as imagined by Weaver, from 1945 to 1995. The conclusion they reached is similar to Weaver's: the social sciences need to (a) reorganise themselves according to a post-disciplinary structure; (b) situate themselves in a complexity science framework; (c) embrace a mixed-methods toolkit, based on the latest advances in computational and complexity science method; and (d) work in interdisciplinary teams.

Such a 'restructuring', however, is not focused on diminishing, for example, the intellectual or disciplinary power of sociology or social science. In fact, quite the opposite: it is focused on widening their respective power and influence, by pushing their relevance and utility across the computational, natural and physical sciences, where many of the latest advances in data mining and big data are taking place – while simultaneously pushing back on sociology and the social sciences to 'catch-up' with the latest advances in method – and for scientists to work better together in teams!

And what was the response in the social sciences? For the most part, as we have been indicating, nothing much in methods education has changed. And this failure to effectively respond has come at a great cost to the field. As Byrne and Callaghan (2013) explain, while a lot of work is being done in the fields of computational modelling, data mining, big data and complexity science, unfortunately, and despite the best of intentions, most of it lacks a proper knowledge of social science and, as a result, has sometimes 'gone off the deep end', as they say. One quick example (which we will explore in Chapter 3) is the whole big data push, which dangerously veers, in many instances, into *a-theoretical modelling* (Burrows & Savage, 2014;

Uprichard, 2013). Another is the whole social physics push, which is nothing more than old-school, hard-science-is-best reductionism, where the fundamental laws of social reality are sought through high-speed computers and their data mining, computational algorithms. And it is, in many instances (but not all!), mostly wrong-headed.

Changing the social life of data analysis

Hopefully, as these examples suggest – and as Duncan Watts pointed out in a 2004 article for the *Annual Review of Sociology* – while the overwhelming majority of physicists, mathematicians and computational scientists involved in the fields of data mining, big data, computational modelling and the complexity sciences are incredible technicians and methodologists, most are not very good social scientists, particularly in terms of social theory. In turn, however, by today's standards the overwhelming majority of social scientists are not very good technicians or methodologists. And both sides are at fault for not extending their reach, and both are foolish for not doing so – and with all sorts of negative and unintended consequences for how we deal with the global social problems we currently face.

Still, building on the recommendations of the Gulbenkian Commission, lots can be done to overcome this problem. In particular (as suggested to us by our colleague Adrian MacKenzie), we need to change the social life of data analysis. But, we will have to save our exploration of this point for our final chapter, as we need to turn our current attention to the topic of big data.

Chapter Summary

- The history of statistics and social science methods is one of incredible accomplishment, but the world has changed considerably in terms of its massive data complexity.
- The result is that current social science methods are limited in their ability to effectively analyse or model complex big data.
- There are a host of reasons why social science methods have not updated, including a lack of training and an unwillingness for social science departments to adapt to the new data world.
- Data mining and the computational and complexity sciences emerged in the 1990s as a way to improve social science methods, offering a fresh new approach to deal with complex and big data. Given their utility, the next three chapters will quickly survey these new areas. Part II of the book provides an in-depth review of key methods from these fields.

Further Reading

Capra, F., & Luisi, P. L. (2014). *The systems view of life: A unifying vision.* Cambridge University Press. https://doi.org/10.1017/CBO9780511895555
This book deals with the shortfalls of conventional statistics in modelling complexity.

Weaver, W. (1948). Science and complexity. *American Scientist, 36*, 536–544.
This article addresses the limitation of conventional statistics to disorganised complexity.

3

WHAT IS BIG DATA?

Chapter Overview

While the term *big data* may at first seem obvious, it is not. In fact, in 2021, debate over big data looms large. And there is good reason. To begin, as we alluded to in Chapter 1, it is not clear what big data is; or, should we say, what big data are? In fact, by our count, big data can be simultaneously conceptualised as (a) a paradigm shift in data analysis, (b) a metaphor for our new data-saturated global existence, (c) a key component in the advance of post-industrialisation and global society, (d) or, alternatively, an over-the-top term for little more than the latest advances in data acquisition, management, modelling and analysis. Given such diversity in perspective, our job in this chapter is to review these conceptualisations to see which of them makes sense. Our suspicion, however, is that they all make sense, but only when viewed in combination with one another . . . so, let us proceed.

Big data as information society

Of the various conceptualisations, the one least often discussed (but the one most historically accurate) is big data as *post-industrial society* – or what is alternatively referred to as information society or the knowledge economy (Bell, 1976). Whatever the term used, they all refer to a major technological shift that began in the 1970s (and culminated in the 1990s) across many advanced industrialised countries, which fundamentally altered their respective economies and eventually the world. According to the American sociologist Daniel Bell, the emergence of information society was distinct in several ways:

- First and most important, it constituted a shift from mechanical industry to information technology, including advances in computers, cyber-infrastructure and information and communications technologies.
- In turn, information and data began growing the economy the same as manufacturing and goods had previously, which led the former to become high-valued commodities and a new form of capital. All of this created a shift from the production of goods to the delivery of services, which eventually (during the 1990s) turned large segments of these advanced industrialised countries into service-sector economies.
- In terms of definitions, a service-sector economy is one based on providing consumers and citizens a variety of professional services, including financing, medical care, data management and analysis, banking and real estate, business services and utilities, social and personal services (i.e. travel, dining, hotels, etc.), computer systems and communication technologies, cyber-security and big data. As such, post-industrialisation also led to the increase in professional labour, especially jobs requiring high levels of education and expertise, from computer programmers and physicians to data analysts and policy evaluators to stockbrokers and financial managers.

- In turn, however, this professions-focused service-sector shift helped to advance the forces of globalisation, as labour and manufacturing were outsourced to the rest of the world: Mexico, Taiwan, China, India and so on.
- This outsourcing also led to the decline of manual labour in these post-industrialised societies, as automation and technology made blue-collar jobs obsolete or too low in income to sustain a certain standard of living.
- This outsourcing also led to the cheapening of goods and services, including information and communications technology and cyber-infrastructure. (For example, the iPhone components are produced all over the world and assembled in China.) All of this allowed for more inexpensive ways to collect, store, manage and analyse larger and larger reservoirs of data.

And it is here, in this list, that the story of post-industrialisation links to the smaller storylines involved in the development of computers, cybernetics, communications technologies, systems science and artificial intelligence (Capra, 1996; Castellani & Hafferty, 2009; Hammond, 2010). And, in turn, it is also through these links that post-industrialisation brought about the internet, the World Wide Web, Microsoft, Apple, Google, Facebook, Twitter, Amazon.com and the worldwide proliferation of software systems, apps, social media, information architectures, communication networks and our ever-expanding global, digital landscape and its warehouses of data. In short, it brought about the emergence of big data. And let us also not forget the latest advances of globalisation.

Big data as global network society

Globalisation – that is, the idea of the world becoming a smaller and more interconnected and interdependent place – is not new. In fact, it has been going on since ancient times (Held et al., 2000; Held & McGrew, 2007; Ritzer & Dean, 2015). The big difference today, however, which we just discussed, is a matter of technology, more specifically the development of the computer and all such related advances in cyber-infrastructure and information and communications technology.

While each of these advances is worthy of its own chapter – or better yet a series of books – they all have to do, in one way or another, with creating data, capturing data, storing data, using data, sharing data, transferring data, visualising data, searching data and linking up (the world over) very-small-to-very-massive warehouses of otherwise disparate and disconnected data, as well as connecting up our planet's global expanse of communication networks (the internet, World Wide Web, cell phones, satellites, fax machines, telephone lines, etc.) and, more recently, the internet of things, smart grids and the deep web. And all of it done with the goal of data becoming superhero BIG! As our colleague the British sociologist Emma Uprichard (2013) puts it,

> Big data. Little data. Deep data. Surface data. Noisy, unstructured data. Big. The world of data has gone from being analogue and digital, qualitative and quantitative, transactional and a by-product, to, simply, BIG. It is as if we couldn't quite deal with its omnipotence and just ran out of adjectives. BIG. With all the data power it is supposedly meant to entail, one might have thought that a slightly better descriptive term might have been latched onto. But, no. BIG. Just BIG. (p. 1)

In this BIG way, then, globalisation is about the expanding reach of information society; or what Manuel Castells calls *global network society*. Like any explorer discovering new planets, Castells's (2011) sociological research has revealed an entirely new world; but he found it, oddly enough, right here on planet Earth. Castells's new world is a virtual matrix situated within, between and amongst the telecommunications lines and cyber-infrastructure overtaking our globe. And the essential structure of this matrix, which is crucial to our understanding of big data, is the network.

The socio-cybernetic web of big data

As we will examine in depth in the second half of our book, a network is a mathematical object, defined as a set of things and the connections amongst them. The objects in a network are called nodes or vertices and are drawn as points; the connections amongst these nodes, in turn, are called ties, edges or links and are drawn as lines (see Figure 3.1).

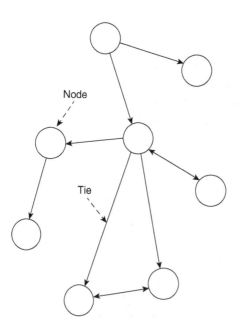

NETWORK GRAPH: The complete set of nodes and ties being studied.

NODE/EDGE/VERTICE: The object in a network (person, group, organisation, country, etc).

TIE/LINK: Defines the relationship between two nodes.

DIRECTED TIES: Show the direction of the relationship with an arrow. A double arrow means the relationship is reciprocal.

Figure 3.1 Basic social network graph

Of the various networks that exist, Castells focuses on two: the cyber-networks we just discussed and, in turn, the social networks entwined with them. For Castells, the past 50 years of globalisation are a direct result of the worldwide impact that information society and cyber-networks have had on global society (Castells & Kumar, 2014). What makes these socio-cybernetic networks so powerful is their novelty and reach, both in terms of their technical structure and their social dynamics, which Castells outlines as follows.

First and most important, these socio-cybernetic networks constitute a novel form of global communication. And, this novelty is not just amongst humans or peer-to-peer networks. It is also amongst the artificial intelligence machinery of which these networks are made. For example, researchers at Facebook recently found some of their bots talking in a language of their own invention, and the researchers could not understand it.[1]

Second, these socio-cybernetic networks take the form of complex systems. In other words, they are not only comprised of billions of nodes and their corresponding information and communication networks, but they are also highly dynamic, distributed, emergent, self-organising systems, as well as nested, meaning they are comprised of networks within networks within networks.

Third, these socio-cybernetic networks are highly flexible. If a node or some other aspect of the system is disabled or no longer of use, others can take its place. For example, if Amazon.com were to go bankrupt, something would emerge to take its place. And, if the telecommunication lines go down in Umbria, Italy, due to weather, the internet will eventually find a way around them.

Fourth, the speed of these socio-cybernetic networks, including the massive amount of data and information they move – think for example of the speed and size of massive global Twitter feeds – is redefining conventional notions of time and space. In fact, it has created a new form of time, which Castells calls timeless time: a condition where time zones no longer matter. A good example is the stock market. When does trading begin and end? In response, machines making use of big data are starting to do 24/7 trading, including spotting trends, forecasting and so forth, with the humans supervising them desperately trying to keep up.[2]

Finally, because of the global speed and presence of these socio-cybernetic networks, global network society is redefining conventional notions of geography: it matters slightly less, now, where in the world you are (although it still does matter), and a lot more about where in the matrix you link in. Castells (2004) refers to this redefinition as the shift from *spaces of places* to *spaces of flows*.

---

[1] See www.fastcodesign.com/90132632/ai-is-inventing-its-own-perfect-languages-should-we-let-it.

[2] See www.wired.com/2016/01/the-rise-of-the-artificially-intelligent-hedge-fund.

Still, as concerns global network society, a few caveats are necessary – with which even Castells agrees (Castells & Kumar, 2014). First, the entire world is not part of network society; instead, it is a type of worldwide system, a global web of socio-cybernetic relations. And, in terms of big data, this is key. As Jan Van Dijk (2012) has argued, we need to be careful how far we push the story of global network society; or we should at least know its limits. The concept of globalisation, as one would guess, presents a series of difficult historical, empirical and conceptual challenges, as it is used to describe something that is rather complex, heterogeneous and multidimensional, which has (over the last 45 years) emerged and manifested itself somewhat differently throughout the world (Giddens, 2001; Van Dijk, 2012; Walby, 2009; Wallerstein, 2000).

Consider, as illustration, the global digital divide. A rough indicator of inequality throughout the world, it is based on the uneven spread of cyber-infrastructure and, in turn, uneven access to and usage of information and communications technology. Such an indicator is useful because it reminds us to be careful in making common 'big data' claims that the world has been saturated in data. All of this takes us to our next point. When discussing globalisation, one must also be careful of what sociologists call technological determinism: the idea that only shifts in industry or economy drive the major changes in societies. In other words, contrary to the hype of big data, global society is not just about the worldwide spread of cyber-infrastructure coming to a neighbourhood data warehouse near you.

Still, despite these important caveats, Castells and other authors (Giddens, 2001; Held et al., 2000; Held & McGrew, 2007; Ritzer & Dean, 2015; Van Dijk, 2012; Wallerstein, 2000) generally agree that the world has become thoroughly saturated in data, creating a virtual planet of ever-increasing and endlessly flowing information. In this way, then, big data has less to do with the size of any one **database** and more to do with the fact that we live today in a globalised 'big data' world. In other words, big data is a globalised worldwide socio cybernetic web of networks upon networks upon networks. But, again, that is not the entire picture. All of this takes us to the issue of the databases themselves.

Big data databases

To reiterate: like globalisation, collecting large amounts of data is not a new endeavour. For example, one can go all the way back to the censuses of ancient India, Egypt, Rome and China to find large amounts of data being collected on people. As such, in some ways the term *big data* is a misnomer. In other ways, however, it is not, as the databases of today look like nothing in recent or ancient history. (As illustration, see Tarani Chandola and Cara Booker's *Archival and Secondary Data Analysis*, which is part of the *SAGE Quantitative Research Kit*.)

To make this point clear, consider what researchers call the *five Vs* of big data, which, when combined, account for what makes a big data database unique. One must point out, however, that the five Vs of big data remain open to debate, as it is not clear if most large data sets meet their criteria (Konys, 2016). Still, let us quickly review them, as they do constitute a shorthand for what makes big data unique:

- *Volume:* To begin, big data often exceeds current capacity for storage. In fact, over the last few decades, as storage capacity has exponentially increased, what was previously considered big data is no longer seen as such a threat; still, the sheer volume of information available today is, at least analytically speaking, overwhelming. For example, in the *Forbes* article we mentioned earlier about how big data is changing the airline industry, its author explained that 'today, through thousands of sensors and sophisticated digitised systems, the newest generation of jets collects exponentially more, with each flight generating more than 30 times the amount of data the previous generation of wide-bodied jets produced. . . . By 2026, annual data generation should reach 98 billion gigabytes, or 98 million terabytes, according to a 2016 estimate by Oliver Wyman.'[3]
- *Variety:* Big data today is also generated through a wide array of types and formats: structured and unstructured, relational, transactional, longitudinal, discrete, dynamic, visual, textual, numeric, audio, geospatial, physical, ecological, biological, psychological, social, economic, cultural, political and so on and so forth.
- *Velocity:* In our big data world, the issue is not just the speed at which massive amounts of data are being generated but also the speed at which they often need to be acquired and processed. Also, there is a significant amount of big data that remains important for very short moments of time: for example, delayed flight schedules, ticket price fluctuations or sudden interruptions in travel that an airport has to respond to quickly. And then there are the complex ways this increased data velocity, in turn, speeds up the decision-making process – forcing decisions, often times, into a matter on nanoseconds rather than days, weeks or months; all of these present major challenges to the hardware and software of companies and users – not to mention the 'knockoff' effects on social life that come from this increased speed in decision-making.
- *Variability:* While the velocity and volume of big data appear constant, in actuality they are rather variable, with inconsistencies in their flow, as in the case of a sudden Twitter trend or online searches in response to a disease outbreak. All of these present major challenges to websites and data management systems, which can (and often do) crash in the face of so much data and demand.
- *Veracity:* Big data is often not in a format that makes it easily explored or linked together. For example, while today's airline industry is overwhelmed with multiple storms of unstructured social media data, the challenge is converting

---

[3]See www.forbes.com/sites/oliverwyman/2017/06/16/the-data-science-revolution-transforming-aviation/#411384ae7f.

and combining these unstructured storms of data into something useful and meaningful for analysis – an issue we will address in greater detail in our next chapter on data mining, which was developed, in part, to advance the collection, management, processing, transformation and analysis of big data databases. The other issue is how trustworthy or accurate these big data are. For example, just because social media on an airline industry are being collected does not mean they are valid or reliable. Also, we know in the social sciences that what people say and what they do are two different things – which has led, for example, to psychologists focusing more on what people do on social media, as opposed to who or what they say they are in their various profiles. Also, now that we live in a world of highly-biased identity politics, social media trolls, covert and overt governmental attempts to control data and the internet, challenges to net neutrality and fake news and internet bots, one has to be highly critical not only of the veracity of the big data being analysed but also its legitimacy and even reality. Which takes us to the final V.

- *Vulnerability:* While not considered part of the usual set, this other V of big data has made its inclusion imminently clear over the last few years. Vulnerability exists in two major forms: vulnerability due to hardware or software breakdown and vulnerability due to hacking, cyber-security and privacy issues. Examples include Russian cyber-attacks on the 2017 presidential election in the USA, WikiLeaks and the Equifax cyber-security debacle along with the endless surveillance of our private lives.

Finally, the six Vs aside, what also makes these databases unique is their architecture, which often (although not always) takes the form, as we discussed earlier, of a distributed socio-cybernetic network. Consider, for example, the OhioLINK library system, which we regularly use to do our research. As stated on its website,

> OhioLINK is comprised of 120 academic libraries, which are distributed among 93 different Ohio colleges and universities, including the State Library of Ohio, 16 public university libraries, 51 independent college libraries, 23 two-year college libraries, 16 regional campus libraries, 8 law school libraries and 5 medical school libraries. In terms of its big data network, it provides users access to: (1) over 46 million books and other library materials; (2) more than 100 electronic research databases – each of which expands OhioLINK's network to global data warehouses the world over; (3) over 24 million electronic journal articles (again, the network expands); (4) over 100,000 e-books; (5) nearly 85,000 images, videos and sounds; and (6) over 58,000 theses and dissertations from Ohio students at 31 Ohio institutions.[4]

And this description does not even take into account the different software packages and data management systems these different libraries use, as well as significant differences in (and quality of) the various mainframes and computer hardware they use.

---

[4]See www.ohiolink.edu.

Another example is the database network of airline social media sites, all downloading and sharing data by the minute on who's where (or not), and when (or should have been), and in terms of how and with what or not (as in the case of luggage!). In all these examples, it seems, these databases/data warehouses constitute an interlinking web of smaller systems and networks and their corresponding cybernetic support structure, all criss-crossing to produce the larger, self-organising and emergent system we call big data – and with the largest big data network of them all being the World Wide Web!

The failed promise of big data

So, now that we understand what makes big data unique, are we therefore to also believe that big data will solve all the world's problems without even trying? Or, is it all just a bunch of hype? The answer most likely exists somewhere in the in-between. But, let us explore the question nonetheless.

Even with all the above advance in big data articulated, there is still an aspect of big data that comes across as hype. And, it is this insight, more than anything else, which helps to clarify the misunderstandings that surround the debate about big data. In terms of the proponents, the biggest misunderstanding is that, despite all of its potential, big data cannot ultimately deliver on its promise. Three reasons in particular: (1) the world is too complex, (2) big data is not equally available to all and (3) big data alone does not drive change. Also, as we will discuss in our review of data mining, there is a major difference between big data and useful or good data – although the two are not mutually exclusive – as well as good data analysis and bad.

Alternatively, however, in terms of the critics, the biggest misunderstanding is that, like it or not, big data and the larger information society and globalisation of which it is a part, despite all their failures and flaws and hype, are not going away, no matter what they say. The more important focus for both advocates and critics alike, then, is to address these failures and flaws and hype, as well as successes and accomplishments and advance, which, in many ways, is why we wrote this book, as we see ourselves as situated somewhere in the middle of the debate, as critical advocates or alternatively supportive critics.

In this way, walking this middle ground places us squarely in what we would like to call a new *complex digital social science*. As three of the key authors in the field of digital social science – Lupton (2014), Marres (2017) and Rogers (2013) – make clear, while it is crucial to be critical of the failed promises of big data, and while it is necessary to be sober about the relative strengths and limits of data mining and digital methods, we nonetheless live today (in 2021) in a global network society and a series of interdependent and interconnected data-saturated world(s). If social scientists are going to be at the forefront of making sense of these world(s), we need to embrace new and different methods and methodologies – including being critical of digital social science – as well as critically advance those we have been using. All of this takes us to the next issue: data mining.

Chapter Summary

- While the term *big data* has become common parlance, experts are still not entirely clear what it actually means.
- In some ways *big data* is a useful term for making sense of globalisation and how information technology has changed the world.
- In other ways, big data refers to a qualitative change in data, which data scientists use the five Vs to describe – volume, variety, velocity, variability, veracity, and (for those who add a sixth dimension) vulnerability.
- Still, in other ways, big data is hype, which has produced the failed promise that once we have all the data we need, then everything can be understood. The truth of big data lies somewhere in the in-between of all these views.

Further Reading

Castells, M., & Kumar, M. (2014). A conversation with Manuel Castells. *Berkeley Planning Journal, 27*(1), 93–99. https://doi.org/10.5070/BP327124502
This article deals with the worldwide impact of information society and cyber networks on global society.

Konys, A. (2016). Ontology-based approaches to big data analytics. In *International multi-conference on advanced computer systems* (pp. 355–365). Springer. https://doi.org/10.1007/978-3-319-48429-7_32
One can refer to this book for the debate on the five Vs of big data.

4

WHAT IS DATA MINING?

Chapter Overview

If *big data* is all about the development and emergence of networks of complex data sets (global or otherwise), then *data mining* is all about pattern recognition and knowledge extraction from these complex data sets. Or, that is at least how it is defined today.

A bit of data mining history

Back in the late 1980s and early 1990s, when data mining first emerged, it was defined as a complete (and entirely circular) approach to data management and analysis, from data collection and preparation to pattern recognition and knowledge extraction to further data collection and analysis and so forth. For example, as shown in Figure 4.1, the actual analysis of data (which is what data mining amounts to today) originally only involved two of data mining's eight major steps, or three if you count the formulation of questions.

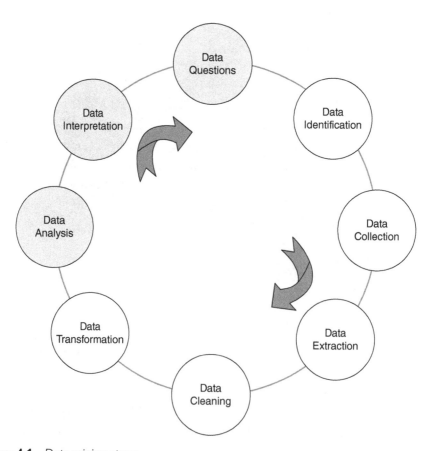

Figure 4.1 Data mining steps

When data mining first emerged, it also had a slightly different name, which was much more explicit about the fact that data mining is a process. It was called knowledge discovery in databases, shortened to KDD. Later, as the field developed, the acronym was dropped and the term *data mining* was used instead.

The other reason KDD was used initially is because, in the 1980s – when it was always argued that research should be guided by rigorous hypotheses and concise research questions – data mining had a rather negative connotation, akin to other related terms such as *data fishing* or *data dredging*, both of which conjured images of untrustworthy and unethical researchers combing through their databases to find something (including anything) of significance. And, as we saw in our review of big data in Chapter 3, this fear of a-theoretical, data-driven knowledge discovery and decision-making remains a major concern to this day – and rightly so – particularly given that many of those skilled in the tools and techniques of data mining are not social scientists grounded in the theories and concepts of social scientific inquiry.

The data mining process

Again, as shown in Figure 4.1, data mining typically involves an ongoing process of data collection, management and analysis that seeks to uncover non-obvious patterns in large databases for the purposes of knowledge discovery. The first emphasis here, in this definition, is on the *non-obvious*. Concerns about a-theoretical data dredging aside, a lot of data mining is resolutely exploratory in nature, seeking to know what we don't know, as well as figuring out the unknown unknowns. And, it is also about conducting such 'explorations' in the face of massive amounts of information – as we have seen several times now in our airline industry example – that otherwise resist being understood vis-à-vis the tools and techniques of conventional statistics or qualitative inquiry (Bar-Yam, 2016).

As such, the quality of the data explored in the data mining process is equally important as the high-powered computational methods used to explore them. Hence the reason that six of data mining's eight steps involve data management issues. For example, in his recent article, 'From Big Data to Important Information', Bar-Yam (2016) explains that while 'advances in science are being sought in newly available opportunities to collect massive quantities of data about complex systems' (p. 73), the real challenge is not analysing these data in their entirety – as such analysis is humanly impossible. Instead, even in the face of big data, the challenge is to frame data mining inquiry 'as an effort to determine what is important and unimportant as a means for advancing our understanding and addressing many practical concerns, such as economic development or treating disease' (p. 73). As such, data mining includes significant attention to what data are studied and collected, as well as how they are cleaned up, prepared and transformed for analysis and, in turn, once a particular stage of analysis is complete, focusing on what data are needed next and how those data will be obtained.

Such concerns about data, however, are not unique to data mining and are, in most ways, the steps involved in any good process of data-driven knowledge discovery. What makes data mining so unique, however, particularly when it first emerged, is that it explicitly ties the data management and analysis processes together, particularly in terms of knowledge discovery leading to the collection of new or different data. In the 1990s, this made its approach rather unique (albeit less today), as data collection, management and analysis are often treated as distinct and separate processes. In contrast, data mining emphasises the idea of how important these three processes are to each other and how one informs the next.

And it is here, in this emphasis on 'process', that data mining highlighted its other key concept, *intelligent discovery*. If the errors of data fishing and data dredging and erroneous conclusions are to be avoided (both in terms of false positives and false negatives), exploratory knowledge discovery needs to be 'intelligent' in its design – particularly given the massive new databases being studied. In other words, the methods used to explore today's big databases in search of new and unknown knowledge require their own degree of programmable learning. Hence the field of data mining's turn to the tools and techniques of computational modelling.

And, it is this tradition of developing algorithmically intelligent, knowledge-generating machines that remains *en vogue* almost 30 years later, as we live now in a world of smart cars and smartphones, artificially intelligent surgical equipment and financial surveillance systems, nudge-wear and health apps, and a myriad of web crawlers and internet bots sending us spam mail, influencing political elections, following Twitter trends, linking up our globalised social media worlds, stealing our online identities and helping start-up companies market their goods and services. In fact, some scholars estimate that more than half of all web traffic on the internet is comprised of bots. The question, however, is what does it mean to call a method intelligent? And, in turn, how much should we trust that intelligence?

The 'black box' of data mining

We think it best, for the purposes of discussion, to begin by clarifying that machine intelligence is to human intelligence what airplane flight is to the flight of birds. Birds and planes both have wings and both do, in fact, fly; but they do so in otherwise massively different ways. The same for machine learning. It is a form of learning, but it is not human learning. And it is this difference that we need to constantly remind ourselves about. Let us explain.

Of the various artificial intelligence camps, we are members of the one that is not worried about any near-future machine uprising! In fact, our worry is the opposite: for us the real fear regarding machine learning is that, to date, most machines are not, on their own, sufficiently 'smart' enough to run things. Or, alternatively, if they are smart enough to run something, it remains often impossible to know how, exactly, they arrived at the conclusions they reached, as the machines are not smart enough, often, to tell us. (In other words, they are equally ignorant of why they arrive at the results or decisions they do.)

As such, machine learning, today, still requires a significant degree of concomitant human intelligence, involvement, management, guidance or control. And, absent that involvement, machines can (and often do) lead us to make bad decisions. Case in point is Cliff Kuang's (2017) recent *New York Times* article, 'Can A.I. Be Taught to Explain Itself?', which addresses the issue that 'as machine learning becomes more powerful, the field's researchers increasingly find themselves unable to account for what their algorithms know – or how they know it' (p. 46).

Keeping things simple, we can basically organise machine learning into two basic types: supervised and unsupervised. Supervised learning involves training a computational algorithm with data for which the cases and their outcomes are already known. Cases in this instance are defined as the input object – which is usually a **vector**, as we will discuss in Chapter 6 – and the outcome as the output object. An easy example is flight schedules. In order to improve brand allegiance, one of the things an airline wants to know (and, in turn, predict) is which flights tend to result in the highest rates of delay or cancellation? To get this information, a data mining expert can feed into a neural net thousands and thousands of previous flights, continually supervising the training of the machine until it can correctly (or reasonably) identify which flights were delayed or cancelled, and how or why. With this neural net trained, data mining experts can then use it to predict which flights in the near future have the greatest chance of being delayed or cancelled.

In turn, unsupervised learning involves training a computational algorithm for which the catalogue of cases or their outcomes are not well known. The goal here is not just to arrive at accurate prediction but to also identify (map) the different types of cases upon which those predictions are based (be they groups or trends).

Of the two types of learning, data mining is mainly involved in the latter, as the exploratory goal is to identify non-obvious patterns in large data sets. (For more on exploratory research, see Scott Jones and Goldring's *Exploratory and Descriptive Statistics*, which is part of the *SAGE Quantitative Research Kit*.) However – and this is a very important point – data mining is actually part of both forms of machine learning, as even in the case of supervised learning, the challenge remains of figuring out how the computational algorithm (be it a neural net, decision tree, genetic algorithm, etc.) arrived at its predictive results. In other words, even though we are the architects of their algorithmic structure, we humans still struggle to understand how machines learn. And that is a problem.

As illustration, Kuang (2017) provides an interesting example in his *New York Times* article. Back in the 1990s, the Microsoft researcher, Rich Caruana and colleagues developed a highly predictive neural net for identifying patients at high risk for pneumonia. When asked by the hospital staff at the University of Pittsburgh Medical Center, however, if they could therefore go ahead and use the net, Caruana said, 'No!' The reason was that he and a fellow graduate student noticed that (contrary to clinical fact) the neural net incorrectly predicted that asthmatic patients had a lower than expected risk for pneumonia. The reason the neural net made this incorrect prediction is that given that asthmatic patients are at such a high risk for pneumonia, they tend to get immediate treatment, giving the false impression they are low-risk candidates. The neural net was technically right but clinically wrong. And, without proper guidance by human intelligence, it was likely to lead to terrible clinical decision-making.

The other challenge with machine intelligence is that bias can be easily built into how an algorithm learns. One illustration is how machines associate words in an online search, linking, for example, the word 'female' to related stereotypical terms such as 'mom' or 'homemaker', while linking the word 'male' with terms such as 'science' or 'money'. Other examples include lending algorithms that discriminate against giving home loans or credit cards to those with excellent credit ratings mainly because they are from the lower socio-economic strata. And then there are the related issues of algorithms overfitting data, as well as issues of finding correct patterns in noisy or messy data. All of this takes us to the issues of validity and reliability.

Validity and reliability

Perhaps one of the biggest challenges to the computational algorithms of contemporary data mining is the anxiety researchers and users have over confirming the validity and reliability of the models they create. As one of the analysts in Kuang's (2017) article put it, 'I don't need to visualise another recommendation. If I'm going to sign off on a decision, I need to be able to justify it' (p. 46). Alternative names used to describe the need for 'justification' are sensitivity analysis, calibration, statistical significance and uncertainty analysis.

This anxiety about justification is not to suggest, however, that conventional statistics are necessarily better off, despite their repertoire of statistical tests and frequentist theories of probability. Nor is it to suggest that the tests for significance in statistics do not apply to data mining, or that the dividing line between statistics and computational modelling is all that clear. For example, cluster analysis is variously catalogued as a statistical technique, a vector quantisation tool and as a data mining classification method; and genetic algorithms have links to symbolic regression, optimisation techniques and decision trees. In turn, confirmatory machine intelligence often relies on logistic regression and Bayesian sensitivity analysis.

Still, our detour into these issues is required to make clear the point that fitting models to data is an extremely important part in the data mining process, and one that continues to require further development. All of this takes us to another issue: the statistical assumption of normality, otherwise known as the central limit theorem.

The limits of normalised probability distributions

As we discussed in Chapter 2, most parametric statistical techniques rely on the assumption that the population or sample they are studying satisfies the normal (or bell curve) distribution in addition to other criteria related to sampling adequately. However, it is to be noted that even though the central limit theorem assigns a very important value to the normal distribution, that is not the be-all and end-all of things. For example, as shown in Figure 4.2, there are other kinds of distributions (too many to list here) that characterise a variety of natural and social phenomena. In fact, as we have identified in our research, many complex distributions are not symmetric but are right skewed (Castellani & Rajaram, 2016).

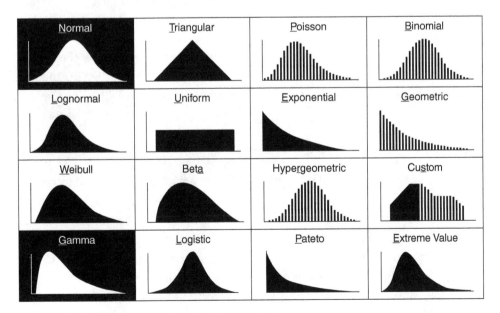

Figure 4.2 Different types of probability distributions

As such, assuming that the population is normally distributed is a major limitation in conventional statistics – particularly given that, with big data, databases are rapidly increasing in size and complexity. All of this takes us to yet another issue: fitting models to data.

Fitting models to data

Most curve-fitting methods, including those used in statistics – as in the case of growth mixture modelling, hierarchical regression and analysis of variance – start with the assumption that the data already fit a particular type of curve. For example, it is well known that a first-order reaction will fit a linear first-order differential equation. However, there are examples of situations where the form of the function is not known a priori. In fact, it is our contention that almost every complex system has this property (Castellani & Rajaram, 2016). As such, assuming a function's form a priori essentially simplifies the complexity, thereby not capturing the more interesting and complex parts of the system.

In contrast, in computational modelling, the goal is to fit functions to data rather than fitting data to known functions. To do the former, techniques such as genetic algorithms (section 'Genetic Algorithms and Evolutionary Computation', Chapter 8) and neural network–based methods ('Artificial Neural Networks', Chapter 8) are state of the art, as they inherently have the capacity to adaptively fit the best function that can capture the complexity in the process or system under study. In addition, they have the capacity to provide multiple models whose degree of complexity is inversely proportional to their ability to capture the complexity in data. Hence, the function that works best will always be somewhere in the middle – that is, one that is not too complex but sophisticated enough to capture most of the complexity in the system. All of this constitutes a different way of thinking about validity and reliability in a way that significantly challenges the conventions of statistics and social scientific method.

Data mining's various tasks

With our basic definition of data mining intact, as a final point we need to quickly review the various tasks it is used to accomplish. Again, as with so much in the fields of big data and data mining, such a list varies according to those creating the list. Despite such variances, there are some commonalities across and amongst them. To begin, while we have highlighted the latter, there are two major approaches to data mining: (1) 'verification or validation focused data mining' and (2) the more common 'exploratory knowledge discovery focused data mining'. The former is focused on exploring user-based hypotheses, while the latter is focused on gaining new or unknown insights. Data mining techniques can also be used to perform a variety of tasks, such as data visualisation, geospatial modelling, association and regression, multidimensional scaling, complex causal modelling, summarisation, classification, case-comparative reasoning, decision tree development, sentiment analysis, textual clustering, anomaly detection, network structural analysis and dynamics, improved learning and pattern detection, agent-based modelling, trend spotting and analysis, mapping non-linear macroscopic dynamics and predictive analytics (which we have mentioned several times now). Still, despite its numerous tasks, data mining was developed, ultimately, to deal with the increasing complexity of the globalised, data-saturated world in which we now live. All of this takes us to the final chapter in Part I: Chapter 5: The Complexity Turn.

Chapter Summary

- Over the last four decades, the field of data mining has changed considerably. Originally, it was called knowledge discovery in databases (KDD) and was correctly hailed as an entirely new approach to data management and analysis.
- Conventional methodologists reacted strongly to data mining, seeing its exploratory approach as a form of data fishing; that is, it was not theoretically driven in a way that pure science is imagined to take place.
- Despite these critiques, data mining took off in the managerial sciences and big business, including sales and marketing. Today, it is the backbone of most major information age companies, from Facebook and Amazon.com to Twitter and Google.
- Given its increasingly widespread usage, data mining scholars inevitably made their way through the main critiques of this approach, and today it has developed into a rigorous approach to data management, modelling and analysis grounded in the latest developments in computational science.

Further Reading

Bar-Yam, Y. (2016). From big data to important information. *Complexity, 21*(S2), 73–98. https://doi.org/10.1002/cplx.21785
This article offers an introduction to data mining techniques.

Kuang, C. (2017, November 26). Can A.I. be taught to explain itself? *New York Times*. www.nytimes.com/2017/11/21/magazine/can-ai-be-taught-to-explain-itself.html
This article explains the tug of war between artificial intelligence and human intervention.

5

THE COMPLEXITY TURN

Chapter Overview

Now that we have a basic understanding of the concepts, histories and criticisms surrounding the conventions of quantitative social science, data mining and big data, it is time to situate our journey within the larger context of the complexity sciences.

Mapping the complexity turn

Figure 5.1 is a macroscopic, transdisciplinary introduction to the complexity sciences. (For a more detailed online version, go to www.art-sciencefactory.com/complexity-map_feb09.html. Also, please cite this map as Castellani, B. (2018). Map of the complexity sciences. *Art and Science Factory*. www.art-sciencefactory.com/complexity-map_feb09.html.)

Moving from left to right, the map is read in a roughly historical fashion – but not literally, as we are compressing an *n*-dimensional intellectual space into a two-dimensional map grid. Also, in order to present some type of organisational structure, the history of the complexity sciences is developed along the field's five major intellectual traditions: (1) dynamical systems theory (purple), (2) systems science (blue), (3) complex systems theory (yellow), (4) cybernetics (grey) and (5) artificial intelligence (orange). Again, the fit is not exact (and sometimes even somewhat forced), but it is sufficient to help those new to the field gain a sense of its evolving history.

Placed along these traditions are the key scholarly themes and methods used across the complexity sciences. A theme's colour identifies the historical tradition with which it is 'best' associated, even if a theme is placed on a different trajectory. Themes were placed roughly at the point they became a major area of study; recognising that, from here forward, researchers have continued to work in that area, in one way or another. For example, while artificial intelligence (AI) gained significant momentum in the 1940s and, therefore, is placed near the start of the map, it remains a major field of study, and is, in 2018, going through a major resurgence.

Also, themes in (brown) denote content/discipline specific topics, which illustrate how the complexity sciences are applied to different content. Finally, double-lined themes denote the intersection of a tradition with a new field of study, as in the case of visual complexity or agent-based modelling.

Connected to themes are the scholars who 'founded' or presently 'exemplify' work in that area. In other instances, however, 'up-and-coming scholars' are listed – mainly to draw attention to scholars early in their work. There was also an attempt to showcase research from around the world, rather than just the global north. Also, while some scholars (e.g. as in the case of Bar-Yam) impacted multiple areas of study, given

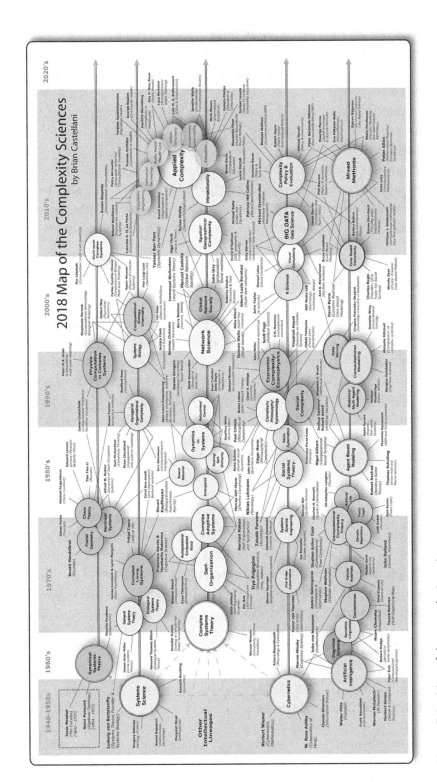

Figure 5.1 Map of the complexity sciences

their position on the map only a few of these links could be visualised – which goes to the next point: unfortunately, there is no way to generate an educational map that has everyone and everything on it! As such, there is always someone who should be on the map who is not!

Also, and again, it is important to point out that the positioning of scholars relative to an area of study does not mean they are from that time period. It only means they are associated with that theme.

Finally, remembering Foucault's famous argument that most history is really a history of the present as it looks back, who or what is considered an important theme or scholar is a function of time and place. Hence the reason this map has gone through so many revisions – as the complexity sciences evolve, so does their history.

Data mining and big data as complexity science

As shown in Figure 5.1, while generally touted as *sui generis*, the fields of data mining and big data are not only part of the larger developments of post-industrialism and globalisation, they are also part of the complexity sciences. As also shown in Figure 5.1, from the beginning of artificial intelligence and systems science to cybernetics and dynamical systems theory – in fact, going all the way back to the 1940s and Weaver's (1948) article on science and complexity – scholars across the entire academy (and around the world) have been fast at work developing tools to make better sense of the increasing complexities of the globalised life we all now live, including the socio-ecosystems in which we and the entire web of life are situated.

Alternatively, however, one can also argue that the complexity sciences had a hand in creating our current global society and its complex global problems, insomuch as the technological advances they helped to create – from computers and artificial intelligence to cyber-infrastructure and big data – also helped to bring about post-industrialism and the current phase of globalisation (which we highlighted in Chapter 3). Either way, or by whatever intellectual or historical journey one seeks to take, the complexity sciences are part of the data mining and big data story.

Top ten list about complexity

Over the past few decades, a rather significant number of books and articles have been written on the complexity sciences – just do a Google search! As such, our focus here is slightly different. Instead of conducting an overview, we will provide our *Top*

Ten List of things about the complexity sciences and the complexity turn, particularly in relation to the social sciences that you may not know, but should. *So, let's get started. Drum roll please.*

Number 1

As we have already suggested, the complexity sciences do not constitute a singular science or theory. Instead, there are numerous (albeit overlapping) complexity sciences and theories, as well as different methodological and epistemological viewpoints. A good illustration is Figure 5.1, which is now in its seventh major iteration.

Number 2

Relative to our first point, it is not clear if the complexity sciences constitute a paradigm shift or revolution, as certain authors have claimed (Wolfram, 2002). For example, in fields like non-equilibrium thermodynamics and dynamical systems theory, the study of complexity is more a recent advance, as scholars have always sought to model the dynamics of systems, as in the case of aviation and flight systems. In turn, in other fields, such as systems biology for example, complexity constitutes both a rapprochement (a return to the past) and an advance. In sociology as well, many 19th- and early 20th-century scholars were systems thinkers. All of this takes us to the next point.

Number 3

While the complexity sciences are relatively new, a wider *systems perspective* is not Hammond (2010). In sociology, for example, one can trace the emergence of a systems perspective to the founding of the discipline, as in Spencer's evolutionary theory, Marx's dialectic, Durkheim's social fact, Pareto's 80/20 rule and Comte or Quetelet's social physics (Castellani & Hafferty, 2009). And this tradition has been carried through to today, through the work of systems sociologists such as Talcott Parsons, Kenneth Bailey, Walter Buckley, Niklas Luhmann and Immanuel Wallerstein.

Number 4

Despite this long history, and perhaps because of it, the tangle between systems thinking and the social sciences has been rather consistently contentious, and, in large measure, for good reasons. As Castellani and Hafferty (2009) point out, a lot of social scientific systems thinking went in the wrong theoretical direction, embracing highly problematic views of society. Examples include an imperialist view of social evolution, as well as a near-hagiographic appropriation of old-school biology and its homeostatic and functionalist view of structure. And, unfortunately, the list of the errors made by old-school social systems thinking continues from there: conventional, tautological, highly abstracted and therefore void of utility, predictable, unable to deal with power relations or inequality, retrospectively descriptive and therefore causally useless, devoid of an empirically accurate theory of instability or social change and wrongfully focused on grand narrative. And, it keeps going, culminating, for most scholars, in the work of Talcott Parsons – whom we just mentioned above.

Of all the systems theorists, including Luhmann, perhaps Parsons is the best nominee for systems thinking's intellectual errors. Or perhaps not. In short, Parsons was a systems theorist who built his theory out of equal parts old-school, European sociology and (in the 1940s) systems science and cybernetics. What ultimately doomed Parsons, however, was not his embrace of the latter. It was, amongst other things, his abstracted and dogged functionalism and the idea (which he got from old-school sociology, which we just mentioned) that society sought equilibrium and homeostasis. In other words, what got Parsons into trouble was the type of complex system he defined society as, not the idea that society is a complex system. Unfortunately, most social scientists missed this point. Worse, in missing it, they threw Parsons and, in turn, systems thinking into the dustbin of social science history, thereby putting themselves, in 2021, in the position of newcomers to the more recent complexity sciences.

Number 5

Still, the complexity sciences have inevitably made their way back into the social sciences. The British sociologist John Urry calls this re-emergence of systems thinking *the complexity turn* and dates it to around the late 1990s. We generally agree with Urry's date and think a good starting point is Byrne's (1998) *Complexity Theory and the Social Sciences*, published the same year as Cilliers's (1998) *Complexity and Postmodernism*. Or, the Gulbenkian Commission's 1996 report *Open the Social Sciences* (Wallerstein et al., 1996) published the same year as Capra's (1996) *The Web of Life*. The complexity turn is not to suggest, however, that all of the disciplines within the social sciences have gone round the same bend (Urry, 2005). Psychology, for example, is miles behind, and perhaps has not yet even decided if such a travel is worth it.

Still, *the complexity turn* in the 1990s does constitute a sea change in thinking within the social sciences, even if only amongst a small but growing network of scholars.

Number 6

As a result of the complexity turn in the social sciences, the last 10 years has constituted a sort of an intellectual tipping point, resulting in an outpouring of conferences, journals, methods, scientific networks and avenues of study. One of the downsides to this tipping point is that the complexity sciences went from a few key intellectual lineages (which Capra faithfully outlined in *The Web of Life*) to an intellectual movement comprised of numerous and intersecting minor histories. Now, do not get us wrong, as all this interdisciplinary appropriation and collision has been a good thing, as it has pushed scientific inquiry into new areas of thinking (Abbott, 2001; Morin, 2007).

Still, it does lead to a key point one needs to grasp: As Byrne and Callaghan (2013) have warned, not all complexity methods or theories are the same, and all are not equally useful for social inquiry. An excellent example is the difference between what Morin (2007) calls restrictive versus general complexity and what Weaver (1948) calls disorganised versus organised complexity. And, that does not even get us into the issue of methods. As such, one needs to be critically aware of the type of *complexity turn* one is making and the epistemological, theoretical and methodological assumptions upon which it is based.

For example, relative to the current book, it is not enough to say that big data are complex, as if that only meant one thing to everyone. Instead, one also has to put time into what it means to say that, as it has all sorts of implications for the methods one uses, including those of data mining.

Number 7

Relative to our sixth point, there is no one agreed-upon definition of what makes something complex. As such, an alternative name for our seventh point is *How many scientists does it take to define complexity?* For example, in *Complexity: A Guided Tour* (2009), Mitchell explains that in 2004, during the annual summer programme of the Santa Fe Institute, she put together a panel of top scholars in complexity to help commemorate its 20th anniversary. The room was filled with graduate students and post-doctoral fellows, all anxious to ask their questions. Right out of the gate, however, the first question, and the one most obvious to ask, was a showstopper: How do you define complexity? The question ended the show because nobody on the panel could agree on a definition. In fact, a few arguments broke out, students became frustrated and faculty just shook their heads, knowing that despite 20 years of science, the Santa Fe Institute, a leading organisation devoted to the study of complexity, could not define its primary topic of research.

We, however, have a different take on Mitchell's example. Just as there is no one science of complexity, there is no reason to assume there is only one type of complexity; instead, there are multiple types of complex systems, along with multiple ways of defining them.

Number 8

Still, while empirical differences exist, there is nonetheless a core list of characteristics that almost all definitions of complexity share. For example, it is generally agreed that complex systems are causally complex, dynamic, non-linear, comprised of a large number of agents (pieces-parts, etc.), self-organising, emergent, network-like in organisation and evolving. And, it is quite common, given this shared list of characteristics, for complexity scientists to apply the insights gained from the study of one complex system to another. In fact, it is this interdisciplinary exchange of ideas – despite the caveats to be careful in such intellectual transport across fields of study – that makes the complexity sciences so innovative and powerful.

Number 9

Related to our eighth point, it is also the case that despite differences in view, most complexity scientists treat big data as complex. And they have rather consistently seen statistics as only best at modelling disorganised complex systems but not sufficient for modelling the myriad of complex organised systems we are currently up against: from global warming and disruptive climate change to the world capitalist system and pandemics to regional and urban complexity.

Number 10

Finally, it is fair to say that, in 2021, the current cutting edge in the complexity sciences is a combination of methodological integration and policy-oriented application – in other words, applying things and making method generally accessible. Hence the rising importance of data mining and big data and the advances made in the usage of complexity thinking in public policy evaluation, urban development, programme planning, clinical care, healthcare, modelling disruptive climate change and ecological analysis, and marketing, global finance and business. And let us also not forget, the airline industry. The challenge, however, is how to integrate these methods effectively as concerns the effective data mining of big data databases and our data-saturated post-industrial, globalised world(s), which is why we need, now, to turn to the second part of our book.

Chapter Summary

- While generally touted as *sui generis*, the fields of data mining and big data are not only part of the larger developments of post-industrialism and globalisation, they are also part of the complexity sciences.
- The complexity sciences emerged in the 1940s in response to the growing complexity of most scientific study. Weaver referred to this as the shift from the search for simplicity to the need for models of qualitative complexity. It also refers to a shift towards a complex systems view of the world.
- This change in science was not possible, however, without the 20th-century advances in computer technology, including the capacity for computational methods.
- The result was a sea change in methods, resulting in the creation of incredible techniques such as artificial intelligence, genetic algorithms, agent-based modelling, microsimulations, complex network analysis, geospatial modelling, data visualisation and machine learning.
- The complexity turn in the social sciences also created a new framework for thinking about, studying and modelling complex big data, namely 'social complexity theory'.
- To outline the value of social complexity theory and the complexity sciences for data mining complex big data, the chapter ends by reviewing a top ten list of things everyone should know about this area of inquiry.

Further Reading

Hammond, D. (2010). *The science of synthesis: Exploring the social implications of general systems theory*. University Press of Colorado.
This book offers a wider systems perspective.

Mitchell, M. (2009). *Complexity: A guided tour*. Oxford University Press.
This book takes us through a guided tour of complexity.

PART II

THE TOOLS AND TECHNIQUES OF DATA MINING

6

CASE-BASED COMPLEXITY

A DATA MINING VOCABULARY

Chapter Overview

As stated in the introduction, given the significant similarities amongst the methods of data mining, our goal for Chapter 6 was to outline a set of user-friendly mathematical formalisms, including their ontological foundation, which would make our journey across these tools and techniques easier. And, as also stated, the framework we would use to assemble our outline was *case-based complexity* (Byrne & Ragin, 2013; Castellani et al., 2016). So let's get started.

Case-based complexity

Within the world(s) of computational modelling and interdisciplinary mixed methods, *case-based complexity* constitutes one of the major methodologies for modelling complex social systems or, more generally, social complexity (Byrne & Ragin, 2013; Castellani et al., 2016). And, when employed using the techniques of data mining, it is particularly useful for analysing and modelling big data. To date, there are several different (albeit interrelated) approaches to case-based complexity. Here are four:

1   Those employing Ragin's *qualitative comparative analysis* and *fuzzy set analysis* (Rihoux & Ragin, 2009)
2   Those employing Byrne's *case-comparative complexity*, which combines qualitative comparative analysis, complex realism and cluster analysis (Byrne & Ragin, 2013)
3   Those employing Hayne's *dynamic pattern synthesis*, which explores the dynamical relationships amongst cases (Haynes, 2017)
4   And, finally, those employing *case-based modelling*, as in the case of the SACS Toolkit and COMPLEX-IT – which draw on the latest developments in data mining and computational modelling.

Regardless of the method used, a case-based complexity approach to case-comparative analysis is grounded in three core arguments; which also deeply resonate with the majority of computational methods used in data mining big data:

1   The case and its trajectory across time/space are the focus of study, not the individual variables or attributes of which it is comprised.
2   Cases and their trajectories are treated as composites (profiles), comprised of interdependent, interconnected sets of causal conditions, variables, factors or attributes.
3   And, finally, cases and their relationships and trajectories are the methodological equivalent of complex systems – that is, they are emergent, self-organising, non-linear, dynamic, network-like and so on – and therefore should be studied as such.

To this list, case-based modelling (our approach) adds four more points, which situates case-based complexity even more squarely at the cutting-edge of data mining method:

1   Cases and their trajectories are dynamically evolving across time/space and, therefore, should be explored to identify their major and minor trends.
2   In turn, these trends should be explored in the aggregate for key global–temporal patterns, as in the case of spiralling sources and saddles.
3   The social interactions amongst cases are also important, as are the hierarchical social contexts in which these relationships take place.
4   And, finally, the complex set of relationships amongst cases is best examined using the tools of network science and simulation.

Speaking of case-based methods, it would be useful to quickly review a bit more about this approach, as well as its methodological platform and companion software.

COMPLEX-IT and the SACS Toolkit

The utility of case-based modelling is that it is a mixed-methods, computationally grounded approach to modelling complex systems, particularly in terms of large data sets (Castellani et al., 2016; Castellani & Rajaram, 2012; Rajaram & Castellani, 2012, 2014). The methodological platform for case-based modelling is the SACS Toolkit, which provides users with a series of steps and procedures (as well as a mathematical justification) for modelling complex systems in case-based terms. Also, in line with case-based complexity, the purpose of the SACS Toolkit is to model multiple trajectories (particularly across time/space) in the form of major and minor trends, which it then visually and statistically data mines for both key global–temporal dynamics and unique network-based relationships. The SACS Toolkit also data mines its results to either (a) predict novel cases or trends or (b) simulate different case-based scenarios. For an in-depth overview of the SACS Toolkit, including its mathematical foundation, go to www.art-sciencefactory. com/cases.html.

As shown in Figure 6.1, the software companion to the SACS Toolkit is COMPLEX-IT (www.art-sciencefactory.com/complexit.html). The purpose of COMPLEX-IT (which is an evolving project) is to make the otherwise highly complex tools and techniques of data mining accessible to a wider and less technical audience. To do that, COMPLEX-IT improves the user-centredness of data mining by opening-up the 'black box' of computational thinking – which it does in two key ways: functionality and interface design. COMPLEX-IT's *functionality* is unique because it runs a specific suite of techniques that support case-based data exploration, modelling and prediction. In turn, COMPLEX-IT's tab-driven interface provides users a seamless, simpler and visually intuitive platform. Also, advanced users can examine, download or modify COMPLEX-IT's algorithms, results, and code. Currently, COMPLEX-IT is available as both an online and a downloadable platform.

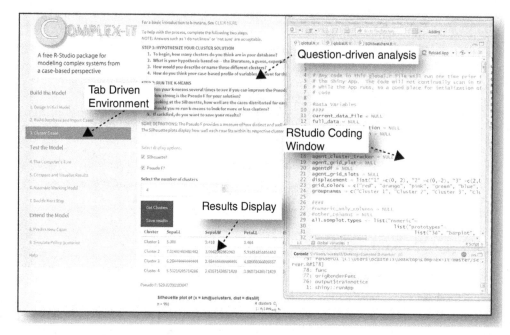

Figure 6.1   COMPLEX-IT and RStudio

COMPLEX-IT's suite includes (a) *k*-means cluster analysis, (b) the Kohonen topographical neural net, (c) a series of data visualisation techniques, (d) case prediction, (e) a platform for case-based scenario simulation and (f) a tab for designing a suite of basic agent-based models, which can be shared with programmers. COMPLEX-IT also includes a step-by-step series of questions that, concurrent with the actual process of data analysis, take the user through the model design process by helping them develop a systems map of their topic – all of which ends with a generated report on the results of one's study.

As should be evident, COMPLEX-IT and the SACS Toolkit integrate a wide range of data mining techniques, including most of the methods we will discuss in the current book. COMPLEX-IT and the SACS Toolkit also make use of qualitative techniques, such as grounded theory and historical analysis. In other words, COMPLEX-IT and the SACS Toolkit are methodologically unique in their ability to bridge the gap between quantitative and qualitative methods, as well as statistics and computational modelling.

And, it is because of their uniqueness that we have mentioned them here, as they function as companions to (and outlets for) the current book and its views on data mining and big data. In other words, for those readers interested in taking the next step, COMPLEX-IT and the SACS Toolkit offer a useful way to data mine big data from a *case-based complex systems perspective.*

But first, before getting there, we need an ontological foundation on which to ground our approach. And so we will turn to that now.

The ontology of big data

> Like geological stratum, many of the software systems running our digital world today are comprised of code built on top of older code; it's like going on an archeological expedition when things crash and you have to dig through the layers of programming language to fix it! (Betsy Schaeffer, personal communication, 5 April 2018)

At its most basic, ontology addresses the question: What is the nature of 'being?' To which one almost immediately asks: The 'being' of what? Are we talking about the 'being' of Being? Or, the 'being' of people? Or, are we talking about the 'being' of physical reality or the mind? Or, perhaps even less profound, are we talking about the 'being' of more concrete things, like computers or software packages or databases?

It turns out that, while most scholars tend to focus on the first couple of questions, ontology actually concerns all of the above. And, if we are going to ever overcome the controversies confronting big data and data mining today, which we outlined in Part I of our travels – particularly how simulated big data is replacing the reality it was created to represent – we need to come to grips with this ontological complexity, sufficient to place our own approach within these wider arguments. In other words, we need to engage in an ontological archaeology of big data.

The archaeology of big data ontologies

Based on the work of the French historian and philosopher Michel Foucault – in combination with fields such as digital sociology and the sociology of technology – one could envision (as my colleague Betsy Schaeffer suggested) a new transdisciplinary field of study, something akin to the archaeology of big data ontologies, which would focus on an investigation of the layers of coding and programming languages through which our big data globalised world is emerging – from machine language up – and the various intersections (or lack thereof) of their corresponding ontologies. For example, such a field would seek to understand (a) how our global cyber-infrastructure and information systems form the colliding and conflicted ontological boundaries (or limits) of our digital and bioecological life; (b) and, in turn, how these contradictory and incomplete collisions (and the power relations upon which they are based and produced) define our epistemological understanding of the contemporary digital and bioecological world(s) in which we live (Konys, 2016; Mackenzie, 2017), as well as the corresponding degree of intellectual passivity we embrace as users of this technology.

Unearthing the layers of ontological complexity

To aid in such an analysis, one would first need a taxonomy. In fact, by our count, the ontology of big data can be organised into five major types, within which multiple subtypes and approaches exist. Here, then, we will review these five, mainly to establish our case-based place within them.

- *Philosophical ontology:* This ontological type is the most classic and is, by definition, what most think of when using the term. This ontology is generally the domain of philosophy, religious studies and the humanities. It is concerned with ultimate truth about the fundamental nature of being, both in terms of life and the universe – that is, spiritual, mental and material reality. The number of different philosophical ontologies is, as everyone knows, rather significant, going all the way back to the ancients. More recent manifestations include neo-positivism, postmodernism, social constructionism, post-structuralism, feminism, critical realism and complex realism – as well as the numerous fissures and factions within and across these subtypes.

    o   While some may find such in-fighting tedious, it is nonetheless massively important, mainly because these ideas have directly and indirectly influenced the fields of data mining and big data, particularly in terms of seriously important discussions such as the following: What constitutes good data? When is enough data enough? How can we be sure our data are valid and reliable? What is the difference between the real world and the simulated world; or, are all such distinctions currently moot? And, related, are digital social trends even real? (Marres, 2017).

    o   For example, as we discussed in Chapter 3, one key camp in the world of big data sees no significant need for social theory, as big data is, in many ways, reality! In turn, others, such as those embracing a complex realism (Byrne & Callaghan, 2013), see big databases as the polar opposite: they are, at best, imperfect, incomplete and partial traces of the actual social complexity being studied and therefore to be held in constant suspicion and concern.

    o   In fact, of the various positions, the one within which we will ground our current mathematical formalisms is complex realism: which, in addition to the above point, basically argues that, while reality can indeed be understood, the epistemological challenge is that no one scientific model is sufficient – no matter how big data driven it is – as reality is ontologically far too complex. Therefore, at best, we only have traces of the complex social systems we study (Byrne & Callaghan, 2013; Williams & Dyer, 2017).

- *Information science ontology:* This ontological type is just as important as the first, but (oddly enough) the least known outside the library and the fields of computer and information science. It is concerned with how best to use information systems to represent some domain of life. In terms of a definition, an information ontology is defined as a logical system (hard copy or electronic) that names and defines the types, properties and interrelationships amongst a domain of entities.

    o   It does this using simple subject–predicate–object statements, which are called *triples.* The most widely used online format for constructing triples is called

OWL (Web Ontology Language). A simple example from the world of airline travel – as in the case of NASA Air Traffic Management Data Integration – would be for the departure and arrival of a plane, which we will call BC525. A triple for this plane might be <BC525 hasOriginAirport JFK>. In this triple, BC525 is the entity in the domain 'Planes arriving and leaving the United States' and it is related to the entity JFK through the predicate *hasOriginAirport*.

o   What is also great about OWL is that the triples forming such an airline ontology can be visualised as a directed network, so that the entire ontology can be examined for logical consistency. Figure 6.2, for example, shows what a graph of a segment of the ontology 'Planes arriving and leaving the United States' would look like.

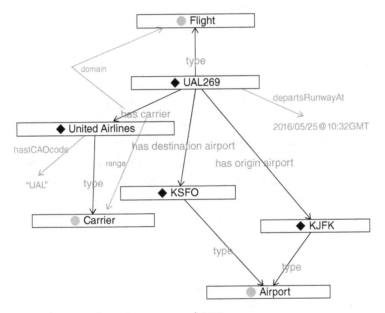

Figure 6.2   Visualisation of graph segment of OWL

Note. OWL = Web Ontology Language.

In terms of big data, however, the ultimate power of an information ontology is its tremendous capacity to link together otherwise disparate and heterogeneous (and ultimately incompatible) databases and software systems into a larger electronic (and potentially global) network. All of this is tremendously powerful because – as we experience every day using our smart phones – it allows for better data/information exchange, communication, integration, query, retrieval, extraction, analysis, reporting and decision-making (Keller, 2016; Kitchin & McArdle, 2016). One example, shown in Figure 6.3, is the ability to map (in real time) all flights around the world based on the simple triple we defined earlier. (For a video of Figure 6.3, see www.nasa.gov/aero/nasa-air-traffic-management-research-tool-shows-new-colors.)

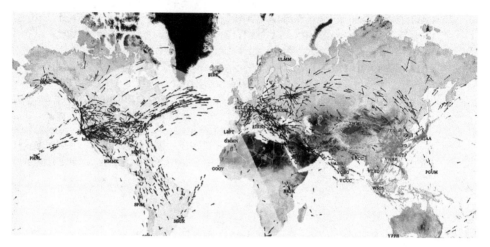

Figure 6.3 Discrete map of all global flights

In short, information ontologies constitute the globalised backbone of big data. In other words, in many instances, big data is only as good as the ontologies upon which it is based, and the ever-present biases, errors, limitations, conflicts, prejudices and imperfections contained within it. As such, in terms of our own formalisms, we will situate ourselves within the ontology of information ontologies. And we do so because we are ultimately concerned with how, from a complex and critical realist perspective, these information ontologies create the big data traces of the complex social systems being data mined and studied.

- *The ontological structure of big data:* The third ontology is the counterpart to the second type. Here, the concerns are the same as those raised in Chapter 3 (e.g. do big data represent reality; or have they become their own reality?) but also, mainly, whether big data databases meet the standards of their own ontology – that is, the five Vs of big data: variety, velocity, variability, veracity, and vulnerability. For example, as most current research shows, many big data databases do not meet these criteria (Konys, 2016). Given such ontological shortcomings, we suggest a useful synonym for 'big data' to be 'complex data', as it seems the more apt ontological description. All of this leads to the next ontology.
- *The ontology of complexity:* This ontological type is concerned with several of the issues discussed in Chapter 5, such as what is the true nature of a complex system (Cilliers, 1998)? Is it, for example, a case of disorganised or organised complexity? Or, is it a matter or restrictive versus general complexity? Also, what are the key characteristics of a complex system? For example, are all complex systems self-organising and emergent? Or is there no such common thing, pointing to the reality that multiple types of complex systems exist? And given the answers to such questions, from an epistemological perspective, are any such complex systems knowable? And, if so, in what ways? Or, alternatively, what are the limits of our knowing?

As should be evident, the answers to these questions have important implications for how one understands the complexities of big data (Cilliers, 1998). For us, given our commitment to complex realism, we will combine Morin's ontology of general complexity with Weaver's view of organised complexity.

- *The ontology of method:* This final ontology has to do with the methodology upon which various methods are based. Contrary to popular opinion, methods have their own ontological viewpoints, the same as the scholars that use them. Unfortunately, as we suggested in Part I of our tour, many of those working in the fields of data mining and big data give little thought to such issues. For example, it is crucial to realise that, in many instances, the big data answers we get from our models come from the data mining questions we ask. Case in point, if I use a network toolkit to analyse a database, I am going to find a network; if I cluster these same data, I will find key trends; and if I reduce these data to their most salient three or four variables, I will find them. How do I know if any of these ontological assumptions about the reality of these objects of study are right?

Given such concerns – and how we have positioned ourselves relative to the above ontological debates – in terms of methodology, we will embrace an interdisciplinary mixed-methods perspective, pitting the relative advantages and limits of their various ontological positions against one another, all in the effort to develop a more rigorous model process.

The formalisms of case-based complexity

The utility of our case-based ontological position is that it allows us to create a series of mathematical formalisms that underlie (and therefore help to explain and link together) the majority of the tools and techniques of data mining. These data mining formalisms, which we will outline now, concern the following nine issues:

1   The primacy of cases
2   The twin concepts of a vector
3   Cataloguing and grouping case-based profiles
4   Measuring the distance between cases
5   Cataloguing case profiles
6   Understanding the diversity of case profiles
7   Defining the concept of time and the study of static and longitudinal databases
8   Understanding the concept of velocity and knowing the difference between discrete and dynamic modelling of time and change
9   Grasping the concept of a vector field

What is a case?

As we have suggested already, a **case *c*** is simply an abstract description of the qualitative and quantitative characteristics of some object under study (Castellani et al.,

2019; Castellani & Rajaram, 2012). In this way, cases also constitute the building blocks of a set of complex data or, in turn, a larger complex system. Also, in those instances where dynamics or interactions are being studied, cases are the agents that drive change. We will denote by c_i, the ith case in a system consisting of N cases, where N is usually a large number. As such, i is an index that can take on values from 1 to N.

The state of a case c_i is described by its profile, as measured by one or more variables x_{ij}, where j can take on integer values from 1 to k. In other words, each case has a profile that can be described by the values taken on by the k variables $(x_{i1}, x_{i2}, ..., x_{ik})$. This arrangement of the variables in the form of a row is called a row vector. Hence, $c_i = (x_{i1}, x_{i2}, ..., x_{ik})$ denotes the profile of the ith case c_i.

We envision a large database D consisting of row vectors $c_i = (x_{i1}, x_{i2}, ..., x_{ik})$, where each element x_{ij} is a measured variable for some **case profile** $c_i(t)$, as defined for a particular instant of time t. Suppressing the dependence on time t, one can represent such a database D in matrix form as shown below:

$$D = \begin{bmatrix} c_1 \\ \vdots \\ c_n \end{bmatrix} = \begin{bmatrix} x_{11} & \cdots & x_{1k} \\ \vdots & \ddots & \vdots \\ x_{n1} & \cdots & x_{nk} \end{bmatrix}. \tag{6.1}$$

In Equation (6.1), each row in the database D is a case c_i, whose instantaneous profile is given by the k variables that constitute the vector c_i. If the case profile has only two variables, then the profile can be plotted on graph paper with its profile $c_i = (x_{i1}, x_{i2})$ as the x- and y-coordinates, respectively. In big data databases, however, where we have more than two variables describing the profile, the case profile often cannot be plotted per se but has a similar interpretation as a generalisation of a two-dimensional (2D) vector.

Two definitions of a vector

As we have already suggested, a vector is a mathematical object that contains a number of elements, each of which takes on numerical values. A vector can be written as a row (as above in Equation 6.1) or a column. For example, $c_i = (x_{i1}, x_{i2}, ..., x_{ik})$ is a row vector that describes the profile of the case c_i. This has k elements and each element can take on numerical values. Vectors that have the same length can be added or subtracted. So, row vectors c_i are synonymous with cases from a mathematical (statistical) standpoint.

Furthermore, every point in two dimensions has an x-coordinate and a y-coordinate and hence can be represented as (x, y), where x and y can take on numerical values.

Therefore, every point in two dimensions is actually a vector. And conversely, every vector in two dimensions is equivalent to a point which has an x-coordinate and a y-coordinate. This second insight is a key because, as in physics, we can use it to introduce the idea of vectors as quantities that have a magnitude and a direction.

As shown in Figure 6.4, to visualise the magnitude and direction of a vector (a.k.a. case) given by (x, y) in two dimensions, we imagine drawing an arrow from the origin $(0,0)$ to the given point (x, y) with its tail at $(0,0)$ and head at (x, y). The length of this arrow is the magnitude and the direction given by the arrow head is the direction of the vector (x, y). In this way, then, vectors in physics are equivalent to vectors in conventional statistics, as introduced above. And this link extends to k-dimensional space as well. A case profile given by $c_i = (x_{i1}, x_{i2}, ..., x_{ik})$ is simply a k-dimensional vector with numerical elements for each of its components. Even though we cannot visualise this as a vector with magnitude and direction in two dimensions, the intuition carries over. Each choice for the component variables x_{ij} fixes a single profile for the case. And a change in the value or values of the components x_{ij} changes the profile of the case.

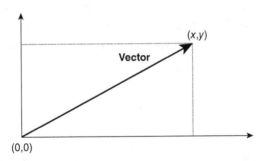

Figure 6.4 Example of an individual vector plotted in two dimensions

In terms of data mining, our formal linkage of these two concepts of a vector is crucial because – as we will see later – it allows us to connect, for example, data mining methods that **cluster** or catalogue cases with those that study aggregate trends across time/space, as in the case of modelling the increases or decreases in the velocity of Twitter trends for different airlines based on how they respond to weather-based flight delays.

Cataloguing and grouping case profiles

As we will see with many of the techniques of data mining, a major focus is on grouping similar cases and then, in turn, using those groupings to predict the membership of new or novel cases. Case in point: clustering the best and worst airports into their respective groups to see what makes them the best (or worst), and then looking at the profiles of other airports to see into which of the two they fall and why.

Also, although we cannot address this issue here, data mining techniques also exist for clustering relational databases (obtained from networks – see Chapter 12) and geospatial data (see Chapter 11). Also, these techniques apply to both static and longitudinal data (see section 'The Notion of Time t'). In the latter case, the database is written as $D(t)$, and the clusters of cases will also vary with time in a dynamic fashion. Understanding the relationships between the case clusters and the reason for their complex dynamics across time t is, in short, the main goal of studying the complexity of a database D.

In this chapter, we will focus on clustering cases based on the distance matrix. However, in Chapters 11 and 12 – as just suggested – we will take a glimpse into other types of data sets and profiles.

Mathematical distance between cases

In terms of clustering, the idea of similarity of case profiles can be mathematically quantified using the **Euclidean distance** $\|.\|_E$. Given that case profiles are nothing but vectors (or equivalently points with coordinates in space), the Euclidean distance between two cases $c_i = (x_{i1}, x_{i2}, ..., x_{ik})$ and $c_j = (x_{j1}, x_{j2}, ..., x_{jk})$ is given by the following formula:

$$\| c_i - c_j \|_E = \sqrt{(c_{i1} - c_{j1})^2 + (c_{i2} - c_{j2})^2 + \cdots + (c_{ik} - c_{jk})^2}. \tag{6.2}$$

The Euclidean distance satisfies the following three general conditions:

1   $\| c_i - c_j \|_E > 0$. This says that distance between two distinct cases has to be positive.
2   $\| c_i - c_j \|_E = \| c_i - c_j \|_E$. This says that the order between the cases does not matter while measuring distance between cases.
3   $\| c_i - c_j \|_E + \| c_j - c_k \|_E \geq \| c_i - c_k \|_E$. This is the triangle inequality which states that, if we consider cases as points, then the sum of two sides of a triangle is always larger on the third side, with equality happening only when the points are collinear.

In general, any notion of distance that satisfies the above three conditions is termed a *metric* in mathematics. A set, along with such a metric is termed a *metric space*, and the study of such metric spaces is a called *point-set topology*. Using the idea of metric, one can talk about *convergence* of a sequence of cases and the idea of *closeness* of cases as well.

In two dimensions, given two case profiles $c_A = (x_{A1}, x_{A2})$ and $c_B = (x_{B1}, x_{B2})$, the distance between the two profiles c_A and c_B is visualised as follows. Plot the two points with x- and y-coordinates (x_{A1}, x_{A2}) and (x_{B1}, x_{B2}), and draw a line joining the two points on graph paper. The length of this line is simply given by $\|c_A - c_B\|_E$ as shown in Equation (6.2) above. It is to be noted that there are several other notions of distance between cases, but the Euclidean distance is the easiest to visualise and the one most often used in data mining.

Cataloguing case profiles

Given a large database D with case profiles c_i forming its row vectors as shown in Equation (6.1), the idea of cataloguing case profiles can be understood using the Euclidean distance as follows. First, we would want to divide the set of cases (rows of D) into groups or clusters C_i that have similar case profiles – that is, the cases c_i in clusters C_i are closer to each other in Euclidean distance than cases in a different cluster C_j where $i \neq j$ (i.e. clusters are essentially disjoint sets of case profiles that are closer in Euclidean distance to each other and farther than cases in other clusters).

There are a number of data mining methods available for clustering similar case profiles. The k-means and the self-organising map, upon which case-based methods are based – including our software, COMPLEX-IT (www.art-sciencefactory.com/complexit.html) – are two such methods.

So, clustering is simply a mathematical technique that lets us group together cases that have similar profiles – as well as position them away from groups of cases with different profiles. Also, in terms of position, the concepts of 'closer' and 'farther' are generally measured according to the Euclidean distance given in Equation (6.2). Once the clustering operation is completed, one can then catalogue and name each cluster depending on the value or range of values of the profile variables. For example, all short-route flights that belong to the cluster which has minimal delays or technical problems could be classified as the reliable flight group.

In terms of data mining to explore a database, the number of clusters that make sense is arrived at by doing iterations between mathematical convergence and expert opinion. Sometimes, the clusters of case profiles that mathematics gives us may not be meaningful, and at other times, it might indicate a new grouping that was not previously observed in the study.

One can visualise the idea of cataloguing case profiles using the idea of a network or graph. If we imagine each case as a point in space (node) and lines connecting cases, with the closer cases having smaller line lengths (links), then case profiles that are similar in Euclidean distance will be near to each other, and case profiles that are very dissimilar will be farther away with large link lengths. In this way, clusters of similar cases can be identified as hubs in the network (a collection of crowded nodes all with very small link lengths). Different clusters that are very dissimilar from each other will be far away from each other in the network graph.

The idea of cataloguing case profiles using clustering techniques is very fundamental to studying the complexity of a large database D without throwing away any of the cases. This is because, after the cataloguing process, each cluster can be studied separately for its own characteristics both from a static and a dynamic viewpoint. By clustering similar case profiles, we have streamlined the analysis into sub-problems of analysis of clusters. The key point here is that we don't neglect any of the clusters simply because it has a smaller number of cases but treat that cluster separately and try to understand its characteristics – which is one of the main ways that data mining differs significantly from conventional statistics, with its focus on aggregate averages!

Once the clustering process is complete, one can compute the mean (or centre) of each cluster C_i by 'averaging out' the values of the profile variables for all cases c_i in the cluster C_i, giving us the profile of the cluster center $\bar{c}_i$. One can then talk about the distances between the clusters using the similarity or distance matrix. If we assume that there are p number of clusters $C_1, C_2, ..., C_p$, then the p by p Euclidean distance matrix D_E is given by

$$D_E = \begin{bmatrix} d_{11} & d_{12} & \cdots & d_{1p} \\ d_{21} & d_{22} & \cdots & d_{2p} \\ \vdots & \ddots & \ddots & \vdots \\ d_{p1} & d_{p2} & \cdots & d_{pp} \end{bmatrix}. \tag{6.3}$$

The distance matrix D_E is symmetric where $d_{ij} = d_{ji}$, and d_{ij} gives us the distance between the cluster centres $\bar{c}_i$ and $\bar{c}_j$ of clusters C_i and C_j, respectively.

As we have hinted at a couple of times now, the number of clusters is usually a trade-off between the ability to easily classify the clusters using practical considerations and keeping the variation of profiles within the clusters to a reasonable number. For example, how fine-grained does an airline need its analysis of highly unreliable short-route flights to be? Does it need only a couple of clusters or dozens?

Finally, assuming the process of iteration between the mathematical process and consultation with experts has been done, the mean of each cluster $\bar{c}_i$ will serve as a typical profile in that cluster and, hence, can be utilised for further modelling purposes. Again, it is to be noted that one can go back to the individual case profiles whenever needed, and no case is eliminated. However, given that the clustering process subdivides the database D into multiple clusters with similar profiles, using the mean case profile $\bar{c}_i$ at this stage for any further mathematical modelling or validation does not reduce the complexity in the database D from the standpoint of method.

Diversity of case profiles

As with our example of searching for highly unreliable short-route flights, we cluster and catalogue case profiles with the goal of cataloguing the desired level of diversity of the case profiles in a database. Mathematically, **diversity** refers to 'richness' and 'evenness' of case profiles. For example, one can plot a histogram of some set of clusters, with their relative frequency of occurrence on the y-axis. The highest diversity is achieved if all case profiles occur with the same relative frequency, and the lowest diversity is achieved if all the cases belong to the same cluster – that is, there is a single case profile that can describe all the cases in D. And so, all clustering techniques, whether static in time or dynamic, lead to a classification and cataloguing of the diversity of case profiles seen in a given database D.

And this point, which we have outlined already, deserves repeating: clustering is an important way to identify and characterise some fundamental case profiles that are repeated in the database with slight variations. By performing clustering, however, we are not reducing the number of cases, but easing our analytical framework to study the complexity in the database D – which is another major way that data mining, and also the complexity sciences, differ from conventional statistics: they do not seek to remove complexity; instead, they seek to organise it! In other words, by studying case clusters we shift our focus from measures of centrality to methods that focus on measures of diversity.

The notion of time t

There are a number of ways one can conceptualise time. However, the simplest realisation is the assumption that there is a stopwatch somewhere, and while measuring the variables x_{ij} in D, time has been allowed to elapse, and a record of the time elapsed is inherently monitored. So in general, D is actually $D(t)$ – that is, for each choice of time instant t_j, the cases $c_i(t_j)$ and their respective profiles will change, thereby giving an entirely different 'snapshot' of the database $D(t_j)$. Even though in practice $D(t)$ can only be measured at discrete instants of time t_j, the goal is to develop methods that will 'fill in the gap' and give us a sense of the underlying dynamics that govern the evolution of the case profiles $c_i(t)$ as time evolves continuously.

Profiles that vary with time

Each case profile $c_i = (x_{i1}, x_{i2}, ..., x_{ik})$ for a time-varying database $D(t)$ is represented at $c_i(t)$ and will have variables $x_{ij}(t)$ that are functions of time. So, formally, the case profiles can be written as $c_i(t) = (x_{i1}(t), x_{i2}(t), ..., x_{ik}(t))$. Like mentioned above, time can be continuous or discrete. For most practical situations, the case profiles are measured only at discrete instants of time t_j, thereby leading to the notation $c_i(t_j) = \left(x_{i1}(t_j), x_{i2}(t_j), ..., x_{ik}(t_j) \right)$.

However, if the original case profiles actually consist of a continuous time-varying process – as in the case of airplane routes and weather patterns – then $c_i(t_j)$ has to be treated as a discrete time sample of the continuous case profile evolution $c_i(t)$. The modelling method then has to endeavour to 'fill in the gap' by taking the samples and modelling the evolution of case profiles as a continuous time process. However, it is to be noted that there are instances where the time evolution is naturally discrete. For example, if one of the profile variables is measuring (say) the resting heart rate of an anxious person before flight, then we are only interested in the discrete time instants when the heart rate reaches the minimum, and measurements at other time instants are meaningless.

Static clustering in time

Given the mathematical description of clustering above, **static clustering** simply means that for a given instant of time t_j, we gather together cases c_i that have similar case profiles given by their trace variables x_{ij} into separate and disjoint sets. Each cluster $C_i(t_j)$ is simply a set of all case profiles that look more similar to each other than profiles in other clusters at the time instant t_j. Hence, if the entire database was measured only at a single time instant t_j, then clusters remain static and do not change. We have discussed the idea behind static clustering in the section 'Cataloguing and Grouping Case Profiles'.

Dynamic clustering of trajectories

While static clustering gives us a sense of the variation in case profiles at a fixed time instant t_j without marginalising them, the ultimate goal of data mining many 'big data' databases is to model the dynamics of cases and how they change across time/ space – think, for example, of geospatial modelling of airline traffic, weather patterns or Twitter feeds. So, instead of asking what case profiles are seen at a given instant of time t_j, the question now becomes: Which case profile trajectories are similar, or in other words, what are some characteristic variations of case profile trajectories? In simpler terms, the questions really are as follows: Which case profile trajectories have similar trends across time? How do the memberships in these profiles vary across time? Are there new profiles that appear at later time instances? And, are there existing profiles that vanish across time?

The first step towards gleaning out interesting dynamics within the case trajectories is to look for some fundamental trends in the trajectories. It is assumed that we
have measured the database at samples of time instants in the form of $D(t_j)$; that is,
we have snapshots of the database at K time instants t_j, where the index j can vary
(say) from 1 to K. By trends, we mean different kinds of trajectories – that is, some
that are oscillating, some that are monotonic and so on. The focus now is to look at
similar trends in case trajectories $c_i(t)$. For example, if we have two variables (x_{i1}, x_{i2}),
then we would append their trajectories as follows:

$$T_i = \left(x_{i1}(t_1), x_{i1}(t_2), x_{i1}(t_3), ..., x_{i1}(t_K); x_{i2}(t_1), x_{i2}(t_2), x_{i2}(t_3), ..., x_{i2}(t_K) \right),$$

thereby obtaining a long string of values when time t is varied across its sampling
points. So T_i would be the ith case profile trajectory. We would now look for sets of
similar trajectories T_i and place together trajectories that are similar.

We denote the ith trajectory cluster by $C_i^T(t)$, and this will contain all trajectories
that follow the same trend. Clustering this way, we will arrive at a set of mathematical case profile trajectory clusters $C_i^T(t)$, and each of these trajectory clusters needs
to be classified with the help of experts in the field of study. Once again, just like in
the static clustering method, the number of trajectory clusters will be arrived at using
a process of trade-off between interesting dynamics and practical use. The mean of
each cluster $C_i^T(t)$, denoted by $\bar{c}_i(t)$, is the mathematical trend in the cluster. If the
clustering is done well, then the mean will be a good representative of all the trajectories in the cluster $C_i^T(t)$ and will mimic the same variations seen in the trajectories
belonging to the cluster.

A vector field

Although we have repeatedly relied upon the concept of a vector field, we need,
finally, to outline it formally. And so, as our last formalism, we will do that now.

The state space

Assuming that we have two profile variables for the case profile $c_i = (x_{i1}, x_{i2})$, the trajectories $c_i(t) = (x_{i1}(t), x_{i2}(t))$ with samples $c_i(t_j) = (x_{i1}(t_j), x_{i2}(t_j))$ in the database $D(t_j)$,
can be plotted in two different ways. In the first kind of plot (called the *time domain
plot*), we can plot the time t on the x-axis and the value of the variable $x_{i1}(t)$ on the
y-axis, thereby showing the trajectory of the first variable x_{i1} as a function of time t.
The same can be done for the second variable trajectory $x_{i2}(t)$, and in this way we have

two graphs each showing the trajectory of a particular case profile variable, and hence the case profile trajectory $c_i(t)$ itself. This is the traditional viewpoint of trajectories.

As shown in Figure 6.5, the second kind of plot (also known as *trajectory in state space*) involves plotting the x_{i1} on the x-axis and x_{i2} on the y-axis as ordered pairs $(x_{i1}(t), x_{i2}(t))$ for each time instant t_j. **State space** here refers to the rectangular region (with x_{i1} on the x-axis and x_{i2} on the y-axis) that spans the range of values of the variables x_{i1} and x_{i2}. In the state space trajectory plot, time is implicit and cannot be seen from the graph, but interesting dynamics can be visualised better. For example, if a particular **case trajectory** $c_i(t) = (x_{i1}(t), x_{i2}(t))$ remains in a part of the state space, or if it oscillates for example, these can be identified more easily in the state space plot than in the time domain plot. In Figure 6.5, for example, we identified a saddle point and a spiralling source.

A discrete vector field of velocities of trajectories

For the next few paragraphs in this section, we will introduce the idea of a **discrete vector field** first, and then explain the need for such an object in the next section. So, for now, take the time to grasp the concept before we explain why it is useful for data mining big data.

We imagine a case profile as a 2D point, and we also assume that the range of case profiles in the database D can be enclosed within a rectangular region in 2D space. The same idea can be extended in higher dimensions as well. With this in mind, modelling the motion of the clusters in continuous time would require the knowledge of the instantaneous **velocity** of each case – which takes us back to our twin notions of a vector discussed earlier!

For example, in two dimensions $c_i(t) = (x_{i1}(t), x_{i2}(t))$ is a trajectory of the case c_i. Like this, there are multiple case trajectories within the database $D(t)$. Its instantaneous velocity is simply the first derivative denoted by $\dot{c}_i(t) = (\dot{x}_{i1}(t), \dot{x}_{i2}(t))$. There are several methods to compute the instantaneous velocity given the trajectory $c_i(t)$. Since the velocity $\dot{c}_i(t)$ is also a vector, the information about the instantaneous velocity can be visualised as an arrow $(\dot{x}_{i1}(t), \dot{x}_{i2}(t))$ which is placed at the coordinates $(x_{i1}(t), x_{i2}(t))$.

If we suppress the dependence on t, then every point in 2D space (x_{i1}, x_{i2}) represents a case profile from the database D, and we can place an arrow $(\dot{x}_{i1}, \dot{x}_{i2})$ representing the instantaneous velocity of the case profile with its tail at (x_{i1}, x_{i2}). The length of the arrow $(\dot{x}_{i1}, \dot{x}_{i2})$ is the Euclidean distance between $(0,0)$ and $(\dot{x}_{i1}, \dot{x}_{i2})$, and the direction is the same as the arrow with tail at $(0,0)$ and head at the point with coordinates $(\dot{x}_{i1}, \dot{x}_{i2})$, except once the magnitude and direction are known, we now place this velocity vector with its tail at (x_{i1}, x_{i2}). With this procedure – and this is key! – we can now imagine the entire range of case profiles in two dimensions located at $c_i(t_j)$ filled

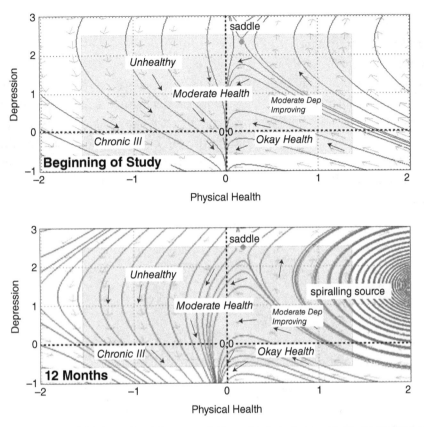

LEGEND: This vector field shows the state-space of all possible trajectories at the beginning and 1st year of our study on co-morbid depression and physical health. All possible trajectories are visualised in the form of arrows (shown in grey between the trend lines), which show direction and velocity; the larger the arrow the faster the trajectory. For the purposes of normalisation, all data were converted to z-scores; as such, coordinate (0,0) is the centre; with the majority of the data falling within two standard deviations (the inner grey area on each graph).

Figure 6.5 Vector field at two time points for co-morbid depression and physical health

Note 1: The graphs were cropped at three standard deviations, in order to visualise more fully the globally dynamic behaviour of the model; while none of the data actually fell outside the first two standard deviations. In other words, this model does not show the trajectories of specific cases and should not be read as such. Instead, it is read as a map of all possible trajectories, with the focus on identifying (as the results sections does) major global dynamics. Note 2: The x-axis is physical health (with poor physical health on the left and good physical health on the right); the y-axis is depression, going from low to high levels of depression as one moves upward along the axis. Note 3: Two key global-dynamic behaviours were identified: a saddle point and a spiralling source. The graph for time = 0 was likewise labelled to give the reader a rough sense of the different quadrants, from high physical health and low depression to low physical health and high depression.

with vectors $c_i'(t_j)$ for a fixed time instant t_j. As time evolves, with different values for t, these arrows will change magnitude and direction. This arrangement is termed as a 2D vector field and has an analogous extension in higher dimensions as well, which cannot be plotted.

Why is it called discrete?

We note that we only have access to a discrete number of cases, N of them to be exact. However, there are infinitely many points in any 2D rectangular area that spans the range of the case profiles in the data D. Hence, there is a gap in the profiles, as not all mathematically possible case profiles within the rectangular range are present in the database D. Also, as we mentioned before, in practice we only have access to samples of the case profiles $c_i(t_j)$. So in addition to the gap in the profiles, assuming that we are modelling a continuous time process, there is a gap in time t due to the discretely sampled time instants – as shown, for example, in Figure 6.6. Due to these two inherent gaps, we term the vector field discrete.

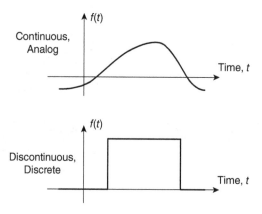

Figure 6.6 Visualisation of discrete versus continuous time

How do we fill the gap?

The discrete vector field is simply a representation of data, in the sense that $c'(t_j)$ is calculated and plotted at the point $c(t_j)$. To fill the gaps mentioned above, one can use a genetic algorithm-based modelling process (which we will discuss in later chapters) to compute the best fit function $f(c,t)$ that will give us $c'(t)$ (which we know from data D) when we plug in c and t. In other words, we are looking for the best function f that can take the case profile c and the time instant t as inputs and can compute the velocity $f(c,t)$, which is fairly close to the velocity seen in the database D. This, in a sense, fills the gap, because such a function f can take in any point c in the rectangular region and any time instant t (even the ones that are not present in the data D) and can compute a velocity vector c'. In this way, $c'(t) \approx f(c,t)$ where the symbol $\approx$ stands for 'approximately equal to'. Here c' comes from data and f comes from the modelling process using genetic algorithms, for example. This is actually a modelling step in the method, where we are going from the data D to a function f representing the instantaneous velocity vectors. The function f is called a **vector field** (with the tacit qualification using the word 'continuous'). For all practical purposes (assuming that the error in the modelling process is small), we can assume that

$$c' = f(c,t), \qquad\qquad (6.4)$$

which is called a **differential equation**. This differential equation is a model for the database $D(t)$ that captures all the interesting complex behaviour seen in the case trajectories $c_i(t)$. Such a differential equation can be solved for $c(t)$, given an initial profile $c(0) = (x_{i_1}(0), x_{i_2}(0))$ for the case trajectory $c(t)$. Since the model fills in the gaps in time and case profiles present in the data D, one can present novel initial profiles and ask what might be the case profile trajectory $c(t)$ if we start with that novel initial scenario.

Why do we need a vector field?

Mathematically speaking, case trajectories can be visualised as curves in state space as explained in the section 'The State Space'. The vector field, then, is simply arrows that are tangential to the state space trajectories at every instant of time. Hence, solving the differential equation (Equation 6.4) simply means that given the arrows f situated at the points c (which has no gaps since f has filled it in), and at time t (which now varies continuously with no gaps as well), can we draw trajectories in state space so that the given arrows are always tangential to these trajectories at all instants of time t. The answer comes from an existence and uniqueness theorem for solutions of differential equations. Without going into too much mathematics, the theorem says that if f is fairly well behaved then we are guaranteed a solution, and such a solution can be numerically computed.

The need for a vector field as a model for the database D is motivated by the potential of differential equations such as Equation (6.4) to capture a variety of complex behaviour in trajectories $c(t)$ that are observed – again, as in the case of weather, air-traffic patterns or the dynamics of a plane in fight, or the evolving complexities of a social media app and so on. Differential equations are the quintessential models of complexity across time and have been used to study a variety of complex systems that exhibit chaotic trajectories, oscillations and so on. As is clear from Equation (6.4), the vector field f is a fundamental unit of a differential equation, and hence we start with the best fit vector field that captures the instantaneous velocities $\dot{c}_i(t)$ from the data, which then serves as a mathematical model that can capture complex trajectory behaviour of case profiles across time.

Once clustering is completed across time to obtain clusters of trajectories $C_i^T(t)$, typically the mean of each cluster trajectory $\bar{C}_i^T(t)$ is utilised to characterise the cluster qualitatively, and all the trajectories in the cluster are used together to obtain a differential equation model given in Equation (6.4). We note that the complexity in the data is not just in the complex behaviour of trajectories (although that is an important facet) but also in the complexity exhibited across different clusters of trajectories $C_i^T(t)$. For example, each cluster $C_i^T(t)$ can exhibit a different complex behaviour across time and, in turn, could further be subdivided in sub-clusters of complex behaviours. Consequently, each cluster or sub-cluster can be separately modelled using a separate differential equation. The level of detail and hierarchy that is required in the modelling process is usually a matter of discussion between the experts in the field. However, the structural framework presented above allows us mathematically to use a single model for the whole database D, a model for each cluster or a model for each case! The flexibility in the modelling process is an important aspect that can be utilised to model up to as fine a level of hierarchy as is needed.

And, with this final point, we come to the end of our review of our mathematical formalisms. Time, now, to turn to a review of our list of key data mining tools and techniques.

Chapter Summary

- Most data mining and computational methods focus on cases and the profiles of variables that describe them – from clustering consumer purchasing patterns to sorting people based on health conditions and symptoms.
- It is therefore possible to create a set of user-friendly mathematical formalisms, including their ontological foundation, which makes the reader's journey across these tools and techniques easier.
- This set of formalisms is called *case-based complexity*. Its framework is called the SACS Toolkit. Its software platform is called COMPLEX-IT, which readers can use to run a variety of the methods discussed in the book from a case-based perspective (www.artsciencefactory.com/complexit.html).
- These formalisms are as follows:

  o The case and its trajectory across time/space are the focus of study, not the individual variables or attributes of which it is comprised.
  o Cases and their trajectories are treated as composites (profiles) comprised of an interdependent, interconnected set of causal conditions, variables, factors or attributes.
  o And, finally, cases and their relationships and trajectories are the methodological equivalent of complex systems – that is, they are emergent, self-organising, non-linear, dynamic, network-like and so on – and therefore should be studied as such.
  o Cases and their trajectories are dynamically evolving across time/space and therefore should be explored to identify their major and minor trends.
  o In turn, these trends should be explored in the aggregate for key global–temporal patterns, as in the case of spiralling sources and saddles.

- The social interactions amongst cases are also important, as are the hierarchical social contexts in which these relationships take place.
- And, finally, the complex set of relationships amongst cases is best examined using the tools of network science and simulation.

Further Reading

Haynes, P. (2017). *Social synthesis: Finding dynamic patterns in complex social systems.* Routledge. https://doi.org/10.4324/9781315458533
This book deals with dynamic pattern synthesis.

Rihoux, B., & Ragin, C. (2009). *Configurational comparative methods: Qualitative comparative analysis (QCA) and related techniques: Vol. 51. Applied social research methods series.* Sage. https://doi.org/10.4135/9781452226569
This book explains qualitative comparative analysis.

7
CLASSIFICATION AND CLUSTERING

Chapter Overview

Top ten airlines

Go to any major travel website and you are most likely to encounter a top ten list – for hotels, vacation hot spots, credit cards, beaches, restaurants and, of course, airlines. The question, however, is always: how valid or reliable are these lists? And what factors are they based upon? For example, price, safety, quality of food, comfort, destinations to which they travel? And, equally relevant, to whom are these factors relevant? For example, as modestly paid academics who are concerned about our ecological footprint, neither of us can afford to travel first class. Nor can we fly private jets! As such, a top ten list of the most pampered flights in the world would not interest us. We would, however, be interested in relatively cheap flights that did reduce, somewhat, our ecological footprint and save us money. As such, we would look for coach fares, non-stop flights and airlines that use biofuels and offer opportunities to purchase carbon offsets. We would also look for airlines that seek to improve their plane efficiency and flight delays. And so, those would be some of the factors we would use to generate our top ten list. The challenge, however, is how? How would we go about actually cataloguing airlines to arrive at our list?

To answer that question, we would need to turn to the data mining techniques of classification and clustering. For more on these methods, we recommend the following, which we used to write the current chapter: Aggarwal (2014), Bailey (1994), Berkhin (2006), Hand and Henley (1997), Jain (2010), Kotsiantis et al. (2007), Kuo et al. (2002), Lu and Weng (2007), Phyu (2009), Quinlan (1986, 1987) and Yuan and Shaw (1995). Also, please note for those who have not read this book in order, we likewise spend considerable time in Chapter 6 outlining the basic ideas behind classification and cluster analysis, as we use these mathematical formalisms, vis-à-vis a case-based complexity approach, as the framework for our review of the methods in Part II of our book.

Classification versus clustering

While classification and clustering both group cases, often using the same mathematical algorithms, the former uses a training set of known case-based clusters to arrive at its results, while the latter is largely exploratory, seeking to identify groupings that may or may not be known. For example, if you already had a training set that contained the classes of ecologically-to-not-so-ecologically friendly airlines and you used that data to train your clustering algorithm – that would be classification. However, if you did not know which airlines were the most or least ecologically friendly and so you needed to explore to find out – that would be more in the realm of clustering for knowledge discovery. Let us explain.

In general, given a database D, the idea of classification entails subdividing the given set of cases $\{c_i\}_{i=1}^n$ into p pre-defined *classes* (hence the name classification), based on a certain characteristic profile. These classes are known a priori, due to the usage of a well-conditioned training set of cases used (which are used to train the classification algorithm), or due to prior knowledge of the characteristic profiles of the cases c_i at hand. The key point here is that the classes (i.e. clusters) are already known and each case is known to fit into one of the classes C_i a priori, and the only unknown is the membership information for all cases c_i.

Another angle of explanation here is when the entire database D is subdivided into a disjoint partition of sets C_i. Disjoint means that there is nothing in common amongst the classes C_i (or mathematically $C_i \cap C_j = \emptyset \ \forall i \neq j$), and partition means that the C_i s put together give back D (or mathematically $\bigcup_{i=1}^p C_i = D$). The idea here is fundamentally similar to assigning letter grades to different airlines, for example, based on some set of factors. The letter grades for the airlines are classes, and each company will automatically be classified according to a letter grade based on the grading scheme. The letter grades are the predefined classes, and the grading scheme is the rule that assigns each letter grade to an airline.

However, when one does clustering, the characterisation of the clusters C_i (or $C_i^T(t)$, if it is **dynamic clustering**) are unknown a priori. Hence, in addition to clustering the cases (or case trajectories for longitudinal data), one has to spend time trying to identify if there is indeed any contextual meaning associated with the clusters. In doing so, it might make sense to combine a few of the clusters, or subdivide an existing cluster into sub-clusters if there is sufficient delineation in the characteristic profiles (or trends if we are clustering trajectories).

An example here is a study of customer loyalty to an airline across time as it changes its awards policy. There might be several different classes of trends (some major and some minor) that characterise customer loyalty trajectories, and the number and character of these trends are, again, unknown. So the study would follow a large number of customers and cluster their loyalty trajectories, and then after expert consultation, these clusters (classes) will be contextualised, in addition to possible combination or splitting of existing trajectory clusters. With this general distinction in mind, we turn now to some of the actual techniques.

Classification schemes

Despite their differences, most classification schemes involve training an algorithm to identify classes based on some known data set. This is followed by using the classification algorithm to examine new data and classify the new cases c_i based on closeness of the profile of c_i to previously trained classes. For this reason, most classification schemes are alternatively termed *supervised learning methods*. Factors considered relevant to which technique is used include (a) reliability and validity, (b) the computational expense and the ease of the process of training, (c) the ability of the technique to handle large data sets, (d) the robustness of the algorithm to replicate the classes to a fair degree and (e) the ability to extract from the technique's 'black box' the rules by which it arrived at these results.

Decision tree induction

One of the more widely used techniques in data mining is the decision tree (Quinlan, 1986, 1987; Yuan & Shaw, 1995). A decision tree is a graph where each node invokes a test on a case, and each link would be an answer. The model training data set is first used to sharpen the tests at each node and also the links so the tree classifies the training data perfectly with no errors. Then the unclassified data is passed through the tree. The cases will pass through links and nodes until the end where there are no more links. This last level will indicate the classes that the tree has assigned to the cases. Decision tree schemes are known to be NP-complete; that is, one can only develop heuristic algorithms that cannot guarantee a globally optimal classification. However, these schemes are known to be robust and have the ability to handle large data sets in a short amount of time. The biggest advantage is that this technique can handle numerical as well as categorical data. Another example of an NP-complete problem is the celebrated travelling salesperson problem, where it is known that the computational time increases exponentially, but there are several suboptimal heuristic algorithms that are available for this problem. For more on decision trees, we highly recommend Quinlan (1986), which has been cited almost 20,000 times!

As shown in Figure 7.1, in the airline industry, decision trees are highly useful, particularly when it comes to deciding when to discount the prices for non-purchased seats (Tirenni et al., 2007). For example, in addition to introducing baggage fees, if an airline decides to discount too late, then it runs the risk that its empty seats will not sell and they will lose money; however, if they decide to discount too early, they likewise will lose money – however, potentially not as much. In these instances, the decision tree is fairly simple and is defined as the probability p of selling a regular ticket if it is not discounted. Obviously, a variety of other factors could be added to this basic tree to make the decision more sophisticated. But, that does give one a basic sense of how it works. And, also, the more valid and reliable the training set, the more confidence one can put in the probabilities it gives.

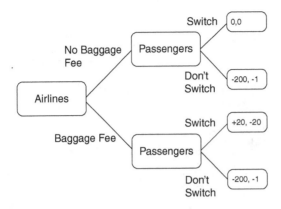

Figure 7.1   Decision tree for baggage fees

Nearest neighbour classifier

In addition to decision trees, there is the nearest neighbour classifier – also referred to as the *k-NN* algorithm. For this technique, once the classes have been trained, each case c_i is assigned the nearest class based on a distance metric. The most commonly used metric is the Euclidean metric discussed in Chapter 6. For text classification, sometimes the Hamming distance metric is used as well. The Hamming distance between two strings of same length is the number of positions at which the corresponding symbols are different. One can show that the Hamming distance satisfies the three conditions for a metric stated in Chapter 6, but it requires a bit of work using the principle of mathematical induction.

Artificial neural networks

These are a collection of techniques – otherwise known as artificial intelligence – that are modelled after the processes of learning in the cognitive and neurological functions of the human brain. The first step in all these techniques is to construct a network of *neurons*, which are elements that can be trained based on an existing data set by adjusting their weights to properly classify the cases. After the learning phase, the network is then ready to classify new data. Figure 7.2 shows an example of a classification solution using a topographical neural net – for more on this net and machine learning, see Chapter 8. Here we hypothetically classify 50 different airlines into seven clusters, from the worst to the best ecologically friendly airlines.

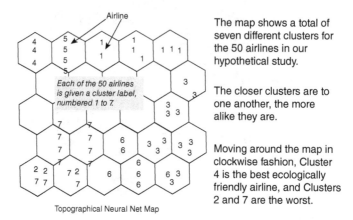

Figure 7.2 Topographical neural net classification for the worst and the best ecologically friendly airlines

Support vector machines

Assuming there are two classes in the data D, support vector machines (SVMs) attempt to draw a line (or hyperplane in two dimensions) that separates the two classes with the largest margin. The margin is defined as the distance between two parallel lines that are closest to the cases from either class (these closest cases are called support vectors). The calculation of the hyperplane is a quadratic optimisation problem which can be easily solved using Lagrangian-based algorithms. Once the hyperplane is computed, given a case c_i all we need to find out is which side of the hyperplane does c_i belong to, something that can be found out mathematically using the sign of the so-called inner-product between the weights of the hyperplane and the elements of the vector profile of c_i. SVMs work very well for binary classifications and have the added advantage of a deterministic solution without the use of heuristics.

Clustering

As we explained in the sections 'Cataloguing and Grouping Case Profiles' and 'The Notion of Time t' of Chapter 6, clustering refers to grouping cases c_i into sets of similar cases called *clusters* (labelled as C_i or C_i^T if the clusters consist of trajectories). However, the contextual meaning of the clusters C_i, if any, can only be determined by studying the clusters posterior. Here, we try to point out some major differences between known clustering schemes. For more information, see Berkhin (2006), Jain

(2010), Kuo et al. (2002) and Uprichard (2009). In particular, we highly recommend Jain (2010), which has been cited more than 4500 times and is a very well written and concise review, including the links between clustering and artificial intelligence.

Hierarchical clustering methods

These methods employ either a top-down or a bottom-up method to recursively construct the clusters. As shown in Figure 7.3 (our hypothetical study of 50 airlines from above), the bottom-up method is called *agglomerative hierarchical clustering*, where each case c_i is considered to be a cluster to begin with, and the clusters are merged in a recursive fashion to construct larger and larger clusters C_i until the required cluster structure is obtained. The top-down method is called *divisive hierarchical clustering*, where all cases c_i belong to one single cluster to begin with, and this cluster C_i is divided into sub-clusters in a recursive method until the desired cluster structure is obtained. The result of a hierarchical clustering method is a *dendrogram* representing the nested group of cases (in this case airlines) and similarity levels at which the clusters change.

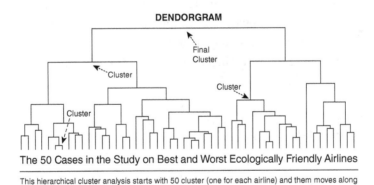

DENDORGRAM

The 50 Cases in the Study on Best and Worst Ecologically Friendly Airlines

This hierarchical cluster analysis starts with 50 cluster (one for each airline) and them moves along until there is one cluster for all the airlines.

Figure 7.3 Dendrogram for decision tree

In both cases, the desired cluster structure can be prescribed in a variety of ways, starting from number of desired clusters to criteria based on the within-cluster (size of each cluster) or between-cluster (e.g. minimum distance between the means of each cluster) distances. The merging or division of clusters is done according to a similarity measure which is chosen in order to optimise some criterion such as sum of squares. There are three main ways the similarity measure is used:

1   *Single link clustering* (also called the minimum, connectedness or the nearest neighbour method): Here, the distance between clusters is taken to be the shortest distance between any member of one cluster to any member of the other cluster. The criterion is chosen to minimise the similarity between clusters. This sometimes leads to a 'chain effect' where the mere presence of a case that bridges two clusters causes the two clusters to combine.

2   *Complete link clustering* (also called the diameter, maximum or the furthest neighbour method): Here, the distance between clusters is taken to be the longest distance between any member of one cluster to any member of the other cluster. The criterion here is to maximise the diameter between clusters, thereby leading to better separation. This method leads to more compact clusters and useful hierarchies.

3   *Average link clustering* (also called minimum variance method): Here, the distance between clusters is taken to be the average distance between any member of one cluster to any member of the other cluster. The criterion chosen here is to minimise the variance of the average distance. This sometimes leads to splitting of elongated clusters and portions of neighbouring elongated clusters to merge.

In general, hierarchical clustering methods are known to be more versatile and can handle non-isotropic clusters (clusters that prefer certain directions). For example, the single-link methods can handle well-separated, chain-like and concentric clusters. Also, hierarchical clustering methods allow the user to choose different partitions according to the desired similarity level using the dendrograms. However, they suffer from an inability to scale well; that is, the time complexity of algorithms are in general $O(m^2)$, where m is the number of cases. Furthermore, they suffer from a lack of a backtracking capability in the hierarchy; that is, they can never undo what was done previously.

Partitioning methods

Here, the number of clusters K is predetermined, and the cases c_i are iteratively assigned and reassigned to the clusters using a non-optimal or greedy algorithm. There are two types of partitioning methods.

The first type is called *error minimisation algorithms*. A perfect example is the K-means algorithm, where we start with K cluster centres, assign all cases based on the nearest centre, recalculate the means of the cluster and keep iterating until the error minimisation criterion is satisfied. This is a *gradient descent* method, because it can be mathematically proved that the sum of squares error actually decreased from one iteration to the next. However, it is not a globally optimal routine. The time complexity for T iterations with K-means, N cases and k variables per case is given to be $O(T * K * k * N)$. The linearity of time complexity is one of the main reasons why this algorithm is very popular.

The second type is called *graph theoretical clustering*, where each case is a node and each edge in the graph represents the distance between cases. A well-known example is the minimal spanning tree algorithm, where edges with large weights (or large distances) are thrown out of the cluster. Another example is based on limited neighbourhood sets, where the idea of neighbourhood sets (sets of cases c_i that are similar to each other) is used to draw boundaries between clusters.

Probability density–based methods

Here, the assumption is that each cluster has cases c_i coming from different probability distributions. The overall distribution is assumed to be a mixture of the individual cluster distributions. The aim of these methods is to identify the clusters and their distribution parameters. The clusters are grown with the addition of cases c_i until the density (number of cases per unit radius) exceeds a certain threshold. The assumptions are sometimes very restrictive in these methods. For example, most methods are developed under the assumption that the clusters are multivariate Gaussian (with each cluster having different parameters) or multinomial distribution. A typical algorithm here is the maximum-likelihood algorithm, where the probability that the data were generated by the distributions and the parameters is maximised. Another example called DBSCAN (density-based spatial clustering of applications with noise) searches for clusters by searching the neighbourhood of each case c_i in the database D and checks if it contains more than the minimum number of objects. AUTOCLASS is a widely used algorithm that covers a broad variety of distributions, including Gaussian, Bernoulli, Poisson and log-normal. The biggest disadvantage is that these methods cannot be used in instances where the cases c_i are not known to conform to known distributions.

Soft computing methods

These methods are offshoots of algorithms from the neural networking discipline. One example is the *fuzzy clustering* method (Ragin, 2008; Yuan & Shaw, 1995), where each case c_i will belong to all the clusters C_j according to a membership function. Larger membership values indicate a higher confidence of the case c_i belonging to the cluster C_j. The *fuzzy c-means algorithm* is a variation of the K-means but with fuzzy cluster membership. These methods are a slight improvement over the K-means in terms of avoiding local minima of the error function, but they can still converge on to local minima with the squared error function. Furthermore, the choice of the membership function strongly dictates the efficiency of the algorithm.

Another example is the *evolutionary approach* to clustering, where genetic algorithms (GAs) are used to evolve existing clusters into newer ones through selection, recombination and mutation of clusters, with the objective of improving the *fitness value* of the overall cluster structure. A higher fitness value indicates a better cluster structure. These have the advantage of achieving globally optimal solutions. Selection employs a probabilistic scheme so that solutions with higher fitness have a higher probability of getting reproduced. There are a variety of recombination operators in use; crossover is the most popular. Crossover takes as input a pair of chromosomes (called parents) and outputs a new pair of chromosomes (called children or offspring). In this way, the GA explores the search space. Mutation is used to make sure that the algorithm is not trapped in local optimum. A major problem with GAs is their sensitivity to the selection of various parameters such as population size, crossover and mutation probabilities and so on.

Chapter Summary

- While classification and clustering both group cases, often using the same mathematical algorithms, the former uses a training set of known case-based clusters to arrive at its results, while the latter is largely exploratory, seeking to identify groupings that may or may not be known.
- The two most widely used classification and clustering techniques are *k*-means and hierarchical clustering.
- Additional examples include decision tree analysis, nearest neighbour classifiers (also referred to as *k-NN* algorithms) and artificial neural nets.
- Assuming there are two classes in the data *D*, another type is support vector machines, which attempt to draw a line (or hyperplane in two dimensions) that separate the two classes with the largest margin.
- Another type is probability density methods. Here, the assumption is that each cluster has cases c_i coming from different probability distributions.
- The final type is soft computing methods, which are offshoots of algorithms from the neural networking discipline. One example is the *fuzzy clustering* method. Another is genetic algorithms.

Further Reading

Jain, A. K. (2010). Data clustering: 50 years beyond *k*-means. *Pattern Recognition Letters, 31*, 651–666. https://doi.org/10.1016/j.patrec.2009.09.011
This article offers a review of clustering methods.

Tirenni, G., Kaiser, C., & Herrmann, A. (2007). Applying decision trees for value-based customer relations management: Predicting airline customers' future values. *Journal of Database Marketing & Customer Strategy Management, 14*(2), 130–142.
This article explains the application of decision trees to the airline industry.

8

MACHINE LEARNING

Chapter Overview

Machine intelligence (a.k.a. machine learning) is not new. In fact, it has been around since the 1940s or earlier, depending upon how one defines the term, reaching its earlier zenith during the 1980s and 1990s, mainly based on major advances in key fields such as distributed artificial neural nets, cellular automata, fuzzy set theory, GAs and Bayesian networks. Most, however, date its first formal usage with Arthur Samuel, who coined the term in 1959 while at IBM (readers may also remember Samuel for developing some of the first checker-playing computers). For more on machine intelligence and learning, see the following: Blum and Li (2008), Burke and Kendall (2005), Fogel (2006), Huang et al. (2015), Jang et al. (1997), Kennedy (2006), Kohonen (1990, 2013), Kosko (1992) and Sharma et al. (2012). In particular, we recommend Burke and Kendall's edited book *Search Methodologies: Introductory Tutorials in Optimisation and Decision Support Techniques*, second edition (2014), which we drew upon to organise our chapter.

Of late, however, machine intelligence and learning appear to be everywhere, and there are several good reasons why, including recent advances in computer hardware, natural language processing (NLP), chatbots, computer vision, computational power, voice recognition, search and exploration and decentralised computing (i.e. *the cloud*) – the last one allowing software applications such as Uber, Facebook or Google to stream to off-premise devices. And, as one can imagine, all of these advances have been pivotal in the technological advances of the airline industry.

The smart airline industry

From check-in kiosks and visual scanning devices to smartphone apps and fully autonomous luggage – of all the various data mining techniques currently available, machine intelligence has probably had the biggest impact on the airline industry. And that is not the end of it. Let us also not forget the list of expert systems on any given airplane, including its navigation devices and autopilot features, as well as the machine intelligence used for air-traffic control, information exchange and telecommunications coordination amongst the numerous airports and airlines all around the world. In fact, we should probably just make the claim for what it is: from our global cyber-infrastructure to the internet of things, machine intelligence has become one of the most important backbone technologies used to run our daily lives on planet Earth. And yet, despite its widespread usage – which we discussed in Chapter 4, section 'The "Black Box" of Data Mining' – most people know little to nothing about what machine intelligence actually is or how it works.

What is machine intelligence?

Machine intelligence refers to two basic (albeit interrelated) forms of computer reasoning: machine learning and artificial intelligence. In both instances, however, we can think about things in a slightly simpler way, as both forms of reasoning are types of optimisation problems. Let us explain.

Many data mining methods – including those we refer to as machine intelligence – can be reformulated as optimisation problems. Roughly speaking, a clustering technique, for example, is simply an optimal rearrangement of the cases c_i into clusters C_i so that the Euclidean distance between members in a cluster is always lesser than the distance between the clusters themselves. Hence, the clustering technique (which one might use, e.g. for a visual scanning device) is equivalent to the minimisation (optimisation in general) of a distance function (objective function in general) subject to constraints. Some of these constraints – as in an airplane device being on or off – are hard constraints that have to be met no matter what, that is, a case cannot belong to more than one cluster; while some constraints might be soft – as in an airplane's slight 'fuzzy' adjustments in response to turbulence.

The set of all possible rearrangements (cluster solutions) that satisfy the constraints constitutes the search space of feasible solutions, and the optimisation algorithm (some form of machine learning) is essentially a way to parse through the search space to reach the optimal solution – for example, quickly reducing a list of all possible music to those few songs you want to listen to keep you calm during your flight's turbulence.

Machine intelligence for big data

So, how does all of this machine intelligence help us more effectively data mine big data? One of the biggest problems associated with data mining in the era of big data is the size and complexity of the optimisation problems. For example, the search space for a travelling salesperson problem (TSP) with 50 cities is of the order of 10^{60}, and hence a brute-force parse through the feasible solutions is simply not possible. It is for this reason that machine intelligence methods have proven so useful.

What machine intelligent algorithms do differently is engage in a form of learning. By this, we mean that they start, initially, with a quick but useful suboptimal solution, which does not optimise the objective function. Quickly, however, they evolve, mainly through repeated iterations, to find an increasingly optimal solution; which is why these data mining techniques are referred to as *learning algorithms* and why, often, we use the term *intelligence* to describe them.

Machine learning has two components typically: (1) a learning element and (2) a performance element (see Yao & Liu, 2014). The learning element uses the environment to modify the performance element so that it can make better decisions in selecting actions to perform its task. *Supervised* learning involves algorithms that take inputs and outputs in the form of data and learns the unknown function that transforms the input to the output. If the outputs are discrete, then it is called a classification problem, and if the outputs are continuous, then it is called a regression problem. *Unsupervised learning* methods, on the other hand, don't have any outputs, and the learning process essentially involves finding patterns or relationships between the input stimuli, thereby resulting in a grouping of related inputs. Clustering is a classic example of an unsupervised learning method where the cases c_i are the inputs, and depending on the relationships (closeness) between the cases c_i, each of them may or may not be placed in the same cluster.

Examples of data mining methods based on machine intelligence

So as not to turn this brief chapter into a book, we need to limit our review of machine intelligence to three of the most popular techniques: artificial neural networks, GAs and swarm intelligence. However, for those interested in a deeper understanding and a broader collection of methods, we recommend, in addition to our earlier references, Burke and Kendall (2014).

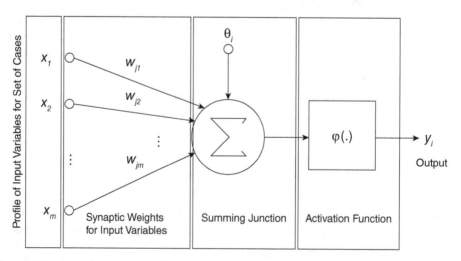

Figure 8.1   A single neuron model

Artificial neural networks

As outlined by Yao and Liu (2014), artificial neural networks try to emulate the inner workings of the human brain, specifically nerve cells or *neurons*. Figure 8.1, for example, shows a single neuron (also called a perceptron), as it was originally developed in McCulloch and Pitts (1943).

Neural networks

In order to train a single neuron using a feed-forward algorithm – a highly popular approach – inputs $x_i, i \in \{1,...,m\}$ and output y_i are given, and the unknown weights $w_{ij}, j \in \{1,...,m\}$ are to be trained according to the following:

$$
\begin{aligned}
w_{ij}(t+1) &= w_{ij}(t) + \Delta w_{ij}(t), \\
\Delta w_{ij}(t) &= \eta\left(y^p - O^p\right)x_j^p, \\
O^p &= \mathrm{sgn}\left(\sum_j w_{ij}x_j^p - \theta_i\right),
\end{aligned}
\tag{8.1}
$$

where θ_i is the threshold, t is the iteration step counter, η is the learning rate, x_j^p is the jth input in the pth example, y^p is the target or desired output in the pth example and sgn(x) is the sign function given by

$$
\mathrm{sgn}(x) = \begin{cases} 1 & \text{if } x \geq 0, \\ 0 & \text{if } x < 0. \end{cases}
$$

There are several other choices for the activation function instead of the sign function above (McCulloch & Pitts, 1943). The main idea behind the training algorithm is to start with a random assignment of weights w_{ij} and update the weights according to Equation (8.1). The updating goes on until either the weights converge $(\Delta w_{ij}(t) = 0)$ or the number of iterations reaches a certain maximum. This type of learning algorithm is called back-propagation method, where the forward pass propagates the activation values from inputs to the outputs, and the backward pass propagates the error, which is the term $(y^p - O^p)$, and the training continues until a stopping criterion is satisfied. There are mathematical theorems that guarantee the convergence of such back-propagation learning algorithms for a variety of activation functions and types of data sets (Rumelhart et al., 2017).

As shown in Figure 8.2 – which was created by Alp et al. (2007) – a neural network (on the other hand) is a parallel connection of multiple neurons, where the learning algorithm updates weights for each of the neurons at each iteration. If the network has several hidden layers, where the hidden layers are typically used to non-linearly extract different features using non-linear mapping functions (akin to independent principal components but much more involved), and other layers try to fit a linear combination of the extracted features using an optimisation, such a learning algorithm is called *deep learning*, which is one of the latest developments in neural networks.

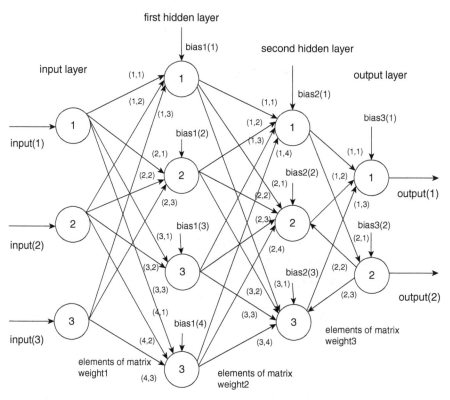

Figure 8.2 Example architecture of a back-propagation model

The greater the number of hidden layers (or the deeper the learning algorithm), the greater the number of independent features that are extracted, and the better the mapping is between the inputs and the outputs. One of the reasons for using the feature space to fit the function instead of the original inputs is because the feature space is typically low dimensional compared to the original input space and hence the convergence of the learning algorithm is faster. Once again, the back-propagation algorithm has been mathematically shown to converge to a steady set of weights w_{ij} for multilayered neural network (Rumelhart et al., 2017). Neural networks are known to be robust, fault-tolerant and noise-tolerant and have parallel computational implementations that make them very fast. They have been used in a wide range of applications, such as pattern recognition, function approximation and system identification.

There are two phases in the modelling process using a neural network:

1 *Training phase:* In the training phase, an architecture for the neurons is chosen, hidden layers and network connectivity needs to be decided upon, and a suitable training algorithm is used to train the network using training data.
2 *Generalisation phase:* The trained network is then subject to new (never seen before) inputs to see how well it generalises the mapping between the inputs and outputs (or how well it clusters the inputs if it is an unsupervised learning algorithm).

Self-organising maps

The neural network learning algorithms described in the previous section were all *supervised;* that is, there were inputs and outputs and the task was to train the network to model the unknown function that maps the inputs to the outputs. The self-organising map (SOM) – which we use extensively in our own research, and which is used as the basis for the SACS Toolkit and COMPLEX-IT (see Chapter 6) – is an example of an *unsupervised* learning algorithm. As shown in Figure 8.3, for their neural net, a two-dimensional grid of nodes is trained to mimic models for the input data (over a large number of iterations), and unknown input elements are then placed on the node that is closest in Euclidean distance – although other distances can also be used (Kohonen, 2013).

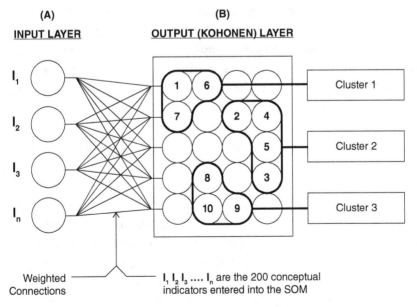

Figure 8.3 Simplified neural architecture of a self-organising map

The SOM is based on *brain maps*, which are local assemblies of single neural cells that were found in the brain, which responded selectively to specific sensory stimuli. The topographical location of the brain maps corresponded to some feature value of a specific stimulus in an orderly fashion. An SOM neural network is modelled after brain maps where neurons closer to each other on the topographical map (which is a hexagonal or rectangular array) correspond to similar models for the input data and vice versa.

Borrowing from Kohonen (2013, p. 56), the SOM learning algorithm for stepwise learning is as follows:

$$\mathbf{m}_i(t+1) = \mathbf{m}_i(t) + h_{ci}(t)[\mathbf{x}(t) - \mathbf{m}_i(t)]$$
$$c = \arg \min_i \{\|\mathbf{x}(t) - \mathbf{m}_i(t)\|\}, \tag{8.2}$$

$$h_{ci}(t) = \alpha(t)\exp\left(-\frac{\|(\mathbf{m}_c(t) - \mathbf{x}_i(t))\|^2}{2\sigma(t)}\right), \tag{8.3}$$

where $\{\mathbf{m}_i(t)\}$ is a sequence of n-dimensional model vectors at iteration t, $\{\mathbf{x}(t)\}$ is a sequence of n-dimensional input data vectors, $h_{ci}(t)$ is a neighborhood function which is a Gaussian centred at $\mathbf{m}_c(t)$, $\alpha(t)$ and $\sigma(t)$ are monotonically decreasing functions of t that do not tend to zero (it should remain at least more than half of the grid spacing). At each iteration, the best matching model $\mathbf{x}_c(t)$ is computed as the solution of Equation (8.3), then the neighbouring neurons are modified according to Equation (8.2) with decreasing rates of modification according to the neighbourhood function $h_{ci}(t)$. The iteration is repeated until all the input vectors $\mathbf{x}(t)$ are exhausted, and starts again, until the neurons stabilise (or don't change any more). The same algorithm can be modified to treat the input vectors in batches instead of one by one with a similar learning process, which is a little faster than the stepwise algorithm.

Figure 8.4, for example, shows the utility of the SOM for clustering massively complex data, as well as its ability to 'reveal' the black box of neural nets, which is done by visualising its output layer. Here we used the SOM to identify different primary care trends for patients with co-morbid depression and physical health issues (Castellani et al., 2016). As a final solution, we settled on 11 major and minor trends. However, as shown in Figure 8.4, this solution was a reduction of the k-means 18 cluster solution – which is why all three maps above show 18 different cluster numbers and their respective cluster names (which is one of the final 11 clusters). In terms of reading Figure 8.4, it presents three different (and also more complex) versions of the 'output (Kohonen) layer' from Figures 8.2 and 8.3, which researchers call the U-matrix. In terms of the information they provide, the bottom-left map is a three-dimensional (topographical) U-matrix: for it, the SOM adds hexagons to the original map to allow for visual inspection of the degree of similarity amongst neighbouring map units; the darker areas indicate neighbourhoods of cases that are highly similar; in turn, brighter areas, as in the lower right corner of the map, indicate highly defined cluster boundaries. The top-right map is useful because it gives a more visually intuitive sense of the topography of the bottom-left map. The bottom-right map is a two-dimensional version of the other two maps, and it is useful because it allows for simpler visual inspection of how the SOM clustered the individual cases. Cases on this version of the U-matrix (as well as the other two) were labelled according to their *k*-means cluster membership. For more on our work using the SOM, see Castellani et al. (2015, 2016), Castellani and Rajaram (2012) and Rajaram and Castellani (2012, 2014).

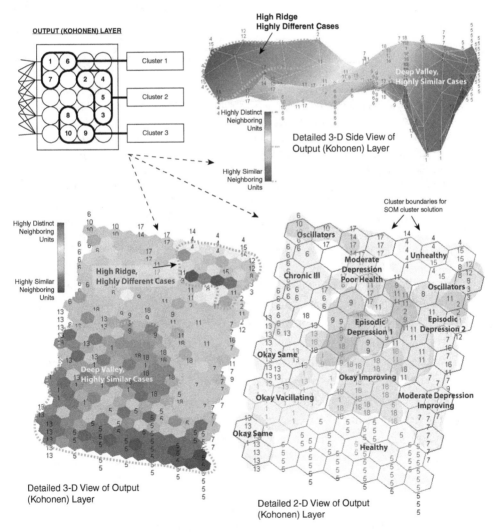

Figure 8.4 Self-organising map for clustering trends of co-morbid depression and physical health in primary care – showing three different versions of the output layer

Genetic algorithms and evolutionary computation

As outlined by Sastry et al. (2014), GAs are optimisation routines based on the principles of natural selection and genetics. A GA starts with a population of feasible solutions to the problem. The candidate solutions are called *chromosomes*. The decision variables that are part of the solutions are called *genes*, and the values of the decision variables are called *alleles*. A fitness measure (typically and objective function) is used to evolve solutions into better ones. For example, in a TSP, a chromosome represents a route and a gene represents a city.

Once an optimisation problem is coded in a chromosomal manner and a fitness measure has been formulated for discriminating good solutions from bad ones, the solutions are allowed to *evolve* using the following steps – which we borrow from Sastry et al. (2014):

1 *Initialisation:* The initial population of feasible solutions is created at random from the search space of solutions.
2 *Evaluation:* The fitness values of each of the solutions in the population are evaluated.
3 *Selection:* A rule is developed (e.g. the tournament selection rule; Holland, 1975) to select a fitter subset of solutions from the population.
4 *Recombination:* Recombination combines solutions developed thus far to create new solution candidates (children) so that the offspring will not be identical to any particular parent but parental traits are combined in a novel manner.
5 *Mutation:* Unlike recombination which requires two parents, mutation refers to a change in a solution starting from a single parent.
6 *Replacement:* The offspring population created by selection, recombination and mutation is used to replace the original parent population using specialised replacement techniques – for more, see also Goldberg (2002) .

Steps 2 through 6 above are repeated until one or more stopping criteria are met. A typical stopping criterion is one which specifies error tolerances between the current and the next solution. GAs are known to produce quick locally optimal solutions and are widely used for optimisation problems that are large in terms of scale.

GAs can be used as learning algorithms in a neural network to train the neurons in a supervised environment. In a sense, as shown in Figure 8.5 – which comes from our research on the health trajectories of countries, amongst other topics (Rajaram & Castellani, 2012, 2014) – the main objective in a GA is similar to a supervised neural network, where an unknown function is sought that can map the inputs and outputs provided.

Swarming travel routes

Suppose you realise that your airline is not maximising its usage of cargo space on the majority of its planes – perhaps, for example, only 20% of the space on most planes

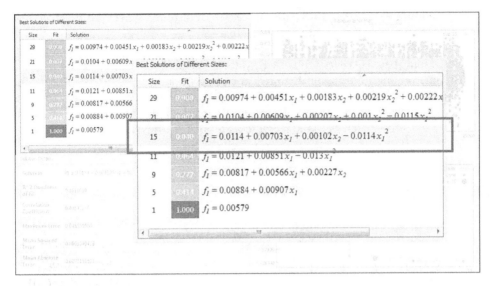

Figure 8.5 Example of a genetic algorithm computed for a study of country-level longitudinal health

*Eureqa – which is the software we used to generate this genetic algorithm – gives multiple models for the vector field of velocities. The Figure shows several optimal solutions. The best fit model (#15 in our case, shown above) is usually the one that has a mid-level complexity in terms of number of polynomial symbols and error values in the mid range amongst all models.

is used. Furthermore, you realise that trying to correct for this problem by overloading planes taking a direct route from one location to the next is also slowing down operations, which is leading to flight delays and the delivery of cargo, all of which is costing you money. Your need a more effective optimal solution.

That is where swarm behaviour comes into play. Contrary to popular mathematical belief, the shortest (and most cost- and time-effective) distance between two points is not always a straight line. Sometimes it is the path taken by an ant, bird or bee.

Overview of swarm intelligence

As outlined by Merkle and Middendorf (2014), swarm intelligence-based optimisation methods are heuristic algorithms for combinatorial optimisation problems that are inspired by the behaviour of ant colonies, bees or flocks of birds in solving shortest route problems such as the TSP. There are two broad categories of methods here:

1   *Ant colony optimisation (ACO):* This is based on the fact that given a long and a short path to food, ants always choose the shorter path based on the pheromone concentration left behind by previous ants that chose the path. The initial few ants that choose the shorter path get to the food and back to the nest faster, smell the pheromones and choose the shorter path again, thereby increasing the concentration

of pheromones in the shorter path over a period of time, thereby leading to more ants choosing the shorter path over time. In a TSP, 'the problem is to find for a given set of n cities, with distances d_{ij} between each pair of cities $i, j \in \{1,...,n\}$ a shortest closed tour that visits every city exactly once' (Merkle & Middendorf, 2014, p. 217). The pheromone information is stored in an n by n matrix τ_{ij} which expresses the desirability to assign city j after city i in the permutation. At the first step, all n are placed in the set S and sequentially removed once a city is chosen. The probability that a city j is chosen is given as (which we borrow from Merkle & Middendorf, 2014, p. 218):

$$ p_{ij} = \frac{\tau_{ij}}{\sum_{z \in S} \tau_{iz}}. $$

Starting with m ants, m solutions are constructed in a single iteration. All m solutions are evaluated for fitness using the total distance travelled and the best solution π^* is found. The pheromone matrix – which we quote from Merkle and Middendorf (2014, p. 218) – is then updated in two ways:

a   *Pheromone evaporation:* All pheromone values are reduced by a fixed value ρ using $\tau_{ij} = (1 - \rho) \cdot \tau_{ij} \forall i, j \in \{1,...,n\}$.

b   *Pheromone intensification:* All pheromone values for cities in the solution π^* are increased by a value Δ using $\tau_{i\pi^*(i)} = \tau_{i\pi^*(i)} + \Delta, i \in \{1,...,n\}$.

Finally, the iterations continue with an update on all m solutions (one corresponding to each ant) until a stopping criterion is satisfied. Typical stopping criteria are given by number of iterations, quality of solution or non-changing best solution after a specified number of iterations. For more on ACOs we refer the reader to Dorigo and Caro (1999) and references therein.

2   *Particle swarm optimisation (PSO):* PSO-based algorithms are typically used to optimise function values without constraints. In contrast to an ACO, a PSO-based optimisation method is modelled to simulate how a flock of birds or a school of fish forage for food. A PSO maintains a swarm of particles, where each particle represents the location in a multidimensional search space, and the particles move in the search space to find the optimal value of the objective function. The movement is determined by the instantaneous velocity of the particle, the current optimal location found by the particle itself (local optimum) and also the current optimal location found by its neighbours or the entire swarm (global optimum).

The key difference between a PSO and an ACO is that in a PSO the global optimal location plays a role in updating the movement of every particle, whereas in an ACO, typically only the local pheromone concentration level of the ant determines its movement. For example, if the function f is being optimised over a D-dimensional space – as outlined by Merkle and Middendorf (2014, p. 229) – then to explain a typical velocity update the following notations are used: The location of a particle $i \in \{1,...,m\}$ is given by the vector $\mathbf{x}_i = (x_{i1},...,x_{iD})$, the velocity of the particle i is given by $\mathbf{v}_i = (v_{i1},...,v_{iD})$, the lower and upper bounds of the particle in the dth dimension where $d \in \{1,...,D\}$ is given by l_d and u_d, the best previous position of the ith particle is given by $\mathbf{p}_i = (p_{i1},...,p_{iD})$ and, correspondingly, the best current global optimal position of the swarm is given by $\mathbf{p}_g$. The particles start at random initially, and at each iteration, if $f(\mathbf{x}_i) < f(\mathbf{p}_i)$ then $\mathbf{p}_i = \mathbf{x}_i$, and if $f(\mathbf{x}_i) < f(\mathbf{p}_g)$ then $\mathbf{p}_g = \mathbf{p}_i$. Then the new velocity v_{id} is calculated based on a weighted average of the previous particle velocity, the difference between current particle position and the current local optimal position and the difference between current particle position and the current global optimal position. Finally, the particle position is updated with $x_{id} = x_{id} + v_{id}$ and the iteration continues until a stopping criterion (similar to the one in ACO) is met. For a more detailed description and applications, please refer to Kennedy and Eberhart (1999).

Chapter Summary

- Machine intelligence refers to two basic (albeit interrelated) forms of computer reasoning: machine learning and artificial intelligence.
- In both instances, however, we can think about things in a slightly simpler way, as both forms of reasoning are types of optimisation problems.
- To achieve optimisation, what machine intelligent algorithms do differently from other methods is they engage in a form of learning. By this, we mean that they start, initially, with a quick but useful suboptimal solution, which does not optimise the objective function.
- Quickly, however, they evolve, mainly through repeated iterations, to find an increasingly optimal solution, which is why these data mining techniques are referred to as *learning algorithms* and why, often, we use the term *intelligence* to describe them.
- In this chapter, several types of machine learning are reviewed, including several that other chapters have also discussed (albeit not in as much detail as here). These include artificial neural nets, the self-organising map neural net, genetic algorithms and swarm intelligence, including ant colony optimisation.

Further Reading

Burke, E. K., & Kendall, G. (2014). *Search methodologies: Introductory tutorials in optimisation and decision support techniques*. Springer. https://doi.org/10.1007/0-387-28356-0

This book offers a broader collection of methods based on artificial intelligence.

McCulloch, W. S., & Pitts, W. (1943). A logical calculus of the ideas immanent in nervous activity. *Bulletin of Mathematical Biophysics, 5,* 115–137. https://doi.org/10.1007/BF02478259
This article explains the original development of the perceptron.

9

PREDICTIVE ANALYTICS AND DATA FORECASTING

Chapter Overview

If you are an airline company, making predictions about the future is one of your biggest challenges. What if, for example, you introduce a new discounted fare for midweek travel? Will it increase revenue? Or, alternatively, what happens if you move one of your highly travelled flights from 8.30 am to 9.00 am? Will it increase or decrease delays in other flights? Or, given what we know about cyber-attacks, can you better predict when and where such attacks will take place next? Alternatively, can you use existing data to differentiate between simple cyberattacks (e.g. spambots) versus a serious cyberterrorist threat? To answer such questions, experts turn to a class of methods known as predictive analytics or, alternatively, data forecasting.

For more on predictive analytics and data forecasting, see the following: Bernardo and Smith (2001), Fogel (2006), Gelman and Shalizi (2013), Lee (2012), Olson and Wu (2016), Wagenmakers (2007) and Waller and Fawcett (2013). In addition, we also recommend Blum and Li (2008), Burke and Kendall (2005), Huang et al. (2015), Jang et al. (1997), Kennedy (2006), Kohonen (1990, 2013), Kosko (1992) and Sharma et al. (2012).

Predictive analytics and data forecasting: a very brief history

Predictive analytics (a.k.a. data forecasting) is a collection of tools that uses current or historical facts (data) to make educated guesses about future or unknown events. In fact, one can go all the way back to the ancients to find such tools, from consulting oracles, gurus and sages to reading tea leaves and divining dreams. More recently, however, these techniques have become more 'scientific', including the usage of historical analysis, market research, expert opinion, game theory and statistics.

In terms of statistics, for example, some of the most widely used techniques include linear regression, time-series models, logistic regression, survival curve analysis and probit regression. (For more, see Martin's *Linear Regression: An Introduction to Statistical Models*, which is part of the *SAGE Quantitative Research Kit*.) Or, alternatively, experts have turned to risk models (based on actuarial concepts), as in the insurance industry, for example, which seeks to determine the insurance premium for a flight, car or health plan.

In terms of data mining, while experts continue to use statistics, they also have turned increasingly to the field of machine intelligence. Here the techniques include all of the methods discussed in Chapter 8 (i.e. neural networks, *k*-nearest neighbours, etc.), as well as recent developments in Bayesian statistics (which we have yet to discuss). As our earlier review of machine intelligence methods (and their potential) suggested, the utility of these tools is their ability to learn from data, which is something the other methods cannot do, and which (hopefully) is what allows artificial intelligence techniques to 'get better' at predicting the future – or at least that is the sales pitch! However, as we saw in Chapter 4, the 'reality' of their promise resides somewhere in the middle.

Still, despite their differences, all of the above statistical and data mining techniques can be grouped into one of two types: classification and clustering techniques, where the goal is to predict class membership of a case c_i, for example; or regression models, which predict either the value of a variable or its probability distribution.

Overview of techniques

Given how extensive the field of predictive analytics is – as well as the degree to which its techniques overlap with other chapters in this book – we will limit ourselves to a short review of a handful of the most widely used methods, including decision trees, neural networks and regression (linear, non-linear, logistic). We will, however, devote slightly greater time to a set of techniques we have yet to discuss – namely, Bayesian statistical parameter estimation and Bayesian hypothesis testing. What has made these latter techniques so popular is their inferential power: using their core formula of inference (known as Bayes's theorem), experts can use these techniques (in real time) to update the probability of their predictions (i.e. hypotheses) in response to more, new or different data. In the world of real-time big data (particularly if plugged into machine intelligence), one can see how such a 'Bayesian' approach is appealing! So, let us turn to these techniques now.

Bayesian statistics

The Bayesian school of thought treats the probability of events to be associated with 'epistemic uncertainty', that is, uncertainty due to lack of knowledge, rather than 'aleatory uncertainty', which refers to uncertainty due to randomness (Wagenmakers, 2007). In other words, for a Bayesian, the probability of an event is simply a quantification of the amount of belief that the event will occur and, hence, does not require the notion of repeatable events or the idea of relative frequency either.

For example, we might believe that during major holidays the probability of a spambot attack on our airline website will be high. The question, then, for a Bayesian is: how strongly do you believe this hypothesis? In other words, the inspiration here is to use *known information* about certain data or a model (prior probabilities) – along with information from data (likelihood function) and the Bayes's rule – to compute the *posterior probability* of the parameter, given the data (in the case of parameter estimation);

or to compute the *posterior probability* of the models from null or alternate hypotheses given the data.

And it is in this inspiration that we arrive at the nuanced difference between a Bayesian and conventional (also called frequentist) statistical approach to inference and prediction. In the former, the focus is on the probability of the model being correct, given some prior data; while in the latter, the focus is on the probability of the data being correct, given some model. For example, returning to our concerns about spambots during the holidays, a frequentist prediction would be: during 'Holiday A' spambot attacks will be high; 'Holiday A' took place; how accurate was our prediction given the data? In contrast, a Bayesian prediction would be: in the past, spambot activity during 'Holiday A' was low; however, in recent past, spambot activity during 'Holiday A' has increased; we therefore predict that there will be an increase in spambot activity; how accurate was our prediction? And, more important, how does this new data help us adjust or change (i.e. learn from) our prior probability?

All of this should make even clearer (to make the point one more time) why this approach works so well in conjunction with machine learning and big data. Since the output of the Bayesian procedure is actually a probability distribution – be it for the parameter or the model, depending on whether it is a parameter estimation or hypothesis test – one has the advantage of precisely computing probabilities of parametric values or events in the future using the posterior distribution. Secondly, as more big data arrives, the posterior probability can be automatically updated using the Bayes's rule by considering the posterior probability from the previous data set as the prior for the current update. For a detailed comparison of the two methods and the advantages of Bayesian methods over frequentist methods, again, we recommend Wagenmakers (2007). Also, a very useful tutorial can be found online at http://blog.efpsa.org/2015/08/03/bayesian-statistics-why-and-how. Finally, we recommend the work of Eric-Jan Wagenmakers, who has written some excellent papers on Bayesian statistics. In fact, we draw on his work for the current chapter, and suggest that readers explore this work as well – see www.ejwagenmakers.com.

Bayesian parameter estimation

Bayesian parameter estimation involves the prediction of the probability distribution of a parametric uncertainty from a data set. Suppose the parameter of interest that we want to estimate is given by θ, and D stands for data, the simplified Bayes's rule states the following:

$$P(\theta \mid D) = \frac{P(D \mid \theta) \cdot P(\theta)}{P(D)}$$

(9.1)

$$P(\theta \,|\, D) \propto P(D \,|\, \theta) \cdot P(\theta), \tag{9.2}$$

where $P(\theta|D)$ is the probability distribution of the parameter conditioned on the data D (or posterior probability), $P(D|\theta)$ is the likelihood function and $P(\theta)$ is the prior probability of the parameter θ.

Equation (9.2) is a better representation of the Bayes's rule since $P(D)$ is simply a normalising constant independent of the parameter θ. In the context of parameter estimation, Equation (9.2) states that the posterior probability is proportional to the product of the likelihood and the prior.

It is important to note that in Equation (9.2), we are going from 'effect' (data) to the 'cause' (model). Also, we are computing the probability of the model (given data) as opposed to the other way around – as used in classical frequentist approaches. In simple cases, the prior and posterior probability distributions are of the same type (e.g. Beta distribution) for a certain combination of the 'likelihood' and 'prior' (such combinations are called conjugates). However, for situations where the 'likelihood' and the 'prior' are not conjugates, the posterior distribution is harder to compute analytically. However, with recent advances in Markov chain Monte Carlo (MCMC) simulation techniques, the posterior distribution can be computed numerically with considerable accuracy. Finally, once the posterior distribution is known, one can then compute the mode, median and summary statistics to state the most probable value of θ; or one can compute, for example, a 95% *Bayesian confidence interval*.

Again, this approach is in contrast to the classical frequentist confidence interval approach. In the last of the latter, the confidence in the range of values is no more than the 'capture rate' of the method that is used to compute the interval; and, therefore, it is not related to the probability of the occurrence of the parameter values. Finally, two additional points about this approach, particularly in terms of big data – which are important to note:

1 *Dependence on prior probability vanishes with more data:* At first glance, it might seem like the posterior distribution depends on the choice of prior probability of the parameter θ. However, it can be proved that with more samples in the data – that is, bigger data sets – the evidence from the data overshadows any lingering effects remaining from the prior distribution. This is a very useful property of the posterior distribution $P(\theta|D)$ because it allows us to choose a variety of distributions for the prior depending on the a priori knowledge of θ.
2 *Dependence of the likelihood function on the way the data are obtained is non-existent:* This means that the posterior probability distribution does not depend on whether the data are obtained in four sets of 25 samples (or any permutation of those) or a single set where the same 100 samples are collected. In the end, the posterior distribution will look exactly the same for both data collection methods.

Bayesian hypothesis testing

In the context of Bayesian parameter estimation, for hypothesis testing one assumes an underlying model (e.g. the binomial model for tossing of a coin) and updates the value(s) of a parameter in the model after new data arrive. But, more often than not, data mining is interested in testing the validity of a model – that is, whether a model M_1 or a model M_2 better describes the data.

The Bayesian approach can be extended to such a hypothesis testing scenario where the hypothesis H_1 would be that the data follow model M_1, and vice versa. Using the Bayes's rule, given data D, we can update the prior probability of the model given by $P(M_1)$ to a posterior probability given by $P(M_1|D)$ as given by Equation (9.3) – which we borrow from Wagenmakers et al. (2010, pp. 164–165).

$$P(M_{1,2} \mid D) = \frac{P(M_{1,2}) \cdot P(D \mid M_{1,2})}{P(M_1) \cdot P(D \mid M_1) + P(M_2) \cdot P(D \mid M_2)}, \tag{9.3}$$

$$\frac{P(M_1 \mid D)}{P(M_2 \mid D)} = \frac{P(M_1)}{P(M_2)} \cdot \frac{P(D|M_1)}{P(D|M_2)}, \tag{9.4}$$

$$BF_{12} = \frac{P(D \mid M_1)}{P(D \mid M_2)}, \tag{9.5}$$

$$P(M_1|D) = \frac{BF_{12}}{BF_{12} + 1} \text{ if } P(M_1) = P(M_2). \tag{9.6}$$

Similarly, a posterior probability for models $\left(\frac{P(M_1)}{P(M_2)}\right)$ multiplied by the likelihood ratio $\left(\frac{P(D \mid M_1)}{P(D \mid M_2)}\right)$ gives the posterior odds ratio. Therefore, if the prior odds of the model is 1 (giving equal probability to both models), then essentially the likelihood ratio (called the Bayes's factor given by Equation (9.5)) can be used to compute the actual posterior probability for the model M_1 (and M_2 as well using a similar formula) as shown in Equation (9.6).

In other words, the Bayes's factor is an important number to calculate in the context of Bayesian hypothesis testing. For example, if $BF_{12} = 2$, then it means that the data is 2 times more likely to occur under model M_1 than under model M_2. For simple situations (e.g. the distributions that occur as conjugate pairs etc.), the marginal likelihood $P(D|M_1)$ (and $P(D|M_2)$) are easy to compute (Wagenmakers et al., 2010). However, in general the marginal likelihood is given by the following equation:

$$P(D \mid M_1) = \int P(D \mid \theta, M_1) P(\theta \mid M_1) d\theta. \tag{9.7}$$

Equation (9.7) is hard to compute in general if the prior probability of the parameter θ is complex. However, there is a neat trick called the Savage–Dickey density ratio (see Wagenmakers et al., 2010) that reduces the computational complexity by a lot.

Finally, as with Bayesian parameter estimation, here are some additional points about this approach, particularly in terms of big data, which are important to note:

3 *Bayesian model averaging:* The posterior probabilities $P(M_1|D)$ and $P(M_2|D)$ can be used to average the uncertainty in the models for prediction. For example, if one model M_1 predicts a certain survival rate of a particular flight that depends on price, fuel consumption, distance and frequency of use, and another model M_2 uses two additional predictors such as competition for flight by other airlines and number of empty seats, and we compute the posterior probabilities to be $P(M_1|D) = 0.6$ and $P(M_2|D) = 0.4$. For a given airline, let's assume that model M_1 predicts a 90% survival rate for the above flight, and model M_2 predicts an 80% survival rate. Because (on first glance) $P(M_1|D)$ is larger, one thinks to go with the 90%, as M_1 is the preferred model according to the posterior probability value of 0.6. However, the Bayesian solution would be to compute $0.6 \cdot 0.9 + 0.4 \cdot 0.8 = 0.86$ to mean that the survival rate is 86%, taking into account the uncertainty of occurrence of both models.

4 *Coherence is guaranteed:* Suppose we have three models M_1, M_2 and M_3, then the corresponding Bayes's factors are multiplicative as follows:

$$BF_{13} = BF_{12} \cdot BF_{13}. \tag{9.8}$$

This means that, 'when the data are five times as likely to occur under M1 than under M2, and seven times as likely under M2 than under M3, it follows that the data are $5 \times 7 = 35$ times as likely under M1 than under M3. No comparable result exists in classical statistics' (Wagenmakers et al., 2010, p. 166).

5 *Parsimony is automatically rewarded:* Complex probabilistic models have a relatively large parameter space and are, therefore, able to make many more predictions and cover many more eventualities than simple models. However, the drawback for complex models is that they need to spread out their prior probability across their entire parameter space. In the limit, a model that predicts almost everything has to spread out its prior probability so thinly that the occurrence of any particular event will not greatly add to that model's credibility. Ockham's razor or the law of parsimony explains that *when all is equal one should choose the simpler model.*

One of the attractive features of Bayesian hypothesis testing is that it automatically determines the model with the best predictive performance. 'Bayesian hypothesis testing therefore incorporates what is known as an automatic Ockham's razor' (Wagenmakers et al., 2010, p. 166).

6 *Actual evidence can be obtained in favour of one of the hypotheses:* The posterior model probabilities $P(M_1|D)$ and $P(M_2|D)$ are actual evidence for or against one of the two models M_1 or M_2, as opposed to the frequentist hypothesis testing procedures where a low (or high) p-value only suggests that the null model is false and does not say

anything about whether or not the alternate model is true. The two hypotheses have equal importance in the Bayesian setting, and hence, one can definitely conclude whether the data are more likely to occur from M_1 or M_2.

7   *Choice of prior heavily influences the test:* Unlike Bayesian parameter estimation, the choice of the prior has a lasting impact on the result of the hypothesis test. This can be a disadvantage if the prior chosen is very complex – and hence spanning a large parameter space. However, there are methods that increase the robustness of the test to the vagueness of Wagenmakers et al. (2010).

Decision trees

In Chapter 7, section 'Decision Tree Induction', decision tree induction was introduced as a classification scheme. Given its approach to organising data, it is also highly useful for data prediction and forecasting. One example is decision tree analysis – which is used extensively, for example, in clinical decision-making – where, the main objective is to increasingly classify (and subclassify) cases c_i into more and more refined classes (or groups), based on some given set of profile factors or desired outcome. Given the focus of the current book, we cannot say anything more about the actual method except that it also falls under predictive analytics. Once a set of test cases (usually a subset of the original data set) is used to sharpen the classification tests at each node, new cases from the data can be introduced which can then be classified (the prediction step).

Neural networks

In Chapter 8, section 'Artificial Neural Networks', we provided a basic overview of neural networks, in particular the self-organising map (SOM). As is currently the rage (in 2021), using neural nets for prediction and forecasting of novel or new cases is highly powerful. Similar to decision trees, neural networks can be first trained using a small data set (or sometimes multiple training data sets) to train the functional relationship between inputs and outputs. Then the untested inputs can be used to predict the outputs (the prediction step).

Regression (linear, non-linear and logistic)

Regression analysis fits parameters of known functional models between input and output data sets, based on minimising the sum of the squares of the residual errors. If the response variable (output) is categorical and can only take on a finite set of values, then the regression is called logistic. If the model is assumed to be linear or non-linear, then the method is termed as linear or non-linear regression, respectively. Regression models are very useful when the form of the functional relationship can be ascertained a priori (linear, polynomial of a certain degree etc.).

Still, these approaches, while useful, lack the robustness of machine intelligence – particularly in the case of GAs (Chapter 8, section 'Genetic Algorithms and Evolutionary Computation'), where the best function is found and fitted to the data rather than fitting the data to a known function. Nevertheless, regression models are widely used in data that arise from phenomena that are inherently known to be non-complex. Once the model is fit, the predictive step involves using an unknown input to compute the value of the response variable.

Chapter Summary

- Predictive analytics (a.k.a. data forecasting) is a collection of tools that uses current or historical facts (data) to make educated guesses about future or unknown events.
- In terms of statistics, for example, some of the most widely used techniques include linear regression, time-series models, logistic regression, survival curve analysis and probit regression. Or, alternatively, experts have turned to risk models, based on actuarial concepts.
- In terms of data mining, key techniques include many we have so far reviewed, such as machine intelligence.
- Another key area, which has really developed in the last decade, is Bayesian statistics, which this chapter devotes considerable time to reviewing. This chapter is specifically interested in Bayesian statistical parameter estimation and Bayesian hypothesis testing.
- The Bayesian school of thought treats the probability of events to be associated with 'epistemic uncertainty', that is, uncertainty due to lack of knowledge rather than 'aleatory uncertainty', which refers to uncertainty due to randomness. For a Bayesian, the probability of an event is simply a quantification of the amount of belief that the event will occur and, hence, does not require the notion of repeatable events or the idea of relative frequency either.
- This is what makes this approach different from frequentist probability theories, which the final part of the chapter attempts to further elucidate.

Further Reading

Wagenmakers, E. J. (2007). A practical solution to the pervasive problems of p-values. *Psychonomic Bulletin and Review, 14*(5), 779–804. https://doi.org/10.3758/BF03194105

This article deals with a comparison of the frequentist and Bayesian methods.

Wagenmakers, E. J., Lodewyckx, T., Kuriyal, H., & Grasman, R. (2010). Bayesian hypothesis testing for psychologists: A tutorial on the Savage–Dickey method. *Cognitive Psychology, 60*, 158–189. https://doi.org/10.1016/j.cogpsych.2009.12.001
This article is a tutorial on the Savage–Dickey method.

10

LONGITUDINAL ANALYSIS

Chapter Overview

Suppose you are asked by your airline to make a prediction. You told them how you read Castellani and Rajaram's *Big Data Mining and Complexity* and how you now understand the latest advances in predictive analytics. So now they want you to help them predict a few things. Mostly, they want to know what the future holds for them financially, relative to their two biggest competitors, Airline B and Airline C. And so you begin collecting your data on all three airlines. The question, however, is across what time period?

If you recall, in Chapter 6, sections 'The Notion of Time *t*' and 'A Vector Field', we addressed the issue of time, discussing such key formalisms as discrete versus continuous time, the dynamic clustering of case-based trajectories, vector fields and state spaces and global–temporal dynamics. However, despite this review, the issue of time has remained in the background. It is time, therefore, to bring it to the foreground of our analyses.

Time matters

The fact remains that, in our information-saturated world of real-time big data, most social scientists (and, by extension, policy evaluators and health researchers) remain horrible at prediction, and in large measure because, historically speaking, despite the temporal reality of most social phenomena, the vast majority of the databases that we study are static – that is, they are a single snapshot of a particular moment in time/space. Or they are, at best, comprised of a couple time-stamps, usually in the form of some pre- and post-analysis. In other words, despite our best efforts to study data as relatively static, causality is resolutely grounded in time/space. And so the only way, often, to know where something really is headed (and the reasons why it is heading that way) is to explore our data's memory to see where they have been.

Consider, for example, Figure 10.1, which shows three versions of the same financial data collected for your airline and its two biggest competitors. Along the *x*-axis is time, going from zero months to 84 months (7 years). Along the *y*-axis is financial success, with zero being bankrupt. On this graph are three airlines: Airline B, Airline C and then yours. For all three versions, everything is the same – except time.

For example, version 1 provides a small window of time: 10 months. Based on these data, it appears that not only is your airline doing the best, but Airline B looks like it is financially falling apart. But then there is version 2, which provides a much larger window of time – suggesting that your airline is not doing nearly as well as you thought! Also, it appears that, at least potentially, whatever happened to Airline B seems to have happened to your airline. Furthermore, it looks like, eventually, both airlines bounce back, but only slightly. And then there is version 3, which provides

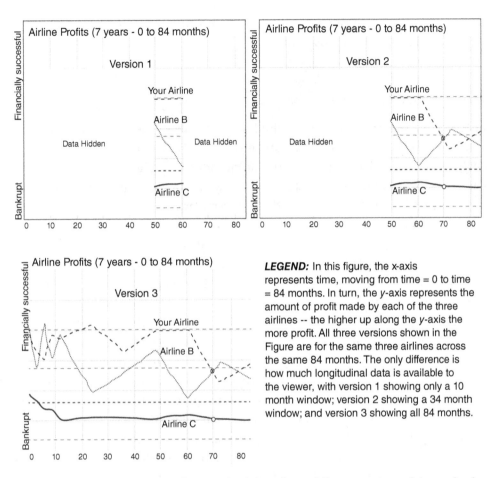

Figure 10.1 The importance of longitudinal data: three different versions of the profits for three airlines

the largest window of time. Here we see an even more complex picture. Not only are there periods of intense financial fluctuation in your airline and Airline B – which is not fiscally healthy, but, in stark contrast, while Airline C does not do as well, it is financially very stable. Also, in corroboration with version 2, it seems that whatever happens to Airline B also often happens a few months later to your airline, albeit to a degree less.

And so we see that when it comes to examining the causal patterns in our data (be it for understanding, let alone making predictions), time does indeed matter. In fact, it matters greatly! Why, then, do social scientists continue to study mostly static or highly limited temporal databases? There are a lot of reasons (Castellani et al., 2015; Rajaram & Castellani, 2012, 2014). Here, for example, are some of the more important, which can be grouped into two major types: (1) the complexities of data and (2) the limitations of method.

The complexities of data

In terms of the complexities of longitudinal data, one of the first and most problematic challenges is that such data are often expensive to collect, retrieve, extract, analyse and update. For example, in the airline industry, while the internet of things has created an information-saturated world of real-time big data (which we discussed in Chapters 3 and 4), data mining all that data remains costly in terms of time, talent, resources and money.

Second, as Chapters 3 and 4 also highlighted, despite all the big data currently available, deciding on the 'right' data remains difficult. For example, which financial data best illustrate the economic success of an airline company? In turn, which data give you the best insight into what customers really want?

Also, even when collected in real time, a lot of temporal data are incomplete or missing. How, for example, is one supposed to gain insights from customers who fly with a different carrier for a year and then suddenly come back to your airline?

Also, again even with real-time data, often the time-stamps chosen are not well-considered or too close together or too far apart. For example, what is the best time frame to truly understand customer opinion on an issue? In other words, despite all of the 'big data' hype about real-time information, it may be that making a reactive decision in response to immediate fluctuations in opinion (e.g. as we see in day trading) is actually financially reckless and rash; in other words, wrong.

And then there is the issue of attrition. For example, how does one study customers who no longer fly with an airline or participate in a social media app?

Also, even though temporal data is the key to causality, it remains difficult to know if some set of events (or, alternatively, from a policy perspective, one's manipulation of a causal factor) actually had its intended effect – particularly outside the confines of a controlled clinical trial. For example, amongst all the factors impacting the lives of travellers, how does one know that a sudden 'discount rate' actually improved sales? And, equally important, how long an effect did the sudden 'discount rate' have? And would it have been longer or more effective had the 'discounted rate' been longer or shorter in duration?

And, finally, longitudinal data – be they cohort, time-series, continuous and so on – seldom follow a singular common trend; instead, they self-organise into multiple major and minor trends, which, when modelled microscopically, are highly dynamic and complex – often taking the form of a variety of complex behaviours. All of this makes curve fitting, prediction and control (e.g. achieving financial stability in the airline industry) very difficult. Furthermore, these continuous trends (which we made clear in Chapter 6) are often a function of different measurements (k-dimensional vectors) on some profile of factors and the complex set of qualitative interactions and relationships amongst these variables (Castellani et al., 2015).

The limitations of method

The other major issue is method. As we have argued for continuously throughout this book, how one understands a social issue is (in large measure) a function of the methods used to study it. All of this has direct implications for (a) the complexity of the dynamics one is able to 'detect' in data, (b) as well as the complexity of the causal models one is able to 'identify'. Relative to this insight, as we discussed extensively in Part I of our book, the methods of conventional statistics – linear regression, time-series analysis and so on – are not exceptionally great at providing useful insights into the complexities of longitudinal data (Castellani et al., 2015; Rajaram & Castellani, 2012, 2014).

Case in point. It is very difficult for conventional statistics to (a) model the aggregate non-linear dynamics and complex trajectories of cases or their densi-ties in continuous time, (b) detect the presence of multiple trends (i.e. major and minor) across time, (c) identify and map complex steady-state behaviours (i.e. transient sinks, spiralling sources, periodic orbits), (d) explore and predict the motion of different trajectories and time instances, or (e) link these different trends to the complex k dimensional vectors/profiles upon which they are based, so that (f) they can construct a multilevel theoretical model of their topic of study (Castellani & Hafferty, 2009; Castellani & Rajaram, 2012; Rajaram & Castellani, 2012, 2014).

New methods are therefore needed! Enter data mining and the latest advances in computational and complexity science methods (Byrne & Callaghan, 2013).

Choosing the right method

As we have hopefully made clear, all of the methods reviewed in Part II of our book can be used with longitudinal data, from cluster analysis and artificial neural networks to GAs and Bayesian statistics to geospatial modelling and complex net-works. It is really, then, about choosing the right method. In the case of prediction, for example, one would choose the methods outlined in Chapter 9; in turn, if one were focused on classification, then one would use the methods in Chapter 8 and so forth.

Here, in this chapter, we want to focus on two methods we have yet to discuss: growth mixture modelling (GMM) and dynamical systems theory (i.e. differential equation modelling), as they serve two very specific functions in the analysis of longitudinal data. They are both very useful for modelling multiple case-based trajectories and their corresponding global–temporal dynamics. For more on these two methods, we recommend the following: Bar-Yam (1997), Hirsch et al. (2012), Jung and Wickrama (2008), Muthén and Muthén (2000) and Nylund et al. (2007). Also, for those interested in a more general overview of the data mining tools and techniques available for modelling longitudinal data, see Baker and Yacef (2009), Brown and Kros (2003), Fitzmaurice et al. (2008, 2012), Gulati (1995) and Wei (2013).

Growth mixture modelling

There are several variations of GMM in the literature. Ram and Grimm (2009), however, follow a main theme, which we will explain in this section. Given the database $D(t)$ (where the functional dependence on time t is written explicitly in this notation), and the various case trajectories $c_i(t)$, the idea of GMM is to use *growth curves* (call them $g_i(t)$) to model the growth (or change in general) in $c_i(t)$ as a function of t. We first explain what a growth curve is in what follows, and then explain what a *growth mixture* means.

Growth curves

A growth curve in general can be written as follows:

$$c_i(t) = g_{0i} \cdot g_0(t) + g_{1i} \cdot g_1(t) + e_i(t),$$

(10.1)

where g_{0i} and g_{1i} are constants, and $g_0(t)$ and $g_1(t)$ are growth curves (also called basis vectors – a terminology adopted from linear algebra) that the case trajectory $c_i(t)$ is expected to follow from prior expert knowledge in the field or can be estimated from the data itself.

In *growth curve modelling*, the entire database $D(t)$ is assumed to be sampled from a single population, and hence all case trajectories are assumed to follow the growth basis vectors $g_0(t)$ and $g_1(t)$ with varying degrees depending on the value of the coefficients g_{0i} and g_{1i}. We note, once again, that $c_i(t)$ is from the data $D(t)$ (the columns), and $g_i(t)$ are mathematical functions that model $c_i(t)$ with a reasonable error $e_i(t)$. For each case trajectory $c_i(t)$, the coefficients g_{0i} and g_{1i} are fit so that the error $e_i(t)$ is minimised (e.g. a least squares fit is one possible way to compute the coefficients). There are three important aspects of a growth curve:

1   *Pattern:* This refers to the structure of the growth basis vectors $g_0(t)$ and $g_1(t)$ – that is, whether they increase, decrease or stay put, and also where such increases or decreases happen across time t. Typically $g_0(t)$ is chosen to be a vector of 1s (i.e. $g_0(t) = (1,1,1,...,1)$) to denote the constant trajectory, and $g_1(t)$ is chosen to be a curve that fits the data well, or a curve that is known to be a good fit from prior knowledge of the field. Since $g_0(t)$ is essentially a measure of constancy of trajectories, the real pattern of the trajectory comes from $g_1(t)$. This formalism is not standard always, and one could choose two different growth basis vectors, both of which represent the pattern as well.

2   *Means:* Given that the coefficients g_{0i} and g_{1i} are different for different case trajectories $c_i(t)$, this refers to the mean of these coefficients (the mean of g_{0i} is denoted by μ_{g0} and the mean of g_{1i} is denoted by μ_{g1}). If $g_0(t)$ is chosen to be a vector of 1s, then μ_{g0} will denote the average starting point of trajectories $c_i(t)$ in the database $D(t)$. μ_{g1} will denote the average change from the initial time instant to the final time instant across all trajectories $c_i(t)$.

3   *Covariances:* The variance of g_{0i} (denoted as σ_{g0}^2) represents the extent of variation in the starting levels of trajectories $c_i(t)$, and the variance of g_{1i} (denoted by σ_{g1}^2) denotes the extent of variation in the change of trajectories $c_i(t)$. In turn, the covariance σ_{g0g1} denotes how the inter-trajectory differences in starting levels relate to inter-trajectory changes.

Multiple group growth curve modelling

If the database $D(t)$ is assumed (or known) to consist of multiple latent groups (sub-populations or classes) of case trajectories – as is often the case in data mining real-time big databases – and the classes are already known a priori (as in the techniques of classification discussed in Chapter 7), then each class can be fit with a different set of basis vectors. For example, the classes could arise naturally based on a categorical variable c (and the case trajectories belonging to the classes will be labelled as $c_{ic}(t)$). The categorical variable c could be gender or eye colour, for example. Then separate growth curve models will be fit for each class. The model will look as follows:

$$c_{ic}(t) = g_{0ic} \cdot g_{0c}(t) + g_{1ic} \cdot g_{1c}(t) + e_{ic}(t),$$ (10.2)

where $g_{0c}(t)$ and $g_{1c}(t)$ are the basis vectors, g_{0ic} and g_{1ic} are coefficients for the the ith case trajectory, and $e_{ic}(t)$ is the error trajectory for the ith case trajectory within the class c, respectively. The three aspects of pattern, means and covariances will now be studied for each class c and possibly compared across classes.

Growth mixture modelling explained

GMM is an extension of the multiple group growth curve modelling, where the grouping variable c is latent or unobserved (Ram & Grimm, 2009). As with cluster analysis (discussed in Chapter 7), here there is no a priori knowledge of how the trajectories group together. This is, instead, one of the outputs of GMM; that is, several different number of subgroups are assumed, and the growth curves are fit for 1, 2, 3 and so on number of subgroups (a stopping point is chosen based on expert knowledge), and the separation of patterns, means and covariances are used to determine the best choice for number of subgroups. Furthermore, for each case trajectory $c_i(t)$, a probability π_{ic} is also estimated, which is the probability that the trajectory $c_i(t)$ belongs to the subgroup c.

The general growth mixture model – which we borrow from Ram and Grimm (2009) – looks as follows:

$$c_{ic}(t) = \sum_{c=1}^{p} \pi_{ic} \left(g_{0ic} \cdot g_{0c}(t) + g_{1ic} \cdot g_{1c}(t) + e_{ic}(t) \right), \tag{10.3}$$

which is simply a weighted sum of multiple group growth models weighted by the probabilities π_{ic}, which should satisfy $0 \le \pi_{ic} \le 1, \sum_{c=1}^{p} \pi_{ic} = 1$.

First, a baseline model with a single class (i.e. the entire database $D(t)$) is constructed. Next, after the expected number of classes for stoppage is determined, for every choice of class numbers (or number of clusters of trajectories), $p = 1,2,3,...$ until the stoppage number, three group-difference models are created: (1) one where the means μ_{g0} and μ_{g1} are allowed to differ, (2) one where both the means and variances μ_{g0}, μ_{g1} and $\sigma_{g0}^2, \sigma_{g1}^2, \sigma_{g0g1}^2$ as well as the error variance σ_{ϵ}^2 are allowed to differ and (3) one where the means and variances and also the patterns $g_0(t)$ and $g_1(t)$ are allowed to differ. The baseline (or invariance model) treats the entire database as a single group; that is, $p = 1$. This stage will yield multiple models, which also have the number of groups p embedded in them as well. To select the best model (and hence, automatically the number of groups), one employs the following – which is further outlined in Ram and Grimm (2009, p. 571):

1 The parameter estimates and the actual models are examined to make sure they make sense. For example, a model with a negative variance means that the model is useless. Also, if the models themselves have similar or same parameter estimates, then that would mean that two or more group number choices for p exhibit identical change patterns. Such models need to be set aside, while models with smaller values of p are considered carefully first. Also, knowledge of the substantive area regarding the distinctiveness of trajectories should be used to inform model selection.

2 The models are compared using relative fit criteria such as the Bayesian information criteria (BIC), Akaike information criteria (AIC) and the adjusted BIC. Lower values in these criteria indicate a better fit (Ram & Grimm, 2009, p. 571). Models that don't fit better than the baseline model can be thrown out, thereby reducing the number of models considered.

3 The models are also evaluated with respect to the accuracy with which individual trajectories $c_i(t)$ have been classified into groups. A statistic called *entropy* is computed (with values between 0 and 1), and high values indicate that individuals are classified with higher confidence.

4 Lastly, an array of likelihood ratio tests (LRTs) are used to compare models with p and $p - 1$ as the number of groups, and if the p-value is less than 0.05 then the model(s) with $p - 1$ groups are rejected (again, see Ram & Grimm, 2009, p. 571, for details).

Still, while highly useful, GMM is not the only approach to identifying multiple trends in a database. There is also differential equation modelling, which has the added advantage of being able to model global–temporal dynamics.

Differential equations and dynamical systems theory

As we discussed in Chapter 6, differential equations are useful for modelling the instantaneous rate of change in a case. We can write this rate of change as $c'(t)$ (known as the derivative from calculus) as a function $f(c(t),t)$ of the case profile at time t – given by $c(t)$ and explicitly as a function of time t as well. Since $c(t) = (x_1(t),...,x_k(t))$, we have that $c'(t) = (x_1'(t),...,x_k'(t))$, where $x_i'(t)$ is the instantaneous rate of change of the profile variable $x_i(t)$.

Differential equations are also useful, as we hope to demonstrate here, whenever complex behaviour is manifested in the form of time-varying phenomena, as in the case of modelling multiple trajectories across time. In terms of details, as we reviewed in Chapter 6, section 'How Do We Fill the Gap?', differential equation modelling permits a certain hierarchical flexibility. For example, a single differential equation such as Equation (6.4) can be used for the entire database D, or we could have as many models as the number of case trajectories N, leaving the researcher with a broad range of possibilities.

Finally, differential equations (i.e. dynamical systems theory) are also very good at modelling global–temporal dynamics, as in the case of identifying chaotic behaviour, periodic oscillations, attractors and repellents and so on. For example, Equation (6.4) $c' = f(c,t)$, where time t appears explicitly as an independent variable in the vector field f, is called a **non-autonomous differential equation**. Alternatively, an **autonomous differential equation** looks like the following:

$$c' = f(c). \tag{10.4}$$

We note that, in both situations, the case trajectory c is a function of time and is denoted as $c(t)$. In both situations, an initial case profile needs to be fed into the model in the form $c(0) = c_0$. The solution (as described in Chapter 6, section 'Why Do

We Need a Vector Field?') is a trajectory that passes through the profile c_0 at time $t = 0$ and is always tangential to the arrows shown by the vector field f.

Examples of global–temporal dynamics

In the following, we describe special kinds of trajectories (global–temporal dynamics) for the autonomous differential equation (Equation 10.4).

Equilibrium point, sources and sinks

A trajectory of the form $c(t) = c_0$ is termed an **equilibrium point**. This is because, for all times t, the trajectory $c(t)$ stays put at the profile c_0. An equilibrium point is termed as a **source** if trajectories nearby move away from the profile c_0. A source is an example of an *unstable* equilibrium point since it *repels* nearby trajectories, which – recalling our discussion of Figure 6.5 (see Figure 10.2, which is a snapshot) – the nearby case trajectories could move away in a radial fashion or in a spiralling fashion (in this case, the equilibrium point is called a spiralling source). An equilibrium that attracts case trajectories nearby is a *stable* equilibrium point and is termed a **sink**. A sink can also be radial or spiralling depending on how it attracts nearby case trajectories. An equilibrium point is called a saddle point – as shown in Figure 10.2 – if it attracts trajectories in one direction and repels in another.

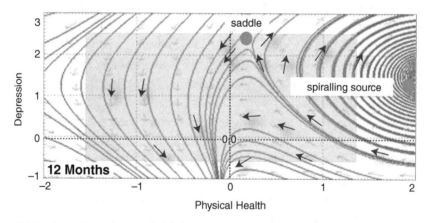

Figure 10.2 Snapshot of vector field discussed in Chapter 6

Periodic orbits

A trajectory which satisfies $c(t + T) = c(t)$ for a given real number $T > 0$ is called a **periodic orbit**. This is because the trajectory returns to its starting point and repeats the cycle for every time period of T. Periodic orbits can be classified as stable or unstable (just like equilibrium points) depending on whether or not they attract or repel nearby case trajectories.

Chaotic attractors

There are examples of differential equations that admit solutions that are chaotic. Of particular interest is a **chaotic attractor**. A famous example is the *Lorenz attractor*, which has two sets of attracting regions in the form of a butterfly. Nearby trajectories can get attracted into one of the two attractors, and it is not known a priori where they will end up. This is due to the fact that small errors due to floating point representations in the initial condition c_0 get propagated into large errors (that are unpredictable), leading to an attraction to either of the two parts of the butterfly depending on whether the larger errors place the trajectory in the attracting region of the left or right wing of the butterfly. The idea of chaos is essentially an unpredictable amplification of small errors in the initial conditions into larger errors, thereby leading to unpredictable and strange behaviour of solutions to differential equations. In other words, small changes in initial conditions due to numerical errors lead to wildly divergent and unpredictable solutions, even though the differential equation is very deterministic, and hence, this type of chaos is sometimes referred to as *deterministic chaos*. The choice of parameters in the vector field f where chaos occurs is referred to as the *chaotic regime*.

Special trajectories for non-autonomous differential equations

First, the vector field for autonomous differential equations is given by $f(c)$. This means that in two dimensions (say), at every case profile c, one can imagine an arrow (which depicts the instantaneous rate of change of the case c). The magnitude and direction of this vector remains a constant, as time t is not an explicit independent variable in f. For a non-autonomous differential equation $f(c,t)$, in two dimensions, we can imagine the same placement of arrows at every case profile c, except, the magnitude and direction of these arrows keep changing according to the equation given by f. So in essence, $f(c,t)$ is a movie, where at each time instant t, we have the instantaneous snapshot of the vector field, with arrows changing magnitude and direction as time elapses.

Non-autonomous vector fields admit similar kinds of special trajectories such as sources, sinks, saddles, periodic orbits, chaotic attractors and so on, except these special trajectories have the potential of appearing and disappearing as time elapses. Once again, this is because time t is an explicit independent variable in the vector field f, and hence, for each choice of f we have a different instantaneous vector field f that may or may not have these special trajectories. Hence, the complexity of possible trajectories for a non-autonomous differential equation is extremely high. Not only does $f(c,t)$ have the ability to capture the motion of case trajectories that change with time, it also has the ability to capture the instantaneous occurrence and disappearance of all the special trajectories mentioned above.

Modelling process

As we have outlined elsewhere, we have developed our own approach to using differential equations modelling for data mining big data from a case-based complexity perspective (Castellani et al., 2015; Rajaram & Castellani, 2012, 2014). Our goal here is to give a quick sense of how such an approach works, primarily to give readers a better appreciation for the utility of these tools. As readers may recall, we mentioned a few steps in our modelling process in Chapter 6, section 'The Formalisms of Case-Based Complexity'.

To begin, we assume that the clustering process has been done and separate clusters of trajectories have been identified and characterised (and possibly named even) after discussions with subject matter experts. Once this is done, we fit a differential equation (non-autonomous, to allow for all complexities) model.

We compute the velocity vectors at each of the case profiles within the range of data, and 'fill the gap' as discussed in Chapter 6, section 'How Do We Fill the Gap?'. This essentially involves construction of a function f. Several things are important here.

First, f is found among the function class of polynomials. This is because polynomials are known to be 'dense' in most practical function classes. This means that given, for example, a square integrable function on a bounded set, and given a tolerance ϵ, one can always find a polynomial that is 'ϵ' away from the given square-integrable function, according to the L^2-distance measure (which is a generalisation of the Euclidean distance to the space of functions).

Second, we search for a polynomial f that best fits the vector field computed from data D; however, we don't specify the degree or the number of terms in the polynomial. Instead, a GA is used to find f, which has the least error. Error is defined in the least squared sense between the computed velocities c' and the polynomial f. In other words $c' \approx f(c,t)$, where $\approx$ stands for 'approximately equal to'.

In short, we do not fit the data to a given function, but instead fit the best polynomial function (among infinitely many choices) to the given data. This is a departure from traditional modelling techniques where the structure of f is already assumed and 'modelling' simply refers to fitting the parameters of the known f. Here, there is no structure assumed except that it is a polynomial – which is a wide class of functions. In fact, the Lorenz chaotic attractor mentioned above is simply a polynomial. Polynomial differential equations have the ability to capture extremely complex case trajectories when used as a model.

Once complete, this model $c' = f(c,t)$ can then be used to identify interesting regions in the state space of case profiles. For example, the occurrence of a saddle equilibrium point would mean that the stable and unstable directions create a partition of the state space at the time instant that the saddle occurs, and trajectories from one portion of the partition cannot cross over into the other portion.

Also, the case profiles in the vicinity of the partition can be investigated to find out why such a crossover is not permitted. The model, however, will automatically capture such partitions. If there are periodic orbits, then those cases on the orbit experience repetitive behaviour and they could be studied separately as to why such repetitions occur. Each of the special trajectories mentioned above lead to a smaller group of special case trajectories that could not have been identified without the differential equation model.

Finally, novel initial case profiles can be fed to the differential equation model, and their trajectories can be predicted with a degree of certainty. The accuracy of such predictions goes back to the accuracy of the clustering operation, which partitions the data D into clusters C_i. The tighter the cluster, the better the fit for the differential equation and the better the accuracy of the prediction of case trajectories for novel initial case profiles.

Comparing and contrasting methods

The main difference between differential equation-based modelling and GMM, as outlined in this chapter, is that in the former, the process of identifying subgroups is separated out from the process of modelling itself. In the latter, the number of subgroups p is actually a part of the modelling process itself and is embedded in the model as well, where selection of a model based on the various methods shown above automatically gives the number of subgroups. It is to be noted that although static (non-dynamic) trajectory patterns $g_0(t)$ and $g_1(t)$ are used as models for GMM, one could also use a differential equation model instead of the two patterns; and hence, differential equations can be 'mixed' with subgroups as well. These differences give differential equation modelling, in the service of a case-based complexity approach – which we call case-based density modelling (CBDM) – several advantages over GMM.

First, as shown in Figure 10.3, rather than fitting data to a function – as is done in GMM and similar statistical techniques – CBDM fits complex functions to data using GAs, which allows for the type of highly refined curve fitting shown in the Chapter 8 neural net figures, as well as the identification of minor (small size) and major trends. While this difference nonetheless allows GMM to do a relatively good job curve fitting the data, as we see with the three lines fit to our earlier hypothetical comparison of the financial success of our three airlines, it is still not as good as CBDM.

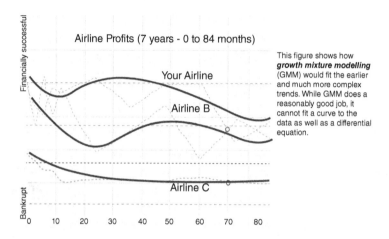

LEGEND: In this figure, the x-axis represents time, moving from time = 0 to time = 84 months. In turn, the y-axis represents the amount of profit made by each of the three airlines – the higher up along the y-axis the more profit.

Figure 10.3 Growth mixture model for earlier hypothetical airline example

Equally important, this curve-fitting approach also allows for the preservation of a data set's complexity, as CBDM can move back and forth between global–temporal patterns, the major and minor trends for different subpopulations and the individual trajectory of a single case within any given trend.

Third, repeated measures (e.g. in the case of co-morbid depression–physical health trajectories) are treated as continuous (as opposed to discrete) so that the modelling process is focused not only on how trends differ but also on how trends change across time, particularly when highly dynamic.

Fourth, memory is built into the model. This is important because it allows the past history of a trend to be directly linked to current and future changes using a differential equation–based model.

Fifth, identified trends can be assembled into a microscopic (vector field) model of all possible trajectories for some defined state-space. As shown in Figure 10.2 earlier, for example, the value of such a model is that it can be data mined for key global–temporal dynamics such as periodic orbits, saddle points, spiralling sources, episodic behaviours and vacillating patterns, as well as the changing velocity of trends across time.

Finally, because of its mixed-methods approach, a technique like GMM can be integrated into CBDM for the purposes of exploration and corroboration. Clustering and classification techniques can also be used.

Chapter Summary

- One of the key features of big data is that a lot of the data are temporal, be these data longitudinal, repeated-measures, time-series or (thinking back to the five Vs) real-time data.
- The temporal nature of big data is a major challenge to social inquiry, as most methods and training focus on cross-sectional data or limited pre–post studies.
- Many of the computational and data mining methods reviewed in the current book can be used with temporal data. The challenge, however, is learning how to do these types of analyses. Examples include dealing with missing data, working with discrete versus continuous data and dealing with issues of collinearity and autocorrelation.
- Another major issue is modelling multiple trajectories and trends across time. One of the more useful techniques for modelling these types of data is growth mixture modelling, which the current chapter reviews in detail.
- The other technique reviewed, which the authors have spent considerable time developing in their own work, is differential equations and dynamical systems theory. Specifically, the authors have developed an approach called case-based density modelling, which has several advantages over other methods, including growth mixture modelling. One example is that it fits trends to data rather than data to trends. Another is that memory is built into the models.

Further Reading

Hirsch, M. W., Smale, S., & Devaney, R. L. (2012). *Differential equations, dynamical systems, and an introduction to chaos.* Academic Press. https://doi.org/10.1016/B978-0-12-382010-5.00015-4
This book deals with differential equations and chaotic dynamical systems.

Ram, N., & Grimm, K. J. (2009). Growth mixture modeling: A method for identifying differences in longitudinal change among unobserved groups. *International Journal of Behavioral Development, 33*(6), 565–576. https://doi.org/10.1177/0165025409343765
This article explains the variations on growth mixture modelling.

11

GEOSPATIAL MODELLING

Chapter Overview

The importance of geospatial modelling

Suppose your airline (along with several others) is interested in potentially moving to a new airport being built, and it is an international one, nonetheless. In the business meetings to discuss the potential move, for which you are providing data, you find everyone discussing an issue one would not normally think, financially speaking, to be highly important: geography!

In the world of data mining big data, geospatial modelling plays a crucial role, as it seeks to reveal (i.e. identify, locate, find, uncover) the relationship that geography and geospatial factors have with other key factors – be they biological, social, ecological and so on. Examples range from identifying key emergency routes in a city or airport to how a natural disaster spreads through a region to predicting weather patterns and global climate change. As further illustration, consider the spread of a disease. As epidemiologists know, our global transportation system provides a highly useful geospatial network by which contagious diseases spread throughout the world. In turn, upon landing those diseases move faster through highly dense cities than rural countrysides, for example; or near water, and so on and so forth. Mapping the geospatial movement of diseases, therefore, is very important. Figure 11.1, for example, is a 2020 map of the global spread of the Zika virus.

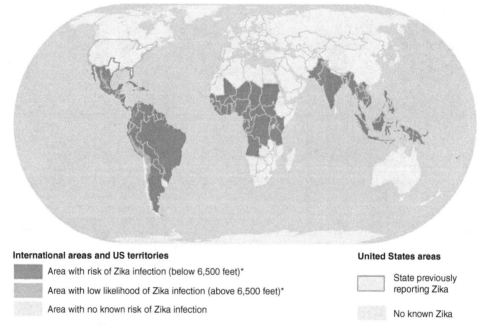

International areas and US territories

- Area with risk of Zika infection (below 6,500 feet)*
- Area with low likelihood of Zika infection (above 6,500 feet)*
- Area with no known risk of Zika infection

United States areas

- State previously reporting Zika
- No known Zika

Figure 11.1 2018 Global map of the Zika virus (wwwnc.cdc.gov/travel/files/zika-areas-of-risk.pdf)

The same is true of mapping socio-economic and ecological deprivation. Figure 11.2, for example, comes from data collected for the Welsh Index of Multiple Deprivation, which is the official measure of small area deprivation in Wales. Here, in this map, is a visualisation of overall deprivation, across several categories, including such key factors as housing, employment, income, fuel poverty, crime and so forth.

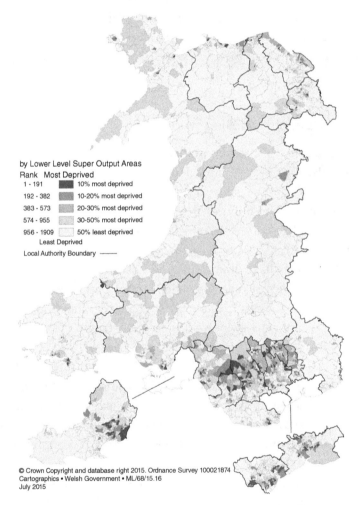

Figure 11.2   2014 Map of overall deprivation in Wales by lower level super output areas

In the airline industry, other geospatial issues range from the geographical information systems in your airplanes to weather pattern analysis to wayfinding – which amounts to a massive amount of 2D and 3D big data! Wayfinding, by the way, is the usage of geospatial information systems to more effectively and efficiently guide people, planes, luggage and so forth through some physical environment – as illustration, think of smart cars, your plane's autopilot or those high-powered computational algorithms that find the fastest route to your destination, as well as the mind-numbing level of data crunching necessary to get those answers. For example, going back to your meeting to relocate to a new airport, one of the issues your colleagues might discuss is airline traffic density at the new airport, which can be high, if not thought through correctly, due to how the airport manages getting all sorts of traffic in and out of the airport, from people and packages to cars and planes to trucks and buses, not to mention how the location of the new airport will improve (or not) your airline's access to its most important or high-trafficked airplane routes.

How does geospatial modelling work?

Okay, so we get a sense of the importance of geospatial modelling. But how do we use these tools? And, related, how does one 'think through' the complexities of geospatial data, let alone deal with the massive amounts of such information being collected, minute by minute, as humanity moves through our worldwide internet of things? These are the questions we asked ourselves in writing the current chapter.

While social scientists have always made use of maps and mapping, as well as considered the importance of geography and its place in their work, the latest computational developments in geospatial modelling are very new and, for most social scientists, sit outside the purview of what is generally taught. As such, we sought in this chapter to provide a slightly more detailed overview of the field, including (a) an overview of key concepts and terms, (b) an introduction to the big data challenges of collecting and organising complex geospatial data and then (c) reviewing the data mining tools and techniques available for modelling and analysing geospatial data. For a good review of geospatial modelling, we refer the reader to Cliff and Ord (1981), De Smith et al. (2007), Fotheringham and Rogerson (2014), Maguire et al. (2005) and Miller and Goodchild (2015).

Of these, however, the best is De Smith et al.'s *Geospatial Analysis*. Originally published in 2007, and with more than 1000 citations, it is currently in its sixth edition (2020). There is also a companion website www.spatialanalysisonline.com/index.html. For the current chapter, we will draw from the *2020 Online Edition* (www.spatialanalysisonline.com/HTML/index.html). And again, as with other chapters, we make use of their organisational structure so that readers can move from our review to their excellent full-length treatment of the topic – which we strongly recommend (as we have before with other works) as necessary reading.

Conceptual framework

Prerequisites

By way of introduction, it is useful to describe some of the basic terminology required to understand geospatial modelling and analysis. All of the definitions below can be found in 'Section 2.1: Basic Primitives' of the 2020 online edition of De Smith et al.'s *Geospatial Analysis*. (Note: For those definitions taken directly from the online version, we have placed them in brackets, noting the section where it can be found):

1   The *place* in geospatial data is described concretely using a coordinate system. Typically, coordinates are used (this is called a *vector* format – remember our discussion of this concept in Chapter 6? – where points, lines and polygons are used to represent a place) or pixels (this is called *raster* format). Both representations have their advantages, with the latter being used when there are multiple layers and computations need to be done. Vector and raster formats can be converted. Places are also sometimes called *objects*.

2   The *attribute* of a place refers to a particular characteristic of the place. An attribute can be *nominal* – where it is used as a qualitative label for the place with no sense of ranking and where arithmetic operations make no sense (e.g. telephone area code); *ordinal* – where labels mean a certain ranking but again no arithmetic operations allowed (e.g. geographical preferences ranked in order of personal preferences); *interval, ratio* – quantitative attributes where differences or ratios make sense (e.g. temperature or elevation above sea level for the former, and acres burnt in a fire for the latter); and finally *cyclic* for attributes that represent cyclic phenomenon (e.g. calendar dates or angles, where 0 and 360 degrees are the same).

3   *Layers* of attributes are used to completely describe a place. Patterns are then found within layers or across layers. The layers may contain information on the same spatial points or not. An example of the latter would be one layer containing the density of disease spread, and the second layer that monitors water quality at points that don't exactly coincide with the geographical location of people affected by the disease.

4   A *field* is a representation that shows the variation (either discrete or continuous) of a measurement across a geographical area. Temperature or elevation fields are continuous, whereas marking isolated incidents of a disease will be a discrete field. Points, lines and polygons are used in both cases.

5   *Density* refers to the number of discrete objects per unit area and is essentially a link between discrete and continuous fields, since density is always continuous. Example is number of cars per unit area represented as traffic density.

6   *Scale* refers to the spatial resolution (rather than true spatial ratios, since scale on digital maps will depend on the size of the screen) that is shown on a map. For example, the spatial resolution of a paper map is usually 0.5 mm at the scale of a map, (500 m on a 1:1,000,000 map, or 5 m on a 1:10,000 map), a figure that takes into account the widths of lines on maps.

7   'A property on a map is said to be *topological* if it survives stretching and distortion of space' (De Smith et al., 2018, Section 2.1.10: Topology). Examples are dimensionality (distinction between a point, line and a plane), adjacency (touching of land parcels), connectivity (junctions between roads) and containment (point lying inside rather than outside an area).

Spatial relationships

1   Places are *co-located* if they have the same coordinates. Attributes of co-located places can be used to identify patterns. For example, as with your airline's consideration of a new airport, a cluster of airlines with high-traffic patterns might be explained by a concentration of industries in the area (leading to large amounts of business travellers), attributes that could be in two different layers.

2   A *spatial weights matrix* W is used to identify relative distances (weights essentially) between pairs of places. For example, the distances between centroids of neighbouring counties, along with the labels for the counties in each row (three entries per row) can be stored in a W matrix. The relationship between the weight and the actual distance is immaterial for the most part compared to the relative weights in W.

3   *Multidimensional scaling* is the idea of representing distances on a map based on the relationship of a variable or a phenomenon and the actual distance. For example, distances on a map can reflect travel times, interactions between community members (based on the idea that interactions decline systematically with distance, i.e. the distance decay model) (De Smith et al., 2018)

4   *Spatial context* can be gained by comparing the attributes of objects with other objects in the vicinity. For example, the price of an airline ticket might be high from an airport in part due to the lack of other airline routes through that airport or the lack of other regional airports nearby (monopoly), or the price might be less because of the presence of multiple airline hubs and also the presence of many airports in the geographical area. *Neighbourhood* can be defined to be within a geometric boundary from a point on a map (a circle, polygon etc.), or as a *convolution* with a decreasing weight as one moves radially outward from a point, or as the number of adjacent cells (in the raster format).

5   *Spatial heterogeneity* refers to the variability in results if the area under study is re-located as well as the lack of generalisation of results to the earth as a whole based from the results of a smaller geographical area. *Spatial dependence*, on the other hand, refers to the remarkable similarity of conditions to persist locally (e.g. lack of rainfall in desert areas, extreme cold in polar regions). *Tobler's law* states that 'all things are related, but nearby things are more related than distant things'. The magnitude of similarity can be measured using spatial autocorrelation statistics (Cliff & Ord, 1981). (For more, see De Smith et al., 2018, Section 2.2.7: Spatial Dependence.)

6   *Spatial sampling* allows us (due to Tobler's law) to obtain a reasonable description of the earth's surface by a few well-spaced sampling points. As explained by De Smith et al. (2018), various methods exist.

7   *Spatial interpolation* refers to computing the attribute of a place based on the weighted average of known attributes of nearby places, with weights depending proportionally on distance. This process of weighted average is called *convolution*, which leads to *smoothing* of properties across places. This again is in accordance with Tobler's law, which suggests that processes that leave a smooth pattern on the earth's surface are more prevalent. *First-order* processes are those that produce a variation in point density due to a single causal variable – for example, the density of cases of unsatisfied airline customers reflects the density of delayed flights for some set of airports. On the other hand, there might be *second-order* processes that result from interactions; and hence the presence of one point makes others more

(or less) likely in its vicinity. For example, the social media spread of a discounted fare for a delayed flight through Twitter interactions amongst people waiting in an airport. It is to be noted that Tobler's law can be false as well (leading to sharper densities rather than smoother), as in the case of competition of space, where the presence of one airport, for example, will discourage other airports from establishing themselves in the vicinity, leading to dispersed patterns rather than clusters.

Geospatial modelling with real data

The field of geospatial analysis is extremely vast (De Smith et al., 2018) with multiple software tools allowing for a variety of computational algorithms. Hence, we have chosen to focus on some main aspects in this book. In general *geographical information systems* or GISs are systems used for input, storage, manipulation, summarising, editing, querying and visualising geographic information. *Geographic Information Science* or *GIScience* is the study of organisations and tools associated with the process of collecting and disseminating geographic information.

Part 1: Collecting and organising geospatial data

As we hope we have so far illustrated, there is a tremendous amount of complexity involved in the analysis of geospatial data. Furthermore, given the *five Vs* of big data, the complexity of geospatial data is also a matter of (a) volume, (b) velocity (i.e. how quickly the volume of data grows) and (c) variety (i.e. the kinds of data coming from simulations, drones and satellite platforms, radio frequency identification tags and geo-referenced social media platforms).

Furthermore, with the deluge of data, the hunt for universal laws and mechanistic explanations (the so-called *nomothetic*) is less of a primary goal in advancing science – but rather deeper descriptions (the so-called *idiographic*) of what is happening at particular places at particular times. However, over longer time scales and larger spatial domains, these deeper descriptions merge into long-term spatio-temporal patterns; and hence, the challenge is one of generalisation. Today's GIS is a combination of both nomothetic (in the form of powerful software and algorithms) and the idiographic (in the form of databases) principles, where neither approach is privileged.

With this complexity in mind, we explain some of the commonly used methods for collecting and organising geospatial data:

1   *Surveying* refers to calculating the precise position of points, lines and angles using geometry. Data collected through such surveys can then be used to create highly precise maps.

2   *Remote sensing* involves the use of satellites orbiting the earth to capture information from regions on the earth's surface, which are then transmitted to receiving stations where they are converted to digital images to be analysed. Through the use of a set of specific calculations on the images, a spatial analyst can then identify and classify features on a landscape such as changes in snow melt and location of sea sponges and so on, without having to set foot in those regions.

3   *Maps* are mathematical representations of the earth's surface that are used as a medium for communicating geospatial information relationships in visual form. *Cartography* is the study of design, construction and evaluation of maps, which utilises graphic design, computer science, mathematics, statistics, psychology and, most certainly, geography.

4   *Volunteered geographic information or VGI* is information collected by users roving the surface of the earth. VGI is the contribution of content regarding local activities in various geographic locations around the world that may traditionally go unnoticed by the rest of the world's media. People now have the ability to share qualitative or quantitative information with an internet-enabled audience about their experience in a specific place in the world. VGI is typically collected and shared through the use of smartphones and the internet of things, and is a very important part of the world of big data today.

5   *Location-based services or LBS* are services that offer information about where a location-aware device user is situated. Examples include popular applications such as Google Maps.

6   *Global Positioning Systems or GPS* is a satellite network that communicates with GPS receivers accessed by mobile users. The GPS receiver needs to connect with four or more satellites orbiting the earth as reference to calculate the precise location of the user within a few metres. GPS satellites were launched by the US military but are also used for civilian use. GPS receivers are widely used in cars and smartphones to provide directions to specific locations. Individual GPS receivers can be purchased and installed on almost anything. Physical geographers and human geographers alike find them valuable for documenting information about a place. Data formats collected by the GPS can be exported from many different file formats to be used in a wide variety of software platforms. GPS sensors can be mounted on drones or UAVs (unmanned aerial vehicles), or on balloons for mapping purposes.

Part 2: Modelling and analysing geospatial data

As with our other chapters, we cannot adequately survey all of the methods presently used in geospatial analysis. We refer the reader to De Smith et al. (2018) and highlight several of the more popular, which are as follows.

Surface and field analysis

The variation of a single variable (e.g. height, temperature, cost or barometric pressure) over a two-dimensional surface is captured by a function $z = f(x, y)$, where $z = f(x, y)$ gives the value of the variable at the point (x, y). As with Figures 11.1 and 11.2 earlier, for example, sometimes multiple values are stored if colour-coded information (with values from $[0, 255]$) or time-dependent information (temperature recorded at hourly intervals) are stored. This is essentially the same idea as the vector field discussed in Chapter 6, section 'A Vector Field'. Field data are stored in the form of *Digital Elevation Models* collected through terrestrial, aerial and satellite surveys. Typically, simpler mathematical functions (e.g. planes of the form $z = ax + by + c$) are fitted for smaller grids on the (x, y) plane.

A *raster* representation is one where a rectangular array of identical grid cells on the (x, y) plane is stored in the form of a matrix, with the rows representing positions from north to south and columns representing positions from east to west (also sometimes called *eastings*). The values stored in the cells is the height $z = f(x, y)$ stored of the variable being recorded (e.g. temperature, height etc.). Collection of raster data sets that are adjacent are referred to as *tiles*, and separate tiles are sometimes combined into a *mosaic* before analysis is started. Once the data are combined and represented, numerical approximations to first and second order partial derivatives are then used to estimate rates of change of z along the x and y directions, and surface curvature measures, respectively. Von-Neumann neighbourhoods are used for calculating these numerical approximations where the immediate eight neighbours are included, and an additional cell is added on the extreme north, south, east and west locations.

A *vector* representation is one where coordinate geometry-based ideas are used to store the vector field. *Contour* representation involves filling the region with lines of equal values for z, with the idea that contours cannot intersect. A *triangulated irregular network* or *TIN* is a collection of irregular (unequal) triangles used to tessellate the (x, y) plane with more triangles used in regions of high variation of z, and vice versa. Each triangle takes a different but uniform value of z. Vector representations typically take up less memory for storage compared to the raster format.

Once the (x, y, z) data are stored either in raster or vector format, a mathematical model is then fit for the function $z = f(x, y)$. This can be done either with (a) a single function for the overall (x, y) region using least-squares approximation methods or (b) piecewise functions for smaller regions using polynomial-based functions. The former is called *approximate* or *non-exact* model and the latter is called an *exact* model simply because of the better ability of the latter model to capture variations. Several GIS packages facilitate the creation of grids or surfaces using statistical functions rather than just mathematical functions. The generated surfaces may then be combined with existing surfaces or mathematically defined surfaces to create new grids, which may be used for a variety of purposes: uncertainty modelling, providing reference grids for comparison or residual analysis purposes, for the generation of idealised terrains or for statistical analyses.

Once the surface is modelled, various mathematical and geometrical aspects can be computed such as gradient, slope, aspect, curvature, directional derivatives, volume calculations and smoothing (or interpolation of values to remove sudden changes of z due to errors), which we omit due to brevity. Please refer to De Smith et al. (2018) for details.

Network and location analysis

A group of problems that combine network theory and geospatial analysis fall under the category of network and location analysis problems. For a somewhat detailed exposition on network analysis please refer to Chapter 12. In this section, we will focus on discussing the kinds of problems and the solution methods that are useful.

NP problems are decision problems (problems with a 'yes' or 'no' answer) that are not known to be solvable in polynomial time but have the property that, given a solution, it can be checked for optimality in polynomial time; that is, the number of steps in the algorithm depends on the size of the problem in a polynomial fashion. *P* problems on the other hand are decision problems that can be solved in polynomial time. The long-standing million-dollar prize issue is whether $P = NP$ or not – that is, whether these two classes of problems are the same or not. This is unsolved. NP-complete problems are those NP problems with the property that given a problem x in NP-complete, any other problem y in NP can be transformed to x in polynomial time, leading to the conclusion that if we know how to solve x quickly, then we automatically know how to solve y quickly.

It is to be noted that most of the problems in this category are of the NP or NP-complete type. Hence, the methods used are heuristic algorithms that lead to suboptimal solutions that can be computed fast.

We list some of the main kinds of problems that arise in this category. For more, see De Smith et al. (2018, Chapter 7).

1   *Hamiltonian circuit problem or HCP:* Given a network (or graph), this problem involves testing the existence of a circuit (or a closed path where the starting and end points are the same) that passes through every vertex exactly once. This problem is known to be of the NP class.
2   *Travelling salesperson problem:* Given a network, find a Hamiltonian circuit that has minimal cost. (As a side note, we will discuss this issue in Chapter 12 as well.)
3   *Eulerian circuit problem:* Given a network, this problem involves testing the existence of an Eulerian circuit, which is a circuit that contains every edge exactly once.
4   *Shortest path problem:* Given two vertices in a network, this problem involves finding a path that minimises a certain metric such as distance or cost. Sometimes the second or third shortest path solutions are also important in such problems.

5   *Minimal spanning tree problem:* Given a network, find a minimum spanning tree, which is a tree (a sub-graph such that every vertex is connected and no cycles are allowed) with minimal total length (or number of edges).

6   *Transportation problem:* As with our new airport example, 'the general problem of completely servicing a set of target locations with given demand levels from a set of source locations with given supply levels such that total costs are minimised is known as the transportation problem. The unit cost of shipping from each supply point to each demand point is a key input to this problem specification. This problem is an example of a Minimum Cost Flow Problem (MCFP)' (De Smith et al., 2018, Section 7.2.1: Overview – Network and Locational Analysis).

Some solution methods

It is to be noted that the travelling salesperson problem is a benchmark to compare the speed and optimality of solution since there is no single algorithm to date that solves the problem entirely. Greedy algorithms are sometimes used (which are also heuristic and suboptimal) that have the property of looking for a local optimum at each step in the algorithm, which may or may not lead to a globally optimal solution. The Prim's algorithm for minimum spanning tree (which is actually in the class P) is one such (De Smith et al., 2018), which actually gives a globally optimal solution. The algorithm involves a construction or growth process as follows: '(i) connect every point to its nearest neighbor; typically this will result in a collection of unconnected sub-networks; (ii) connect each sub-network to its nearest neighbor sub-network; (iii) iterate step (ii) until every sub-network is inter-connected' (De Smith et al., 2018, Section 7.3.1 – Minimum Spanning Tree).

A very simple suboptimal procedure for shortest path problems such as the TSP is the nearest neighbour algorithm, where we start at a vertex and keep adding the shortest link until all vertices are chosen. This is repeated with each vertex as the starting point and the path with the least cost is chosen. This is also sometimes called the repeated nearest neighbour algorithm. The shortest path problems can also be recast as a standard optimisation problem (De Smith et al., 2018), although the resulting solution procedure is not very efficient.

For p > 1, the *p*-median problem can be exactly solved using a branch and bound algorithm. However, for large values of *p*, the solution procedure does not scale well; and hence heuristic procedures need to be adopted that may, once again, yield suboptimal solutions. One heuristic starts with a random choice of *p* points (preferably within the so-called minimum bounding rectangle of the *n* customer locations) and then assigns to each of the *p* points those customer locations that are closest. This partitions the *n* customers into *p* groups. Now compute the median points (using an iterative median calculation) for the *p* groups and repeat until the solution does not change much from the previous step. This is very similar to the *k*-means algorithm except with iterative median calculation instead of the centroids. The arc routing problem can be recast into an Eulerian circuit problem with double edges, where the snowplough needs to traverse the street twice (one for each side). Fleury's algorithm can then be used to compute a solution to the problem, where (assuming all vertices have even degree) we start at a vertex at random and keep deleting edges (and adding those edges to our Eulerian circuit) in a way that does not create disconnected components in the remaining graph.

Geo-computational methods and modelling

Frequently, there are problems in geospatial analysis in which the number of observations is extremely large, as with high-resolution spatial data sets, crowd behaviour and spatial data pertaining to multiple time periods. The kinds of techniques that are used to tackle these problems owe their origins to biological processes. Examples are artificial neural networks, GAs and geo-simulation. We discuss these techniques briefly in this section

> *Artificial neural networks and GAs:* Since these modelling approaches were already discussed in Chapter 8, sections 'Artificial Neural Networks' and 'Genetic Algorithms and Evolutionary Computation', we refer to those sections for details. The only thing we want to mention here is that both these techniques can be used in conjunction with spatial analytical methods in areas such as 'intelligent' financial forecasting, land cover change modelling and so on. However, these methods are yet to find widespread use in spatial analysis and are still considered to be in their infancy with respect to the range and variety of applications in geospatial analysis. Again, for further reading, see (De Smith et al., 2018).

> *Geo-simulation:* Geo-simulation employs cellular automata (CA), which are modelled as a one-dimensional string of cells or a two-dimensional array of cells (usually square), which respond to external stimulus by changing their state of characteristics according to the rules that govern their reaction to the stimulus. John Conway introduced one of the first CA-based model called the 'Game of Life' (http://conwaylife.com).

As found in the popular agent-based modelling software, *Netlogo* (http://ccl.northwestern.edu/netlogo/models), a CA such as Conway's Game of Life consists of four attributes: (1) the *state variables*, which describe the state of the CA which can be binary (0 or 1 like in the Game of Life model) or continuous, such as land-use classifications, demographic taxonomies or surface attributes; (2) the *spatial framework*, which defines the (usually) two-dimensional lattice of cells which are square (or other variations such as Voronoi polygons etc.), with boundary conditions (usually periodic where the square is treated as a torus); (3) the *neighbourhood structure*, which defines the nearby cells from which the CA can obtain stimulus (typically a Moore neighbourhood – the immediate eight cells touching the CA, although other variations are also allowed); (4) **transition rules** that govern the state transition of the CA based on stimulus from its neighbourhood; and (5) **time**, which consists of discrete steps where all the CAs change their state simultaneously (also called 'parallel processing') at each time step.

When the CAs are allowed to move within the spatial framework and interact with one another, they are called *agents*, and the technique is referred to as **agent-based modelling** (ABM). 'Agents are autonomous units capable of processing and exchanging information with other agents in order to make independent decisions' (De Smith et al., 2018, Section 8.2.2: Agents and Agent-Based Models). They are typically heterogeneous (and hence things like average behaviour are not of interest in such simulations). They are active and can be proactive (with goals to achieve, such as finding the exit in an emergency) and reactive (they can be supplied with information such as the location of exits in the building and they can use that information to make independent decisions). They have *bounded rationality* where they are given fettered access to information (they might know the locations of the exits but not whether all of them are accessible or not due to congestion). They have the ability to communicate with their neighbourhood (defined a priori) or with other agents in the neighbourhood to get information and can also be made to neglect information that is less than a certain threshold. Finally, they can be made to be *adaptive* at the individual or the population level giving them the ability to change their state based on their current or past state (memory) or based on the frequency distribution of some property in the population (e.g. how many are close to exits), respectively.

Figure 11.3 An example of Conway's Game of Life after several iterations

Source: website http://conwaylife.com

The main advantage of using an ABM is that it captures emergent phenomena (sometimes referred to as 'aggregate complexity'), which are stable macroscopic patterns arising from local interaction of individual entities and cannot be broken down into individual parts, which make them difficult to understand and predict. The main disadvantage lies in the inability to replicate the multiple properties of agents due to computational limitations (although computing power has been steadily increasing) and also an inherent difficulty in analysing, understanding and communicating the model as it is difficult to provide detailed descriptions of its inner workings. It takes a long time to reach conclusions because testing the robustness requires running the simulation for a large number of initial conditions for the agents.

An ABM can also be used as an *explanatory model*; that is, if agents are programmed with behaviours and interactions with a set of rules that exhibit the same (or close enough) pattern as observed in reality, then this provides a 'candidate explanation' for the observed pattern. However, there is no analytical way of testing the validity of the model or its conclusion in terms of how informative it is for real-world scenarios. Alternatively, an ABM can also be used as a *predictive model* where changes in initial conditions (e.g. rules governing agent behaviours and interactions, such as information available to agents, constraints upon or incentives for particular agent behaviour or movement, etc.) can be used to evaluate the possible effects on the model outcome. Predictive models are designed to mimic real-world systems and are particularly useful for scenario development and policy decisions. Due to heterogeneity and interdependencies, ABMs can reflect important endogenous feedbacks between processes. However, any model with positive feedback can create system behaviour referred to as path dependence; where a path to a process can be very sensitive to both initial conditions and small variations in stochastic processes. The choice between adopting an explanatory or predictive approach is hard because ABMs do not fit under the classical deductive/inductive approaches to modelling.

Still, even with these limitations, ABM is a very useful tool in simulating a variety of geospatial phenomena, such as the spread of a disease, growth of a bacterial colony, archaeological construction of ancient civilisations, company size and growth rate distributions and spatial patterns of unemployment and poverty. As concerns this last illustration, the Nobel prize–winning economist Thomas Schelling, for example, was one of the first to create a one-dimensional spatial segregation model – a variation of which is shown in Figure 11.4, which comes from our research on the negative health impact that outmigration has on poor communities.

In a study we did for SpringerBriefs on community health, titled *Place and Health as Complex Systems* (Castellani et al., 2015), we used geospatial modelling to explore two questions relevant to community health today. First, do the sprawling migration patterns of the heterogeneous agents living in our simulated world, 'Summit-Sim',

Figure 11.4 A geospatial model of negative health impact that sprawl (outmigration) has on poor communities

NOTE: Rich agents = squares; middle class agents = stars: and poor agents = triangles. **Cluster A** identifies one of the dense clusters of rich agents. **Cluster B** identifies one of the dense clusters of poor agents, which complexity scientists would call a poverty trap.

result in the clustering and spatial segregation (distribution) of affluence we found in our actual empirical study of Summit County, Ohio, USA? As shown in Figure 11.4, the answer was yes.

Figure 11.4 is a snapshot of Summit-Sim with a preference rating of 3 for all agents. This rating means that, for each iteration of Summit-Sim, rich agents sought to live in a neighbourhood with three or more rich agents; middle-class agents also sought to live in a neighbourhood with three rich agents; if they could not migrate to such a neighbourhood, they sought to live near other middle-class agents; if they found themselves in a neighbourhood with four or more other middle-class agents, they stayed; finally, poor agents sought to live in neighbourhoods with three or more middle-class agents if they could; if they could not, they stayed where they were.

Of the various preference ratings available for our model, we chose 3 because it is a rather modest preference. What made Schelling's model of segregation so powerful is that macro-level patterns of significant segregation resulted from very mild preference ratings. Sprawl seems to follow a similar pattern. Mild levels of neighbourhood preference should produce significant spatial clustering and segregation.

A visual inspection of Figure 11.4 – which, given the constraints of time and space, will suffice for our analysis of Summit-Sim – shows that, as expected, a preference rating of 3 leads to significant spatial clustering and to even more extreme patterns of segregation than that found in our empirical analysis of Summit County. There are very tight clusters of rich agents (see Cluster A), surrounded by a few middle-class agents; there are large, loose clusters of middle-class agents spread out in the same basic area, moving from the top-right corner of Summit-Sim to the bottom lower-left corner. Finally, there are tight clusters of poor agents (see Cluster B), some of which are very large.

The second question we explored was, If the sprawling migration behaviour of our heterogeneous agents leads to spatial clustering, does this segregation of affluence result in community-level health inequalities, as seen in Summit County? As shown in Figure 11.4, the answer is, again, yes. From the start of the model to its completion, the context-dependent unhealthiness of poor agents never dropped below roughly 50%. Meanwhile, the rich agents had near-perfect health. These healthiness ratings fit with our analysis of Summit County; in particular, our comparison of the poorest clusters with the more affluent.

While our abbreviated analysis of Summit-Sim leaves numerous issues unexplored – for example, how do different preference ratings impact spatial segregation or health? – it was adequate to support the value of geospatial modelling.

Chapter Summary

- In the world of data mining big data, geospatial modelling plays a crucial role, as it seeks to reveal (i.e. identify, locate, find, uncover) the relationship that geography and geospatial factors have with other key factors – be they biological, social, ecological and so on.
- This development coincides with the increasing interest that social scientists have in the spatial nature of human life, from the complexities of place and global health to modelling the social ecosystems in which people live.
- Still, most social scientists are new to the latest computational developments in geospatial modelling.
- This chapter therefore provides a rather detailed overview of the field, including a survey of key concepts and terms; an introduction to the big data challenges of collecting and organising complex geospatial data; and then reviewing the data mining tools and techniques available for modelling and analysing geospatial data.
- Key concepts include field, scale and topography; key data issues involve multidimensional scaling and spatial heterogeneity; tools include geo-simulation, complex network analysis and agent-based modelling.

Further Reading

Cliff, A., & Ord, J. (1981). *Spatial processes: Models and applications*. Pion.
This book offers a review of geospatial modelling.

Miller, H. J., & Goodchild, M. F. (2015). Data-driven geography. *GeoJournal, 80*, 449–461.
This article also offers a review of geospatial modelling.

12

COMPLEX NETWORK ANALYSIS

Chapter Overview

In Chapter 11, if you recall, you had a meeting with your colleagues to discuss moving one of your major hubs (along with several other airlines) to a new international airport being built. What we did not mention was that your rationale for doing so was the recent merger your airline made with these companies to build a larger alliance. What we also did not tell you, since you had yet to learn about network analysis, is that the result of this merger is the opportunity for your airline alliance to fly to more than 500 different airports, involving more than 2000 different routes, across 50 different countries (e.g. as shown in Figure 12.1) – as a side note, if you would like to see maps of these routes, visit the SkyTeam website: www.skyteam.com/en/about. So, which routes do you choose to make the most money, establish a greater level of long-term financial stability and secure a stronger foothold in the airline industry? As Bagler (2008), Choi et al. (2006), Derudder et al. (2007), Song and Yeo (2017), Taylor and Derudder (2015) explain, to answer such a complex question, you need the heavy-lifting tools of complex network analysis.

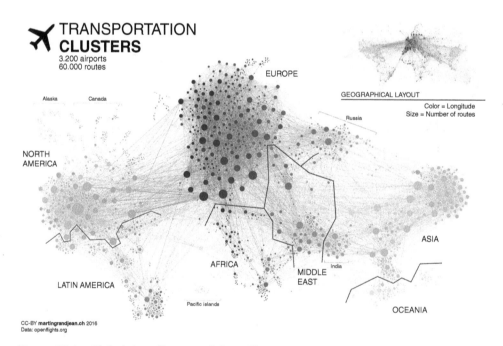

Figure 12.1 Global air-traffic network from Chapter 1

Of all the various data mining techniques presently in existence, the tools of network analysis are probably (at least at present) the most popular, including a significantly long list of books, articles, monographs, handbooks and websites devoted to their review and usage. We therefore do not wish to recreate the field here. Instead, our goal is relatively straightforward. We seek to provide a quick overview of key definitions, explore some important network properties, highlight some of the most classic network models and then review several of the main methods used to study real-world networks.

But first a caveat. Of the numerous writings on networks currently available – for example, Albert and Barabasi (2002), Barabasi (2003) – two authors stand head and shoulders above the rest (at least for us), mainly for the quality of their critical insights into network analysis, which is important, as well as the clarity and accessibility of their writing. Those two authors are Mark Newman and John Scott. Newman is highly useful because he is trained as a physicist and is one of the top scholars in the field of complex networks (Girvan & Newman, 2002; Newman, 2002, 2004, 2006, 2010); in turn, Scott is a sociologist and one of the leading scholars in social networks (Carrington et al., 2005; Scott, 2017; Scott & Carrington, 2011).

They are also useful because, by combining their work, one gains a greater appreciation of the field than either one, on their own, can provide. In other words, while we do not wish, in any way, to solve the debate known as 'Who invented the field of network analysis?', we do want to make clear that studying social networks, today, is best done by drawing upon multiple fields of study, from mathematics and physics to epidemiology and sociology, as well as multiple methods, which is what we do here, in this chapter.

In fact, so useful are the respective reviews of Newman and Scott that the current chapter is divided into two sections: the first based on Newman's (2003) excellent article, which has been cited more than 17,000 times; and the second on Scott's (2017) brilliant book, which has been cited more than 12,000 times! In fact, as we have done in previous chapters, to keep things simple, we will follow the general structure of these two works, as well as use the formulas found in them, so that readers can use the current chapter as a link into their wider reviews – which we strongly recommend as necessary reading. We do, however, as with previous chapters, employ our own examples from the airline industry, of course, to keep our own narrative going, as well as additional references when useful.

What is a network?

As outlined in Newman (2003), a network is essentially a graph consisting of a set of vertices V and a set of edges E. For example, if $V = \{1,2,3\}$ and $E = \{(1,2),(2,3),(3,1)\}$, then we have a three-cycle network (essentially a triangle with vertices at 1, 2 and 3). We will mainly focus on some of the salient features in this chapter. When cases are represented as vertices, the edges between them will represent a relationship between them. This is the main difference between a set of cases that are in the same cluster due to similar profiles and a set of cases in the same network cluster; that is, in the latter it means that those cases are related to each other and hence are connected by edges in the network.

What are some commonly used descriptors of networks?

Here is a quick list of key terms – which can be found in Newman (2003) – that network scholars use:

1   *Vertex or a node:* It is a fundamental unit of a network, represented usually by a dot.
2   *Edge or a link:* It is a line connecting vertices.
3   *Directed or undirected edges:* 'An edge is directed if it runs only in one direction (e.g. in a one-way road between two points), and undirected if it runs in both directions' (Newman, 2003, p. 173). A network in which all edges are directed is referred to as a directed network or graph.
4   *Neighbourhood of a node i in a graph g given by $N_i(g)$:* $N_i(g)$ is simply defined as the set of all nodes that the node *i* is connected to. The usual convention is to assume that *i* is not connected to itself – that is, avoid loops.
5   *Degree:* It is the number of connections (edges) a vertex has. For a directed network, one wants to know the direction of those connections. The connections going out are called 'out-degree', and those coming in are called 'in-degree'.
6   *Component:* The component to which a vertex belongs is the set of all vertices that can be reached from that vertex using existing edges in the network. 'For a directed graph, there is an in-component and an out-component, which are the sets of vertices from which the vertex can be reached and which can be reached from it', respectively (Newman, 2003, p. 173).
7   *Geodesic path:* The geodesic path refers to the shortest route in the network from one vertex to another.
8   *Diameter:* It 'is the length of the longest geodesic path in a network' (Newman, 2003, p. 173).

What are some properties of networks?

Now that we have a basic sense of several of the key terms used in the field, we turn to some of the most classic properties researchers have discovered using these concepts. Again, we turn to Newman (2003) to organise our review.

1   *The small world effect or small diameters:* This is the property that in most networks, most pairs of vertices seem to be connected by a short path through the network. Mathematically speaking, this means that the mean geodesic distance *l* grows as log(*n*) or slower, where *n* is the number of vertices. For networks following the power law (i.e. the frequency of vertices with degree *k* falls off as the inverse of the power of *k*), this dependence is much slower, indicating that the small world effect is true for such networks. This means that on an average the shortest path between

any two vertices does not grow at an alarming rate as a function of the number of vertices n. The following is the formula for the mean geodesic distance for a graph having a single component (i.e. no disconnected sub-graphs):

$$l = \frac{2}{n(n+1)} \sum_{i \geq j} d_{ij},$$

(12.1)

where d_{ij} is the geodesic distance between vertices i and j. Note that the geodesic distance between a vertex and itself (which is zero) is included in the definition of l above. For a graph with multiple components, the harmonic mean is used instead of the arithmetic mean, since in that case, the infinite distance between disconnected components will not contribute to the sum. The diameter of a network is simply the largest geodesic (or the largest shortest path among all shortest paths in the network). This definition is modified to the largest geodesic of the largest component if the network is disconnected. Since this is prone to outliers (a single pair of nodes that has a long path between them would skew the diameter to a large number), sometimes the average geodesic (or average path length) is used to measure the size of a network as well. To understand diameter, consider a circle and a tree network as shown in Figure 12.2. For the circle with n nodes, the diameter will be either n or $(n-1)/2$ depending on whether n is even or odd, since the largest path is reaching half the circle starting from any node. The circle network in Figure 12.2, for example, has a diameter of 7 since $n = 15$ there.

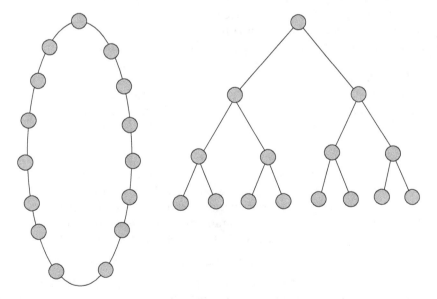

Figure 12.2 A circle and a tree network

The tree network, on the other hand, is much more efficient in terms of accessing nodes. In general, if there are K levels in a tree, then the number of nodes turns out to be $n = 2^{K+1} - 1$ (this can be proved by induction!). Hence solving for K in terms of n, we have $K = \log_2(N+1) - 1$. The largest path is starting from the leftmost node and ending up in the rightmost node in a tree which takes $2K$ links (e.g. the tree network in Figure 12.2 has a diameter of 6 since there are three levels). Hence, the diameter of a tree with $K = \log_2(N+1) - 1$ levels is of the order of $2 \cdot \log_2(N+1)$, which grows much smaller than $n/2$ for the circle network, as n increases. It is to be noted that most real-world networks have very short diameters or average path lengths. The most famous example is Stanley Milgram's (1967) small world experiment with letters, where he found that on an average people were only separated by six links! Facebook, with 725 million users, has an average path length of 3.1, several co-authorship networks have an average path length range of between 5.9 and 9.5, and the World Wide Web with about 50 million web pages, has an average path length of 3.1.

2   *Transitivity or clustering:* This refers to the property that if vertex A is connected to vertex B, and vertex B is connected to vertex C, then there is a high probability that A is connected to C as well. In social terms, a friend of your friend is likely to be your friend. Translated mathematically, this means that there is a higher number of triangles in the network. Hence, the clustering coefficient (where clustering here has the alternative meaning of presence of triangles) is given by

$$C = \frac{3 \times \text{Number of triangles}}{\text{Number of connected triples of vertices}},$$ (12.2)

where a 'connected triple' refers to a single vertex with edges running to two other vertices. The factor of 3 in the numerator is to account for the fact that a single triangle counts as three connected triples. In essence, C is a measure of the fraction of triples that have their third edge filled in. There are some variations of this definition in the literature, but regardless, for real-world networks, it has been empirically found that as the number of vertices n tends to ∞, the probability of clusters is a finite number. However, in the study of random networks, this probability varies as $1/n$ meaning that it tends to zero. This is one among many reasons why random networks (a network model where vertices and edges are added with a defined probability distribution) don't model real-world networks well.

3   *Degree distribution:* The degree of a vertex k is the number of edges incident or connected to the vertex. The relative frequency (or probability) p_k is the fraction of vertices that have a degree equal to k. Random graphs are known to have a binomial (or Poisson in the infinite limit of number of vertices n) degree distribution. However, real-world networks predominantly have degree distributions that are right skewed. More importantly, several networks are known to follow the power law in their tails – that is, $p_k \approx \frac{1}{k^\alpha}$ in their tails. Such networks are also sometimes called 'scale-free' due to the scale-free properties of the power function. Another degree distribution that is seen in many networks is the one with an exponential decay on the tail. Exponential functions decay faster than power laws in general. It should also be noted that even though the overall degree distribution might follow the power law or exponential tails, subnetworks within the network can have other forms of degree distributions.

4   *Network resilience:* This refers to how vulnerable a network is to attacks, when a few vertices are removed from it. Network resilience is measured by looking at how the mean vertex distance changes when vertices are removed. It is well known that if vertices are removed at random with no specified order, then the mean vertex distance does not change much, however, if they are removed in increasing degree of vertices, then the mean vertex distance increases sharply, indicating a higher vulnerability of networks (an increase in mean vertex distance means a disruption in communication). For example, in the airline example, removal of vertices (equivalently shutting down airports) that have higher degree (hubs) might mean that certain cities are not well connected through air routes, whereas, adopting a strategy to remove vertices that reduces redundancy in routes and simultaneously maintains the mean vertex distance can be very cost effective. And hence, a good vertex removal strategy is equivalent to a good airline routing strategy.

5   *Mixing patterns:* This refers to patterns of vertices that have a high probability of having an edge between them. For example, if vertices represent airports and edges represent routes, then an airline network where airports that are hubs for a certain airline forms routes preferentially from other airports that have terminals for that same airline will have a high assortativity coefficient. This type of mixing is sometimes called assortative mixing or homophily. The assortativity coefficient is calculated by first creating a matrix e whose elements e_{ij} represent the fraction of edges between vertices of type i and type j. Then the coefficient is calculated as follows:

$$r = \frac{\mathrm{Tr}(e) - \left\| e^2 \right\|}{1 - \left\| e^2 \right\|}, \qquad (12.3)$$

where $\mathrm{Tr}(e)$ is the sum of the diagonal elements of e, and $\left\| e^2 \right\|$ represents the sum of the squares of all elements in e; r has a value of 0 for random networks and 1 for a perfectly assortative network.

6   *Degree correlations:* This is a special kind of assortative mixing where the question is whether vertices of high degrees always pair (or have an edge) preferentially with other vertices of high degrees. Typically, the correlation coefficient of the degrees of vertices at either end of an edge is the way to measure this, which gives a positive number for networks that are highly assortative and a negative number for disassortative ones. In the airline example, a network where a lot of airline hubs are connected to other airline hubs will have a high degree correlation.

7   *Community structure:* This refers to the presence of a large group of vertices with a high density of edges within them (communities) with a lower density of edges between such groups. Communities are extracted by first assigning a connection strength to all possible $n(n-1)/2$ edges and then performing a hierarchical clustering algorithm by starting with n vertices with no edges between them, and adding edges in decreasing order of connection strength. The process can be stopped at any stage to investigate the presence of communities. A dendrogram is drawn where a cut

at any level will represent a union of vertex sets and hence the communities at that level. In the airline example, hubs in various states are very likely to form communities since there will be a lot more routes between them.

8   *Network navigation:* Apart from the discovery of the small world effect from the famous Milgram experiment, another important observation was made, which was that the short paths that exist between any two vertices can actually be found very easily in real-life networks. In random networks, however, such short paths exist but they are very difficult to find. The focus nowadays is on designing artificial networks that have the same amount of ease of navigation as found in social networks, for example.

9   *Centrality:* Centrality refers to the positional aspect of a node which might be an indication of how influential a node is, or its power structure. The degree of a node is a very simple measure of centrality since a higher degree means higher amount of local connectedness. However, degree is going to miss the positional aspect of a node compared to other parts of the network. There are closeness and decay centrality measures that measure the ease of reaching other nodes, a betweenness centrality measure that captures a node's role as an intermediary or connector, and other centrality measures related to influence, prestige and eigenvector-related measures that capture how well a node is connected to other central nodes. For brevity, we refer the reader to a detailed exposition of these measures.

Some examples of widely used network models

In addition to discovering key properties of networks, researchers have also created some very useful network models. As before, we turn to Newman (2003) to organise our review. However, we also recommend Jackson (2008).

A final point before beginning, here we only focus on those models which have helped to illustrate real-world networks, as there are other models that are entirely mathematical or theoretical in nature (i.e. random graphs). As such, we will discuss the small world model and exponential random graphs. Still, even with these models oriented toward real-world problems, we nonetheless emphasise that none of them captures all the characteristics of real-world networks, only key aspects, which they add to other existing models.

1   *Small world model:* One of the properties that is true of real networks is that they have high clustering coefficients. However, the $G_{n,p}$ random network model (with n vertices and p being the probability of an edge appearing between any two random vertices) has a clustering coefficient of p, which actually tends to 0 for large n (unless the average degree goes to infinity – which is not true of real networks). The small world model was a variation of the random network model due to Watts and Strogatz (1998) to show that it only takes a small number of links starting from a highly regular network to achieve a small diameter, and yet maintain a

high clustering coefficient. To start with, let us consider a ring lattice as shown in Figure 12.3, where there are 25 nodes placed in a ring structure, and each node is connected to its immediate four neighbours, two on each side, hence resulting in 50 links in all. The clustering coefficient for this structure is 0.5, since, for a given node, out of all pairs of its neighbours (excluding itself there are six such pairs), only three (or exactly half) are connected.

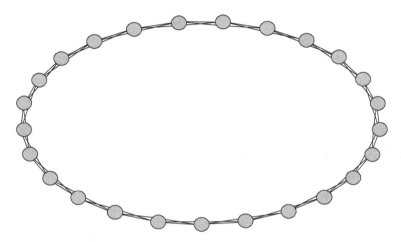

Figure 12.3   Ring lattice on 25 nodes with 50 links

Hence, if we let n grow to large numbers, the overall (and average) clustering will always remain at 0.5. Therefore, this structure (also called the 'small world model') exhibits high clustering but does not exhibit small diameter. The diameter for this network is on the order of $n/4$, since using the same argument as in the case of the circle network in Figure 12.2, the largest path in the ring in Figure 12.3 starting from any given node, is going quarter the distance of the circle (due to the two connections on either side of every node). The main point of Watts and Strogatz (1998) was that by rewiring very few links in this structure, the diameter is significantly reduced but maintaining the original high clustering. For example, in Figure 12.4 only six links were rewired from the original ring lattice in Figure 12.3, and the diameter reduces from 6 to 5 but with minimal impact on clustering.

In fact every node in Figure 12.4 is at a distance of 6 from three other nodes, so rewiring those 6 links actually reduces a large number of path lengths and not just the longer paths. Of course, if we rewire too many links, then the clustering gets reduced as well, and eventually tends to zero, so the interesting range of rewirings is the sweet spot where enough rewiring has been done to substantially reduce the path lengths with minimal effect on clustering. Obviously, such a systematic structure is rarely observed in reality, and hence, this was just a thought experiment towards improving diameters closer to real networks with maintaining high clustering.

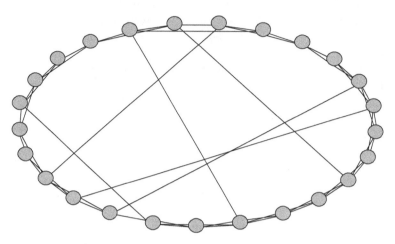

Figure 12.4 Ring lattice on 25 nodes with 50 links with only six links rewired

2   *Exponential random graph models or ERGMs:* Many social networks exhibit local interdependencies (or not) that lead to structures such as stars, hubs, isolated nodes and so on. The ERGMs have the capability of flexibly modelling such dependencies, and also have the additional advantage of being statistically well defined, thereby leading to better estimation or fitting from real-life data. An example of such a local interdependency is to require that link *ij*s probability of occurrence depend on the presence of links *jk* and *ik* – that is, the presence of neighbours. However, this means that a whole range of links get interlocked on such interdependencies; and hence, the network becomes highly correlated (given that one link depends on its neighbours, and its neighbouring link on its neighbours etc.), and all such interdependencies need to be specified in a systematic manner to keep track.

To give a concrete example, we consider a specific example where the probability of a network depends on the number of links present and also on the number of completed triads (or triangular structures) present. If we let $L(g)$ be the number of links in a graph g and $T(g)$ be the number of triangles in g, then a good starting point is to say that the probability of a graph g (denoted as $Pr(g)$) is proportional to $e^{(\beta_L L(g) + \beta_T T(g))}$, where β_L and β_T are weighting factors, and an exponential is chosen to keep the probability a positive number. This is written as follows:

$$Pr(g) \propto e^{(\beta_L L(g) + \beta_T T(g))} \tag{12.4}$$

An interesting (unpublished) theorem by Hammersley and Clifford states that *any* network model can be expressed in the exponential family with counts of graph statistics similar to $L(g)$ and $T(g)$. Hence, the exponential family (Equation 12.4) is a very rich family that captures a wide variety of models. It should be noted that the theorem is just an existence theorem and does not show procedures to explicitly find the required statistics (which might get complicated).

In order for Equation (12.4) to represent a true probability, it should be a number between 0 and 1, so we modify it by dividing by the sum of the same exponential term over all possible networks as follows:

$$Pr(g) = \frac{e^{(\beta_L L(g) + \beta_T T(g))}}{\sum_g e^{(\beta_L L(g') + \beta_T T(g'))}} = e^{(\beta_L L(g) + \beta_T T(g) - c)},$$

(12.5)

where the term c above absorbs the summation terms in the denominator, since the denominator is a positive quantity. One can easily show that the $G_{n,p}$ model can be rewritten in the form of Equation (12.5), where the only statistic that matters is $L(g)$, the number of links. If we include clustering as a second statistic, then we have both the L and the T terms in Equation (12.5). In the general case, if we have several statistics $s_k(g)$ representing several interesting things like triangles, cliques, path lengths and so on, and their corresponding weights β_k, then the ERGM will be as follows:

$$Pr(g) = e^{\sum_s \beta_k s_k(g) - c}$$

(12.6)

The problem then involves estimating the parameters β_k and c. Higher positive values of β_k means that the particular statistic $s_k(g)$ was more important in the formation of the network, and a negative value means the opposite. Typically, maximum likelihood estimation type of techniques are used to estimate the parameters in an ERGM. Larger number of nodes makes the estimation more complicated, and MCMC-based methods are used in such situations, which also fall into convergence problems unless the networks have approximately independent links. So estimation of parameters is a little tricky for larger networks for ERGMs because parsing through a large random sample of networks to get the denominator in (Equation 12.5) becomes harder simply because of the sheer number of possible networks $g'0$. An alternative would be to search in the statistic space instead of the network space, which reduces the dimensionality of the MCMC search.

Key methods used to study networks

In addition to the above models, network researchers also rely on a series of statistical and computational tools (and in some cases qualitative methods) to explore the properties of real-world networks. Here, following Scott (2017), we outline some of the most popular. We do not, however, have time to examine the process of collecting and organising network data. Nonetheless, Scott (2017) does. As such, we refer the readers to his book. In addition, we also recommend Carrington et al. (2005), Knoke and Yang (2008), and Wasserman and Faust (1994).

Also, in terms of conducting network analyses using big data (or any data for that matter!), we recommend Vladimir Batagelj and Andrej Mrvarthe's hugely popular book and corresponding software package *Pajek* – which is Slovenian for spider! There are certainly other excellent software packages available, many of which are also free. However, we have found Pajek to be the best. But, that is just our opinion. For more on Pajek, see De Nooy et al. (2018), which is free to download (http://mrvar.fdv.uni-lj. si/pajek).

Matrices and relational data

In Chapter 6, section 'Cataloguing and Grouping Case Profiles', we mentioned briefly that data mining techniques exist for relational databases. An example of a relational database is the adjacency matrix of a network of social relationships. Alternatively, relationships can also exist between non-social entities. For example, as we mentioned at the beginning of this chapter (and the previous), multiple airlines can belong to an alliance – which means that members of one airline reward programme can earn and redeem reward points for any airline member in the alliance. Alternatively, even airlines that don't belong to the same alliance can enter into code-share or inter-line agreements that allow their members to book tickets with flights from multiple airlines in the same itinerary and also check bags through to a final destination. A network that shows these kinds of relationships between airlines can be represented using an adjacency matrix that shows both the strength and nature of relationships among airlines.

We spend a few moments in this section talking about representing a network using matrices. For a detailed exposition, we refer the reader to the free textbook resource and its accompanying software by Hanneman and Riddle (2005) at http://faculty.ucr.edu/~hanneman/nettext. A matrix is simply a rectangular array of numbers denoted by capital letters. The element in the ith row and jth column of a matrix A is usually denoted by A_{ij}. In a given network of social relationships, where vertices represent people and edges represent the existence of a relationship, the most important matrix is the one denoted as the *adjacency matrix A*, where $A_{ij} = 1$ if there is a relationship between the ith and jth people, and $A_{ij} = 0$ if there is no relationship between them. Adjacency matrices need not be symmetric – that is, $A_{ij} \neq A_{ji}$ always. For example, if the ith person considers the jth person as friend but not vice versa, then $A_{ij} = 1$ but $A_{ji} = 0$. Such networks are represented as directed graphs with edges that can be unidirectional or bidirectional arrows. The adjacency matrix then has the interpretation that rows are origins and columns are targets of relationships. The adjacency matrix A can sometimes have values other than 0 and 1 to reflect degrees of relationships between people, with the idea that a larger value reflects a stronger relationship. In the context of airline alliances for example, direct alliances will have larger values, whereas indirect code-share agreements will have smaller values.

The square of an adjacency matrix $B = A^2$ has elements B_{ij} that indicates the number of pathways between the ith and jth people of length 2. Similarly, A^3 has elements that indicates the number of pathways of length 3 between people – see Hanneman and Riddle (2005) for details. Similarly, the elements of the Boolean squared of the adjacency matrix tell us whether or not there is a path of length 2 between people if the value is a 1, and vice versa.

These are important because information about the number or lengths of relational connections between people (or actors in general) indicate how resilient the network (or the individual actor) is. For example, networks that have very weak connections (A has small values) and actors that are connected by long pathways (A^n has a non-zero element in the ijth position only for large values of n) indicate lower response to stimuli and are less robust than the ones that are not. For the individual actors, the ones that have a large number of short pathways to other actors tend to be central figures of high influence, and vice versa. We will end this part by mentioning that most of the measures of centrality, individual position and overall network structure are related to the number and length of pathways between actors in a network of social relationships. Hence, matrices are the mathematical representation of a network of social relationships and can be used to glean out valuable information about both the entire network as well as individual actors.

Network methods: a basic overview

The contemporary big data network is faced with three very important challenges, as it relates to its study. First, the explosion of data has resulted in networks whose sizes are such that their properties can no longer be studied by conducting a census. This has led to the infusion of statistical inference-based measurements that allow the researcher to predict the property of the whole network by studying a smaller random sample of the same. Second, the same explosion has also led to uncertainties in measurement of network properties due to the sheer volume of data that needs to be parsed. This has led to probabilistic (or stochastic) measurement methods rather than deterministic. Third, the properties of a network are seldom static in time (or in equilibrium), but are evolving. Hence, the methods used to study them are also geared towards understanding network dynamics.

Given these three challenges, the methods used to study such large networks should have stochastic and dynamics components. As such, the development of methods with these characteristics is considered 'cutting edge'. We focus on a brief overview of statistical methods in this section, and then mention a few methods that allow for modelling network dynamics in the next section. For a more detailed exposition, including a review of qualitative approaches for smaller social networks, we refer the reader to Hanneman and Riddle (2005) and Newman (2003).

Before we proceed, however, two caveats are necessary. We wish to make two important points that delineate the kinds of inferential methods used for networks as opposed to the ones used in traditional statistics. First, the inference is about the actors (or cases) rather than attributes (or variables) – that is, we are more interested in questions about the mean strength of associations between actors in the network or correlation between the centrality of position in a network and strength of ties and so on. Second, the samples obtained from a network are not independent due to the inherent possibility of ties (or associations) between the actors in the sampled subnetwork; and hence, the usual assumption of independent samples that is used in a standard hypothesis test is not satisfied. Hence, standard techniques to compute standard errors, p-values and test statistics need to be modified with bootstrapping techniques that compute sampling distributions of statistics through repeated hundreds and thousands of trials of random samples under the assumption that the null hypothesis is true.

Descriptive statistics

Let us consider the adjacency matrix of a network A, say with 10 rows and 10 columns, each depicting an airline. A can either contain binary data simply denoting existence of a tie or not, or valued data indicating the strength of ties. We can simply treat the entries in A as 100 different data values and compute descriptive statistics such as mean, standard deviation and so on. For binary data, the mean will represent the probability of a tie existing between two randomly picked airlines (also called as density of ties), whereas for valued data, it will represent the average strength of ties. Similar meaning can be assigned for other measures. For example, the standard deviation will represent that spread of the strength of ties across the whole network. Furthermore for directed networks, descriptive statistics can be computed for rows and columns separately that depict similar measurements for each actor separately for sending and receiving strengths of ties, respectively.

Hypothesis tests with bootstrapping

Typical hypothesis tests involve the mean (or density) of ties, and also proportion of ties. For example, if we want to test whether a tie exists at all $(H_0 : \mu = 1; H_A : \mu \neq 1)$, or that the proportion of binary ties is different than 0.5 $(H_0 : p = 0.5; H_A : p \neq 0.5)$. The usual intuition from variable-based inferential statistics will carry over except for computing the standard error and test statistic. To compute the standard error, we need to resample a large number of subsamples and find the sampling distribution (of μ or p), and compute the standard deviation of that sampling distribution (which is nothing but the standard error). We can then proceed to compute the test statistic and use the t or normal distribution as usual to compute the p-value. If we did not use bootstrapping to compute the standard error, then we will end up with extremely small p-values resulting in rejecting the null hypothesis when we really shouldn't. Again, the difference in the method is due to the fact that the samples are not independent because of possibility of ties between actors.

With that in mind, we can also ask other kinds of questions involving two relations of the same actors. For example, in the 10 by 10 airline matrix, we could have a matrix A_1 representing financial ties and a matrix A_2 representing airline alliance ties. Then, we could ask questions such as 'Which tie has a higher density?' (this is analogous to difference in means for paired data except now with bootstrapping), 'Is there a correlation between financial ties and alliance ties?' (this is analogous to correlation between two variables, except now with bootstrapping), 'If there is a financial tie, does that mean the existence of an alliance tie or vice versa/' (this is analogous to regression between variables except with bootstrapping). So in essence, all questions regarding hypothesis testing of means and proportions of ties can be asked with the caveat that standard errors need to be computed using bootstrapping methods.

We end by stating that there are software programs available that can conduct the hypothesis tests with bootstrap very quickly, once the number of resamples is specified. One example is the UCINET program that is used in the book by Hanneman and Riddle (2005).

Modelling network dynamics

Up to this point, we have focused primarily (once again – note the pattern!) on static or relatively discrete networks. However, in today's big data-saturated world, networks are constantly evolving, collapsing, forming and changing across time/space. As such, we need to mention a bit about some of the recent advances in modelling longitudinal network data. While many tools and techniques from the fields of mathematics, physics and the natural and health sciences exist for studying dynamics, when it comes to the study of network dynamics, the field is in its infancy. Still, some progress has been made. There are several areas currently being explored, including Markov chains, stochastic processes, epidemiological models and growing networks. Of these, we will focus mainly on the last, and mention a stochastic and an epidemiological model in the passing.

Growing network models

There are examples of networks such as citation networks, the World Wide Web, societies and so on, where the number of links and nodes actually grow or increase with time. Growing network models tend to capture this aspect of growth in networks. We refer the reader to Jackson (2008) for a detailed exposition of growing network models. For example, in the context of citation networks, new articles are born over time, and can form links by citing old articles, old articles can cite new articles, articles are going to accumulate links over time with newer articles having lesser links than older ones, hence leading to a natural heterogeneity. A simple starting case is what is known as the *growing and uniformly random* network, where we start with m nodes that are completely connected, on each date a new node is born and forms m links with existing nodes, each of the m nodes to form new links at each new date is chosen with equal likelihood and hence, the probability that an existing node forms a new link with a new node that is born at time t is m/t. To find an expression for the expected degree for node i born at time $m < i < t$ is given by a summation, where the first term is the original m links that the node i forms plus the expected links from future nodes born after time instant i (for time instant $i + 2$, this would be $m/(i + 2)$):

$$\underbrace{m}_{\text{original}} + \frac{m}{i+1} + \frac{m}{\underbrace{i+2}_{\text{expected at time}(i+2)}} + \cdots + \frac{m}{t} \tag{12.7}$$

$$= m * \left(1 + \ln\left(t / i\right)\right)$$

The sum above can be approximated using the harmonic series as $m * \left(1 + \ln\left(t / i\right)\right)$. To compute the fraction of nodes that have an expected degree of less than d at time t (or $F_t(d)$, the cumulative degree distribution function!), we do the following:

$$m * \left(1 + \ln\left(t / i\right)\right) < d \Rightarrow i > t * e^{-\left(\frac{d-m}{m}\right)}. \tag{12.8}$$

This means that nodes born after time

$$T = t * e^{-\left(\frac{d-m}{m}\right)}$$

will all have degrees less than d, and nodes born before T will have degrees larger than d, which is essentially a preservation of the natural heterogeneity that we explained for citation networks for example, where newer nodes have lesser degree, and vice versa. Hence, the fraction of nodes $F_t(d)$ that have expected degrees less than d at time t is given by

$$F_t(d) = (t - T)/t = 1 - e^{-\left(\frac{d-m}{m}\right)}.$$

(12.9)

Hence, the probability density for expected degree or mean degree (which is the derivative of $F_t(d)$) will turn out to be an exponential degree distribution. Actual degrees will bounce above or below this mean, but using laws of large numbers, one can prove that for large t, the actual degrees will get closer to this exponential distribution of expected degree.

One can use a continuous time approximation (also called mean field approximation) as follows to get to the same result as in Equation (12.7): Let us denote $d_i(t)$ as the degree of node i at time t. Then the instantaneous rate of change of degree is given by

$$d_i' = \frac{m}{t}, d_i(i) = m$$

(12.10)

where the ' denotes derivative with respect to time t. The initial condition is $d_i(i) = m$, or in other words, node i has m links when it is born at time $t = i$. This differential equation is easily solved to give $d_i(t) = m * (1 + \ln(t/i))$ as in Equation (12.7). The point is that by varying the right-hand side of Equation (12.9) based on varying assumptions on how the new links are formed (different than the uniformly random), we could end up with other degree distributions. For example, it is well known that citation networks have fat tails, that is, too many articles with no citations and too many with larger numbers of citations, that is, fatter tails compared to a uniformly growing random network which has an exponential degree distribution for large t.

So to get the fatter tails observed in nature, we impose the additional condition (instead of uniformly forming new links at random) called *preferential attachment*, where the probability of formation of a new link with an existing node is proportional to the number of links that the node already has; that is, the rich get richer! With this preferential attachment rule of forming new links, we have that at each time t, the total number of links is $t*m$ and hence the total degree (sum of degree of all nodes) is $2*t*m$, and hence we require that the instantaneous rate of change of degree d_i' is proportional to the current degree of the node i divided by $2tm$ (where m is the proportionality constant here). Hence, Equation (12.9) changes to the following:

$$d_i' = m * \frac{d_i}{2tm} = \frac{d_i}{2t}, \quad d_i(i) = m.$$

(12.11)

As it turns out, the degree distribution $d_i(t)$ for the differential equation (Equation 12.10) and the solution is given by

$$d_i(t) = m \left(\frac{t}{i} \right)^{\frac{1}{2}}.$$

(12.12)

So as before, to find the cumulative expected degree distribution at time t given by $F_t(d)$, we solve $d_i(t) < d$ for i as shown below:

$$d_i(t) < d \Rightarrow m \left(\frac{t}{i} \right)^{\frac{1}{2}} < d \Rightarrow i > T = t * \left(\frac{m}{d} \right)^2$$

$$F_t(d) = \frac{t - T}{t} = 1 - \left(\frac{m}{d} \right)^2$$

(12.13)

$$f_t(d) = \frac{2m}{d^3},$$

where $f_t(d)$ is the probability density of the degree distribution which is a power law with $\alpha = 3$, the power of the denominator in the power law. This power law on a log–log plot will be a straight line with a slope of -3. If we want to change α to a different number, then all we need to do is change the right-hand side of Equation (12.10). As a result of the power law (due to the preferential attachment), the distribution has a fatter tail than the exponential distribution that resulted from the uniformly at random growth before, because older nodes with preferential attachment will have more links than corresponding older nodes from the uniform random growth assumption. This is just the expected degree distribution, but by performing simulations for larger and larger nodes, it has been proven that the preferential attachment assumption works very well with actual degree distribution in the limit of large number of nodes.

The point is that by changing the rule for formation of new links, we were able to recapture the power law distribution that is seen in reality. Hence, possibly by changing it to other rules of formation, we can hope to capture more general degree distributions seen in real life. For example, the network of co-authorship has a curve that does not fit the uniformly random growth or the power law on a log–log plot. So we can ask, what kind of change needs to be done to Equation (12.9) or Equation (12.10) that might fit this *intermediate* degree distribution observed in a co-authorship model?

A simple modification to the rule would be to say that a fraction a of new links are formed uniformly at random, and a fraction $(1 - a)$ via searching for friends of friends. So of the m links formed, am, are formed uniformly at random and $(1 - a)m$ are formed by looking for nodes that are attached to the am nodes just formed and choosing from these secondary nodes uniformly at random (i.e. uniformly at random from friends of friends). The point here is that the distribution of neighbour's nodes is not the same as the degree distribution, even with independent link forma-tion, because a neighbour is more likely to have a higher degree. For example, if we consider a network with half the nodes having degree k and the other half having degree $2k$, and if we pick a link at random and choose a node at one end of the link at random, then this randomly selected node has a 2/3 chance of having a degree $2k$ and a 1/3 chance of having a degree k. So, if we are trying to find nodes through their friends, then because the nodes having degree $2k$ have twice as many friends, they have twice the chance of being found compared to the nodes that have degree k. Hence, if we look for forming links through friends of friends, then automatically, the higher degree nodes have a larger chance of being found and made links with, so this is in essence a form of preferential attachment, where the fraction $(1 - a)$ of the m links are now forming links with a higher chance of attaching to nodes with larger degree! This type of link formation is called a *hybrid growth network model* since it has both the uniformly at random part as well as the preferential attachment part in different fractions.

This changes the differential equation of formation of new links and its solution to the following:

$$d_i'(t) = \frac{am}{t} + (1-a)\frac{d_i}{2t}; d_i(i) = m,$$

$$d_i(t) = \left(m + \frac{2am}{1-a}\right)\left(\frac{t}{i}\right)^{\frac{(1-a)}{2}} - \frac{2am}{(1-a)}. \tag{12.14}$$

As expected, if $a = 1$, we have the uniformly random growth model, and if $a = 0$, we have the preferential attachment-based growth model; and hence, this model is somewhere in between (or hybrid) for $0 < a < 1$.

We can now follow the same mathematics to find $F_t(d)$ and $f_t(d)$ to give

$$d_i(t) < d \Rightarrow i < T = t\left[\frac{(m + xam)}{(d + xam)}\right]^x, x = \frac{2}{1-a}$$

$$F_t(d) = \frac{(t-T)}{t} = 1 - \left[\frac{(m + xam)}{(d + xam)}\right]^x, x = \frac{2}{1-a} \tag{12.15}$$

$$f_t(d) = F_t'(d),$$

where the ' in the last equation above is the derivative with respect to d, and we have omitted the expression just for simplicity here. As it turns out, this hybrid model has also been shown through simulations to remarkably match several known real distri-butions (with appropriate choice of a – perhaps using a least squares estimation – the process of fitting a to data from real life which we deliberately omit in this exposition).

Epidemiological models

The standard SIR model for epidemiology models the spread of disease in a population of N individuals, where S are susceptible, I are infected and R are recovered individuals, using a coupled set of ordinary differential equations.

$$S' = -\frac{\beta IS}{N}$$
$$I' = \frac{\beta IS}{N} - \gamma I \tag{12.16}$$
$$R' = \gamma I,$$

where ′ denotes the derivative with respect to time. It is to be noted that $S + I + R = N$, or the total number of individuals is a constant and consequently $S' + I' + R' = 0$. In the model above, the rate of change of susceptible population S' is proportional to the fraction infected I/N and the current number of susceptible individuals, and β is the infection rate. The rate of change of infected individuals I' is proportional to the current number of infected individuals, and rate at which susceptible individuals decrease is added exactly into the infected population (through the term $\beta IS/N$) and the rate at which recovered individuals increase has to be subtracted (through the term γI, where γ is the recovery rate). Finally, the rate at which the recovered individuals increase is purely proportional to the current number of infected individuals I.

This model can be adapted to capture the evolution of an online social network with the analogy that 'infection' referring to new users being added, 'susceptible' referring to potential users and 'recovered' referring to users that are opposed to joining the network. However, the main difference is that while the standard SIR model captures a characteristic recovery rate (some individuals recover from the disease eventually no matter what), in an online social network, users don't join the network with the hope of eventually leaving after a predetermined amount of time (or recovering). They rather follow 'infectious recovery' dynamics, where the recovery rate R' 0 is now proportional to the fraction of recovered individuals R/N in addition to the number of infected individuals. Hence, the standard SIR model (Equation 12.15) has to be modified to the infectious recovery SIR model (or irSIR) with R' depicting the process of infectious recovery:

$$S' = -\frac{\beta IS}{N}$$
$$I' = \frac{\beta IS}{N} - v\frac{IR}{N} \tag{12.17}$$
$$R' = v\frac{IR}{N}.$$

The modelling process then becomes fitting the parameters β and v, respectively, from longitudinal data using differential equation and least squares-based curve fitting procedures that are easily available from MATLAB or similar mathematical software. For a detailed exposition, we refer the reader to Cannarella and Spechler (2014). It is to be noted that neither Equation (12.15) nor Equation (12.16) admit explicit analytical solutions; and hence, they have to be solved for S, I and R using numerical algorithms that are again readily available in MATLAB for example.

Markov chain-based models

There are a class of models called *stochastic actor oriented models* that try to capture the evolution of links (social ties) between actors (which are represented as nodes in the network) in a social network. The evolution is treated as a change in 'composition' of the network in the form of a change in the adjacency matrix A whose entries change from 0 to a 1 (or vice versa), indicating the addition of a new tie at a given time instant (or breakage of a tie for a change between 1 and 0). The model is designed to capture dependence of ties between actors such as *density, popularity, transitivity* and several others. The change is modelled as a continuous time Markov process, which means that new ties are formed (or old ties are broken) by one actor at a time only, based only on the current state of the network (i.e. no memory from the past) and based on improvement of a so-called objective function. The modelling process involves fitting the parameters of the Markov process using the method of moments and a procedure known as the Robinson–Monro algorithm. For brevity, we choose not to go into the details but refer the reader to Snijders (2001) and Huisman and Snijders (2003) and the references therein. We will end by stating that this is a probabilistic model that models the probability of a given future state of the network which is computed based on data and the current state of the network (state here refers to the adjacency matrix A, which changes with time depending on addition or deletion of ties).

In the context of our airline network, the three techniques mentioned here will try to capture (1) the dynamics of degree of the network – number of airlines connected to a given airline, (2) the (stochastic) dynamics of the evolution of the probability of new airline alliances (or breakage of old alliances) given the current state of alliances and (3) the coupled dynamics of number of airlines that are potential additions, current members and potential dissolutions (susceptible, infected and recovered), respectively, in that order. The key point to note is that a particular property (whether macroscopic or microscopic) is chosen, along with reasonable assumptions on the mechanisms that drive the evolution of that property, to arrive at a mathematically tractable model.

We end by stating that all three network dynamics-based modelling techniques outlined here try to fit parameters of a known model through data with the objective of capturing some aspect of growth. The models themselves arise out of reasonable assumptions on the evolution of some property of the network (be it degree, ties or populations), and the parameters of the model are fit using data through least squares optimisation routines. In other words, all three techniques 'fit data to a given function (or a model)' rather than 'fitting the best function (or model) to data'. This works well because the mechanisms that involve the formation and breakage of links are assumed as part of the model (and in many instances well justified due to observation).

Chapter Summary

- Of the various tools and techniques of computational modelling and data mining, the study of complex networks is probably the most widely known and used.
- The purpose of this chapter is to briefly survey this incredibly developed field.
- This survey includes a review of key concepts in networks such as vertex, edge and degree.
- It also includes a review of the key properties of networks, such as centrality, network navigation and mixing patterns.
- Next, this chapter surveys some of the more widely used network models. Examples include the small world model and the exponential random graph model.
- Finally, it surveys key network methods, including descriptive statistics, hypothesis testing with bootstrapping and modelling network dynamics, such as growth network models and epidemiological models.

Further Reading

Newman, M. E. (2003). The structure and function of complex networks. *SIAM Review, 45*(2), 167–256. https://doi.org/10.1103/PhysRevLett.89.208701
This excellent article explains the structure of complex networks.

Scott, J. (2017). *Social network analysis*. Sage.
A classic text on social network analysis.

13

TEXTUAL AND VISUAL DATA MINING

Chapter Overview

You are called to a special emergency meeting with your airline bosses and their advertising and social media departments. They are seriously concerned that, as a new airline, they are not doing as well as they would like on the major travel websites, in particular TripAdvisor, Inc. They are also rather concerned about generating more 'buzz' about the excellent flights and services they provide, including a new membership promotion and app that they want to launch in the forthcoming months. They know you are an expert now in data mining big data and want to know what you can do to help. For example, can you develop a larger peer-to-peer network for the airline? And, can you analyse all of the textual data flowing through the various travel blogs and websites (including your own airline) to get a better sense of what the real-time travel trends are and what current and potential customers want? And, can you tell them what degree of trust they should put in your analyses of online life? Also, can you organise your report into something that will make immediate visual sense? Phew! (Figure 13.1)

Figure 13.1   Visualisation of customer satisfaction text

And so to work you go. Fortunately, to answer these questions you will continue, as you have, to employ the tools and techniques discussed in the last seven chapters. In fact, you will basically follow the same circular data mining steps outlined in Chapter 4: data collection, extraction, cleaning, transformation, analysis and so forth – which is why this area is called textual and visual data mining! In other words, the process you will use is the same (relatively speaking), it is just that the data you will 'mine' for your answers differ significantly. And, it is for this reason that the current chapter, similar to Chapter 10 (Longitudinal Analysis), is more about the data than it is about method! Still, as with Chapter 10, there are several additional methods you need to learn – all of which have to do with the specific challenges of unstructured data analysis. So, let's get to our review.

Thinking about textual/visual data mining

While an exact estimate is largely unverifiable, experts guess that roughly 80% of all big data is unstructured, with most of it being textual, audio or visual data, including photos, reports, articles, news, social media, blogs, websites, books, videos, movies, television programmes, audio recordings, music and so forth. The challenge, however, for making use of this data is threefold.

- The first major challenge, which we have already hinted at, is collecting and organising these data into a useful structured format. For example, how would one comb through the billions of photos on Instagram or Flickr or Pinterest, let alone the massive archives of online news found across the internet? And, once done, into what format(s) should these data be cleaned, transformed and organised?
- The second is modifying (or developing) the tools of data mining to more effectively work with textual and visual data, as this data is not the same as conventional numeric data. Examples include the development of sentiment analysis, information visualisation and semantic (concept) mapping to make better sense of policy evaluation and data mining results; as well as web mining the internet for non-obvious patterns and trends; as well as the usage of topographical neural nets for facial recognition, geospatial mapping and predicting musical choices for customers; and also the usage of actor network theory to follow Twitter and Facebook trends.
- The third is determining the extent to which any given analysis of digital social life – in whatever form it be – is valid and reliable, as there is considerable epistemological concern about the 'reality' of digital data, no matter how big it be. For example, as we pondered in the first part of our book, how is digital life (e.g. a Twitter feed) and our analysis of it shaped by the ontologies and technologies that organise it? Or, as another example, is a digital trend a true representation of a social trend? Or are they different? And so on and so forth.

Still, while these challenges are formidable, they are not new. So, before we proceed, let's review a bit of history.

A bit of history

As we just suggested, while the idea of unstructured big data is new, the challenges of textual and visual analysis by computers is not. In fact, these challenges have a rather complex and nuanced intellectual history, going back, for example, to the first electronic card catalogues (Aggarwal & Wang, 2011; Aggarwal & Zhai, 2012; Feldman &

Sanger, 2007; Miner et al., 2012). Or, related, one can go back to the first machines that did basic word counts or abstract summaries on these catalogues.

Or, one can go back to Alan Turing and the now famous 'Turing test' – which is used to tell if a machine can be called intelligent! – as well as fields such as linguistics, physics, computer science, computational modelling, engineering, information science and (perhaps most important of all) natural language processing (NLP). The audacious goal of NLP is to teach machines how to engage in some of the most complex tasks known to humans – namely, how to create computer-understandable data out of unstructured visual, textual and audio information so that these machines can recognise speech, translate and communicate in multiple languages, understand grammar, parse sentences, tag parts of speech, translate text-to-speech, correctly, recognise and spell words, engage in morphological segmentation, extract terminology, search for phrases and identify non-obvious textual and audio patterns.

Then there are also fields such as geospatial modelling (remember Chapter 11), artificial neural nets (Chapter 8) and computer vision and computational image detection, focused on other massively complex tasks such as motion analysis, even detection, visual parsing, tagging parts of an image or video, image restoration, magnification, scene reconstruction and image translation and matching. And now, more recently, we have the extension of these and other fields into the development of machines – that is, self-driving cars, autopilots and drones – that make 'real-time' intelligent decisions in the face of real-world three-dimensional reality, requiring memory, contextual awareness and foresight.

And let us also not forget the more recent developments in *web mining*, which involves the usage of not only the techniques we have so far reviewed during our tour but also techniques such as *link analysis* (i.e. connecting one node of visual, audio or textual activity or communication to another, as in the case of cryptocurrency and peer-to-peer networks), as well as the development of all sorts of web crawlers and internet bots that 24/7 scour the World Wide Web and internet for information, as well as spreading information (be it true or false or somewhere in-between) like viruses.

So, think about all of that history and the incredible intellectual achievements associated with it the next time you quickly grab your smartphone and, speaking directly to it, ask it to do something, including navigating you to your next coffee shop. And who says science is not the magic of the gods! Still, as with all techniques, these methods need to be used with significant caution as they can be easily used as a replacement for (rather than a trace of) the reality they are supposed to help us better understand. For more on textual/visual data mining, we recommend the following, which we used to write the current chapter: Aggarwal and Wang (2011), Aggarwal and Zhai (2012), Fan and Bifet (2013), Fayyad et al. (2002), Feldman and

Sanger (2007), Kanevsky et al. (2003), Keim (2002), Miller and Han (2001), Miner et al. (2012), Soukup and Davidson (2002), Srivastava and Sahami (2009) and Wang et al. (2005). We also recommend, in particular, Miner et al.'s (2012) *Practical Text Mining and Statistical Analysis for Non-Structured Text Data Applications*.

Preprocessing unstructured data

As with several of the other techniques we have discussed on our tour – such as geo-spatial modelling and network analysis – the first step in the process of textual and visual data mining (and in many ways most important) is retrieving and extracting such data into a useful format for analysis.

As Allahyari et al. (2017) explain, currently there are a variety of preprocessing techniques available, which differ depending upon the particular data mining task one has in mind. Given the constraints of time and space, our goal here is only to review a few of them, mainly to give a sense of the types of concerns that need to be considered. For a more in-depth overview, we recommend Aggarwal and Zhai (2012), Miner et al. (2012) and Soukup and Davidson (2002).

One example includes *tokenisation*, which involves deconstructing visual, textual or audio data into smaller pieces, called tokens. This technique – which always makes us think of Star Trek – is also used in data security and cryptocurrency, as it allows information to be broken up into smaller chunks that require a translator to put them back together into recognisable information.

Another preprocessing technique is *filtering*, which involves removing information that is not of importance to the user. An example of this technique is removing 'stop words' from a textual database, such as conjunctions, prepositions and articles.

Lemmatisation focuses on the morphological analysis of words. A good example is the various inflected forms of the word 'walk', such as walks, walked, walking and will walk. 'In other words', as explained by Allahyari et al. (2017), 'lemmatisation methods try to map verb forms to infinite tense and nouns to a single form'.

Another preprocessing technique, which is very important in information retrieval, is *stemming*. Here the goal is to reduce inflected (or derived) words to their word stem, base or root form. For example, in the case of a word search on walking, walked, will walk and so on, the goal is to reduce all versions to the root word 'walk'.

In terms of visual and audio images, three other examples are *rasterisation*, *wavelet transformation* and *wavelet compression*. Perhaps some of the most widely known and classic examples are the various formats in which images come (i.e. JPEG, PDF, PNG, JPEG2000, etc.) and the various image transformation tools found in Adobe Illustrator and Adobe Photoshop.

The tools of textual data mining

Given that, vis-à-vis visual data mining, we have already reviewed the topics of machine intelligence (Chapter 8) and geospatial modelling (Chapter 11), and given the fact that the techniques reviewed in Chapters 6 through 12 can likewise be used to do textual/visual data mining, our focus in this section is on the methods we have yet to discuss. Still, a basic summary of the major areas of textual data mining, including the tasks to which the methods reviewed on our tour are generally assigned, is necessary. And so, let us proceed. As outlined by Miner et al. (2012), textual data mining can be organised in seven major methodological areas.

- *Search and information retrieval:* Here the focus is on key tasks such as 'indexing, searching, and retrieving documents from large text databases with keyword queries' (Miner et al., 2012, p. 32). Methodological examples include word extraction algorithms and basic search engine software. In terms of application, big data examples include Google search, Yahoo and (on a smaller level) just about every single software program or app that has some type of search function. For example, doing an internet search on key destination hotspots.
- *Document clustering:* Here the focus is on clustering documents – or key phrases, sentences, words and so on – to identify non-obvious patterns or connections amongst some set of texts, be they in a pre-existing data set or on the internet and so on. Also, as outlined in Chapters 6 through 8 of our tour, the data mining techniques used for these clustering tasks range from *k*-means cluster analysis to the self-organising topographical neural net to GAs. However, in this case the goal is to explore for unknown or hypothesised ways in which texts cluster together to form different topics, themes, communications or issues. For example, how sentiment analysis can be used to scrape the web in search of key airline terms or phrases such as 'top ten destinations for 2021' to reveal current vacation trends.
- *Document classification:* Here, similar to our review of classification (Chapter 7), the focus is on text for which one already knows, ahead of time, the categories or groups to which some set of documents belong. The goal, then, is to assign these 'known' labels to untagged documents. As outlined in Chapter 7 of our tour, such methods include decision tree induction, nearest neighbour classifiers, artificial neural nets (including deep learning) and SVMs. In terms of application, the most classic examples come from information science and cataloguing, where the goal is to classify new documents according to some existing ontology and lexicon, as in the case of organising scientific research on airplanes and the airline industry according to known headings.
- *Information extraction:* As Miner et al. (2012) explain, 'The goal of information extraction is to construct (or extract) structured data from unstructured text. Information extraction is one of the more mature fields within text mining, but it is difficult for beginners to work in without considerable effort, since it requires specialised algorithms and software' (p. 33). It is also an exceptionally difficult field, given its task, particularly for organising and making sense of unstructured data on the internet and World Wide Web. Methods include conditional random field algorithms and hidden Markov models (see, e.g., our review of Bayesian

statistics in Chapter 9). In terms of the airline industry, examples include creating an algorithm that searches for newswire reports of corporate airline mergers or the economic health and well-being of different airline companies.

- *Concept extraction:* Related (but in many ways not) to information extraction is concept extraction. The reason for this dissimilar-similarity is that 'extracting concepts is, in some ways, both the easiest and the hardest of the practice areas to do. The meaning of text is notoriously hard for automated systems to understand' (Miner et al., 2012, p. 33). Case in point: the title of a recent travel blog that we (the authors of this book) read was 'Yet another "great" travel awards program'. The title, however, was purposely ironic, arguing how most of the awards programmes over the last 2 years (particularly in the USA) have made it near impossible for the average traveller to gain any advantage by joining them. How, in such an instance, would a machine be able to recognise such irony sufficient to correctly catalogue this article?

In other words, and as this example hopefully illustrates, concept extraction still has a long way to go. Fortunately, however, given the structure of natural language, many of the techniques of information extraction can be used to help computers identify the conceptual meaning of text (Allahyari et al., 2017). Also, there are lots of useful ways that computers and humans can interact to help each other. Examples of such machine–human collaborative techniques include concept mapping, supervised machine learning and the semantic web, as well as word clustering and link analysis.

- *Natural language processing:* Related to concept extraction are the numerous triumphs and challenges of natural language processing, which (as a reminder from our above discussion) is the usage of computers to engage in the complex tasks of communication and speech and textual recognition. Methods include decision trees, Bayesian probability, statistical probability, artificial neural nets and a variety of task-specific algorithms (Aggarwal & Wang, 2011; Aggarwal & Zhai, 2012; Fan & Bifet, 2013; Fayyad et al., 2002; Kanevsky et al., 2003; Keim, 2002). In terms of the air industry, examples include verbal communication between pilots, air traffic controllers, GPS systems and their planes, as well as more commonplace tasks, such as using *Google Translate* to help you communicate with an airline agent in another language.
- *Web mining:* As Miner et al. (2012) explain, 'Web mining is its own practice area due to the unique structure and enormous volume of data appearing on the web. Web documents are typically presented in a structured text format with hyperlinks between pages' (p. 34). Related methods include not only those reviewed in previous chapters but also web-crawling techniques such as Scrapy, PageRank, and Apache logs. Web mining comes in three major types: (1) web content mining, (2) web structure mining and (3) web usage mining (which is also often referred to as web analytics).

  o *Web content mining* involves combing through web pages (i.e. scraping, crawling) to discover non-obvious patterns and trends. An easy airline example, going back to our chapter on geospatial modelling (Chapter 11), would be scraping any and all web pages that have something to say about the new airport hub your company is considering, including information on local traffic, congestion, weather and so forth.

o   *Web structure mining* explores the hyperlinks between and amongst some set of web pages. Here the focus is on the underlying complex network of these documents and their links, allowing for the exploration of key ideas such as hubs, degree centrality, small worlds, cliques and so forth – for more, see Chapter 13 of our tour. In turn, one can also generate a topographical network or map of a website's pages, as in the case of your airline company's new website and app.

o   *Web usage mining* explores how people use a website, web pages, or the internet, mainly by combing through web server logs. Such analyses are obviously important, which applications such as Google Analytics use to generate a report on the relative success of one's website. For example, your airline company could use such analytics to know its website's most common landing page, which web pages users tend to click next and which pages are often used to exit, as well as how in-depth the user's exploration of your company's website was, including amount of time spent on each page and so forth.

There are also a lot of ethical issues associated with web mining, as we have seen, for example, in the way various social media companies have been caught web crawling their databases to do more than simply 'understand their customers better', including selling private user data to other companies or trying to influence or nudge users in a particular direction, be it to buy something, support a social cause or vote for a particular candidate. Such issues are further complicated ethically when web mining is used to try and identify someone's sexual orientation, political or cultural views or private peer-to-peer social media interactions, particularly in countries where civil rights are not held in high regard (Lupton, 2014; Marres, 2017; Rogers, 2013).

As Marres and Weltevrede (2013) explain, web mining also comes with other methodological problems, given that the data scraped from the internet is already structured, formatted and linked to ready-made analytics, as in the case of internet searches for 'real-time' issues such as those 'monitoring live content (which terms are current?) and those concerned with analyzing the liveliness of issues (which topics are happening?)' (Marres & Weltevrede, 2013, p. 313).

Sentiment analysis

Of the various text mining strategies available, one of the most popular – which can and often does draw upon most of the above techniques reviewed, as well as many of those discussed in other chapters, including case-based methods (Chapter 6) – is *sentiment analysis* (Gerrits, 2012; Gerrits & Marks, 2017; Liu, 2015; Marres, 2012, 2015; Marres & Moats, 2015; Rogers & Marres, 2016; Teisman et al., 2009). As Pang and Lee (2008) explain,

> An important part of our information-gathering behaviour has always been to find out what other people think. With the growing availability and popularity of opinion-rich

resources such as online review sites and personal blogs, new opportunities and challenges arise as people now can, and do, actively use information technologies to seek
out and understand the opinions of others. The sudden eruption of activity in the area of
opinion mining and sentiment analysis, which deals with the computational treatment of
opinion, sentiment, and subjectivity in text, has thus occurred at least in part as a direct
response to the surge of interest in new systems that deal directly with opinions as a
first-class object. (p. 6)

As with many of the techniques we have explored along our tour, sentiment analysis is almost a field of analysis unto itself, given how relevant it is to the study of
digital life. It is also rife with a number of important methodological challenges
and controversies, the most noteworthy of which are (a) the long-standing sociological insight that what people say – be it on social media, a blog or face to face –
and what they do are often two different things; and (b) sentiments (i.e. opinions, feelings, attitudes, day-to-day views, etc.) are largely subjective and evolving and contradictory, or, worse, untrustworthy, even when sincerely espoused
by someone.

Then there is also the challenge of which data mining methods serve best a particular research question. For an excellent overview of deciding which combination
of methods to use – from machine learning and Bayesian classifiers to decision tree
analysis and feature extraction methods – we strongly recommend 'Sentiment analysis algorithms and applications: A survey' by Medhat et al. (2014). As such, our goal
here is to only give a sense of this technique. For more, in addition to the above references, we recommend Liu's 2015 book *Sentiment Analysis: Mining Opinions, Sentiments,
and Emotions*.

One example, which is of particular interest, is *issue mapping*, which not only explores
the sentiments surrounding an issue or some collective decision-making process – be it
political, cultural or economic; local, regional or global; policy-based, public opinion or
intellectual debate – but also often links these issues and their surrounding sentiments,
as they evolve across time, to key sets of actors (i.e. groups, parties, communities, etc.)
and their complex social networks on a 'big data' scale. It also explores, in turn, the
structural stability of these sentiment networks and their corresponding dynamics
across time/space (Gerrits, 2012; Gerrits & Marks, 2017; Marres, 2015; Marres & Moats,
2015; Rogers & Marres, 2016).

And it is for this reason that these researchers turn to additional methods such as
actor network theory (Marres, 2015; Marres & Moats, 2015; Rogers & Marres, 2016),
complex network analysis (Lupton, 2014; Marres, 2017; Rogers, 2013) and even fitness landscapes (Gerrits & Marks, 2017). One example, in particular – as shown in
Figure 13.2 – is the work of Gerrits and Marks (2017) on collective decision-making
as it evolves across time/space, for which they created a freely downloadable software
app (http://un-code.org).

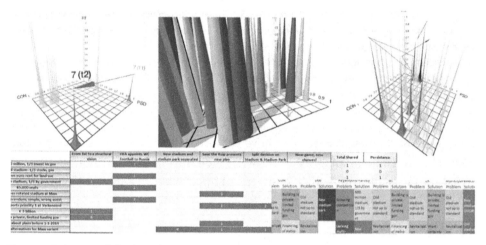

Figure 13.2 Visual display of Gerrits and Marks's Collective Decision Making app

Visualising results

In addition to visual data mining, there are also several interrelated fields devoted to the study of how best to visualise information, regardless of the form. Such fields include data science, information design, software visualisation, statistical graphics, visual sociology, design and illustration and visual complexity. See, for example, the mapping places and spaces website, which is an excellent source on visualisation in science (http://scimaps.org). And, again, as with many of the topics we have explored on our tour, data visualisation requires its own book. We mention it here, however, because data visualisation has, perhaps, never been as important as it is today, in the age of big data, given the tremendous challenges associated with helping not only academics, companies and businesses make sense of their data but also policy evaluators, civil servants, politicians and everyday people the world over!

Chapter Summary

- Given how complex most data are today, a major challenge is how to present information to various audiences, which increasingly are outside academia.
- Another key challenge is how to explore and model textual and visual data. For example, roughly 80% of all big data is unstructured textual or visual data.
- In response to both of these challenge, the intertwined fields of digital social science, data visualisation, data science, data design and visual complexity have emerged.
- One of the major challenges modelling these data is figuring how to process unstructured data. As such, this chapter spends time on this issue. Examples include document classification, web mining and information extraction methods.

- Another challenge is how to study unstructured data. One of the more popular methods, which this chapter reviews, is sentiment analysis.
- The chapter ends with a bit on visualising results.

Further Reading

Aggarwal, C. C., & Zhai, C. (2012). *Mining text data*. Springer Science & Business Media. https://doi.org/10.1007/978-1-4614-3223-4

Miner, G., Elder, J., IV, & Hill, T. (2012). *Practical text mining and statistical analysis for non-structured text data applications*. Academic Press.

Two excellent books dealing with text data mining.

14

CONCLUSION

ADVANCING A COMPLEX DIGITAL SOCIAL SCIENCE

Chapter Overview

As a conclusion to our book, we recommend that everyone involved in data mining big data (regardless of their disciplinary background) engage the complexity sciences, including the specific subfield of digital social science. There are several reasons:

- First, a *complex digital social science* (as we prefer to call it) critically explores and models the expanding big data, digital social world(s) in which we live.
- Second, it takes seriously how digital social life and its big data study are linked to issues of inequality, power relations (domination, exploitation, oppression, etc.), gender, sexual identity, ethnicity, racism, deviance, surveillance and privacy, the digital divide and so forth – something the complexity sciences and the data mining and big data fields have yet to satisfactorily do.
- Third, it also links the worlds of data mining and big data to globalisation and global studies, including global network society, which we discussed in Chapter 3.
- Fourth, it also grounds the study of digital social life in social scientific theory – which is an important counterpoint to some of the a-theoretical trends in big data and data mining; again which we discussed in Chapters 3 and 4.
- Fifth, also, in terms of method, it critically engages the ontological, epistemological, technological and sociological challenges and opportunities that we raised in our review of data mining big data in the first part of our tour.
- Sixth, it also rigorously reflects on and is engaged in the development of the methods and methodologies best suited for studying digital social life, including the fields of numerical, textual and visual data mining and computational modelling – as outlined during the second half of our tour.
- And, finally, it is compatible with both a complex systems view of the world and the methodological framework of case-based methods, as outlined in Chapters 5 and 6 of our tour.

As such, we recommend, as an ending to this chapter and also to this book, that readers continue onwards by reading the various complexity science references we have provided throughout this book, as well as the work being done in the field of digital social science, specifically Lupton's *Digital Sociology* (2014), Marres's *Digital Sociology* (2017) and Rogers's *Digital Methods* (2013). We note, however, that a complex digital social science is not to be taken at face value, as there are significant problems to be addressed, which include the ones discussed in the first part of our book, as in the case of the five Vs of big data and the validity and reliability of digital data. In addition, we offer the following summary points, which we believe help to develop a more rigorous complex digital social science for all those involved in data mining big data.

Changing the social life of data analysis

To begin, one of the most important changes that needs to take place in the world of data mining big data is a shift in the *social life of data analysis*. And, to continue our discussion of this topic in Chapter 2, section 'Changing the Social Life of Data Analysis', of our tour, this needs to happen in several important ways.

First, the social sciences need to do a better job of teaching undergraduate and graduate students the latest advances in both introductory and advanced statistical analysis – which is why our book is part of the *SAGE Quantitative Research Kit*. Examples from the *Kit* include Williams, Wiggins and Vogt's *Beginning Quantitative Research: Literature Review, Design and Data Collection*; MacInnes's *Statistical Inference and Probability*; Ariel, Bland and Sutherland's *Experimental Design*; and Eichorn's *Survey Research and Sampling*.

Two reasons why such training is important. (1) It helps students recognise better when and where such tools are useful and how other tools are also necessary. For example, McBee's *Statistical Approaches to Causal Analysis*, which is part of the *SAGE Quantitative Research Kit*, makes clear that, while students are generally taught what causality is not, they are rarely taught what causality actually is, particularly when causal relationship becomes complex. (2) It will help students see the mathematical links between statistics and computational modelling.

Second, in the social sciences we need to rethink the methodological curriculum at the undergraduate and graduate levels, including developing courses on computational modelling and data mining (from neural nets and agent-based modelling to textual analysis and geospatial modelling).

Third, we need to move past the old divisions of quantitative versus qualitative and social versus natural science to rigorously and critically develop an interdisciplinary mixed-methods framework. As an example, see Olsen's *Multiple and Mixed Methods*, which is part of the *SAGE Quantitative Research Kit*.

Fourth, we need to develop data mining software and apps that challenge user passivity – whether it is a user conducting an internet search or running a statistical package. The reason for this challenge is that technological passivity lulls users into the false sense that the information they are receiving is correct, useful, trustworthy, credible, theoretically valid, methodologically rigorous and sociologically sound. The reality is that, unless critically engaged, it is often difficult to impossible to guarantee such a reliance. Worse, it leads users to make dangerously incorrect assumptions, recommendations or predictions about the complex world(s) in which they and we live – leading to all sorts of potential disasters, such as incorrect policy recommendations or false economic, political or cultural conclusions about some given social issue or global social problem. With a more active and critical involvement in the technology they use, however, such potential pitfalls and disasters can be avoided. All of this leads to our second point.

Fifth, we need to develop user-friendly software for social scientists that stitch together the latest techniques in computational modelling in a more seamless way, so these techniques can be actually used. Unlike the conventional statistics packages available today – which bring together a wide variety of techniques – the majority of current computational modelling programs focus on individual techniques, such as machine intelligence or complex networks or agent-based modelling. We therefore need software that links them together. (One example, which we have developed, is the COMPLEX-IT app; www.art-sciencefactory.com/complexit.html).

And, finally, in the spirit of C. Wright Mills's sociological imagination, we need to put the tools and techniques of data mining in the hands of everyday people, to encourage everyone (particularly those involved in social change) to become citizen scientists so that they can more critically engage the digitally saturated world(s) in which they live. And this can be done, if we so choose, by developing software, in part, that is freely available and user-friendly. A case in point, again, is our development of COMPLEX-IT. Critics be advised: our advocation for the availability of such software does not, however, mean we think that this is the only way to develop a sociological imagination; nor do we think that the public usage of such technologies will not come with its own set of latent problems and new concerns. Even the pencil, as a form of technology, presented people with new and unforeseen problems. Still, we think it is a powerful and important step toward advancing global civil society and our global commitments to one another and the planet.

What does it take to model complex systems?

In addition to changing the social life of data analysis, we also need to develop more rigorous guidelines for data mining big data. Here, then, are some basic guiding principles that will hopefully prevent users from falling into the pitfalls mentioned throughout our tour.

A few methodological caveats

One big pitfall with modelling complex systems and processes lies in the seemingly short-sighted idea that a single modelling technique or process has the ability to capture the complexity of a system in all its glory. Most systems are deemed as complex due to the existence of multiple interacting mechanisms, some of which cannot be explained or captured using models. So one of the main principles behind modelling complexity in big data through data mining techniques is that a multipronged approach with several modelling techniques (or a toolkit of methods) needs to be employed, with the intuition that each approach will capture a different facet of complexity in the mechanisms that are hidden in the data.

Some of the methods, such as machine intelligence and predictive analytics, try to (in a crude way) mimic the thinking of the human brain using adaptive learning algorithms. This is an essential aspect of learning and understanding complex mechanisms, primarily due to the nondeterministic aspect of such processes. The human brain has the capacity to adaptively anticipate and error-correct in real-time. This is something that artificial intelligence and neural network–based methods try to emulate. A network of trained neurons with a training algorithm that adapts to new patterns is a good starting point. Genetic algorithms (GAs) are useful to look for models that cannot otherwise be thought of without prior knowledge of the mechanism involved.

However, we run the risk of overtraining as more and more data show up. A single model for the entire data set might not be able to look for multiple complex processes that are hidden in the data. This is where clustering and factoring type of methods are very useful and important. Clustering divides the data set in subgroups of similar cases c_i (Chapter 6, section 'The Formalisms of Case-Based Complexity') without throwing away any cases, and factoring looks for linear (or possibly nonlinear) combinations of variables that better explain the data (again without throwing away any variables). Once subgroups of clusters with appropriate factors are created, one can then hope to use machine intelligence–based methods to model each cluster, thereby allowing the modelling process to look for multiple complex mechanisms simultaneously.

We also mentioned a few techniques from predictive analytics (Chapter 9), as examples of techniques that can be used to make probabilistic or deterministic predictions of events in the future based on the past history. We want to caution here that prediction is a very tricky subject when it comes to modelling complexity. The assumption while predicting the future is that the current mechanisms and processes found using the models are persistent at least in the near future. Such an assumption can be completely wrong, as complexity by definition has adaptive self-emergent trends that cannot possibly be predicted using past history. Nevertheless, by using proper clustering and factoring techniques prior to building models, one can hope to relatively sharpen the uncertainty involved in such predictions due to self-emergence.

In Chapter 10, we introduced state-of-the-art longitudinal methods, where the focus is on clustering trends of case trajectories across time, and use differential equations as models to capture patterns in those trends for each cluster. Differential equations (even simple ones using polynomials) are known to capture complex trajectory evolutions such as chaotic orbits and so on. However, their use as modelling tools in conjunction with clustering and factoring tools for trajectories seems to be gaining popularity of late. GAs play an important role in providing multiple differential equation models and allow the researcher to choose one which has medium-level mathematical complexity and captures most of the interesting trends seen in the data.

Toolkits rather than tools

Multiple models are the name of the game when it comes to modelling complexity. In addition, multiple modelling techniques motivated by different sources is also a requirement. Hence, toolkits of multiple methods that give multiple modelling paradigms will allow the researcher to explore data mining from multiple angles. Furthermore, having a plethora of techniques for the same data mining objective will allow the researcher to corroborate the results obtained from one method and also allow for the possibility of one method capturing an entirely different complex mechanism or trend that is not captured by other techniques. This makes the subject a truly interdisciplinary field. The modelling techniques are present in mathematics, physics, biology, medicine and sociology. A single platform to explore the ability of all the modelling tools, however, is not a very common occurrence.

Breaking interdisciplinary barriers

A big stumbling block that arises in interdisciplinary research is jargon. Most modelling ideas in the different disciplines are easier to understand if the description is devoid of jargon. A very important step towards building interdisciplinary toolkits of methods is for researchers to break the barrier of jargon and truly understand the intricacies involved in the variety of modelling ideas that stem out of the respective disciplines.

Cross-pollination of complex modelling problems

A complex system that arises in medicine, for example, can sometimes be solved with techniques that were developed to model complex evolutionary processes (e.g. differential equations, GAs etc.). A lot of times, the modelling methods are hidden in a different discipline just waiting to be found, rather than being reinvented from scratch. A repertoire of complex modelling problems that is easily accessed by multiple researchers from different disciplines can improve such cross-pollinations.

Truly developing new methods

As new problems arise, researchers from multiple disciplines can add to the toolkit of methods by developing newer methods that stem from existing methods, or even ones that are completely new. This is easier said than done, since the tendency of researchers to get comfortable with existing methods is a very strong affliction.

As new self-emergent complex processes are created in a nondeterministic fashion, modelling techniques need to evolve at a comparable rate. The need to create and learn newer methods to match with the increase in complexity of processes is of utmost importance. Linear techniques and statistical curve-fitting methods are no longer state of the art due to their inability to capture complexity. Models that are based on adaptive learning or ones that combine deterministic and adaptive learning techniques are a good starting point.

Keeping minor trends

The outliers or minor longitudinal trends are traditionally neglected or ignored by statisticians under the guise of modelling the majority. This notion is no longer acceptable in a complex world and can be a very sensitive issue when dealing with modelling medical issues, as the minority trend could be a single patient suffering from an extremely rare disease. Clustering the trends will put the minority trends in a separate cluster, and those clusters can be delved into further. The number of members in the minority cluster is typically small, and hence that makes capturing the complexity methodologically more efficient.

Divide and conquer scales

Although the whole is much more than sum of the parts in a complex system or some set of complex data, it is not advisable to model the whole. The toolkit should have the ability to have a hierarchical modelling ability that allows for the whole or any part of the system to be modelled. The clustering and factoring allow us to group similar parts and variables of the system. However, the hierarchical ability will allow us to model all clusters together or any number of clusters together. This will allow for mechanisms that exist at a variety of scales to be captured. This is a big part of modelling complex systems, since they can behave differently at different temporal and spatial scales.

Modelling complex causality

There is a lot of debate around if and how computational modelling can identify complex causal patterns in big data, particularly dynamical-temporal data. Relative to this debate, our view is consistent with the one outlined by Moore et al. (2019) in their *Evaluation* article, 'From complex social interventions to interventions in complex social systems: Future directions and unresolved questions for intervention development and evaluation'.

First, we need to be clear that no data mining method, including those grounded in a complexity science framework, 'will ever be able to address the almost infinite number of uncertainties posed by the introduction of change into a complex system' (Moore et al., 2019, p. 36). However, adopting the type of case-based approach as suggested in the current book may help to 'drive the focus of [data mining and] evaluation (i.e. which of the multitude of uncertainties posed by interventions in complex systems do we need answers to in order to make decisions, or move the field forward)' (Moore et al., 2019, p. 36). It can also help to 'shape the interpretation of process and outcomes data' (Moore et al., 2019, p. 36).

Second, 'complex interventions in complex social systems', including exploring computational modelling strategies such as outlined in this book, 'pose almost infinite uncertainties and there will always be much going on outside of the field of vision of an individual study' (Moore et al., 2019, p. 37). 'However, a focus on discrete impacts of system change' as done with our methodological framework (the SACS Toolkit and COMPLEX-IT, 'does not necessarily betray a naïve view of how systems work, but may simply reflect a pragmatic focusing of research on core uncertainties' (Moore et al., 2019, p. 37). And this is, for us, one of the most powerful provisions that our approach provides, given its focus on understanding cases and the complex configurations of which they are comprised – *irrespective of whether* such a data mining study is cross-sectional, pre–post or longitudinal.

Third, we need to strongly emphasise that most data mining approaches are best viewed as learning environments, rather than techniques that uncover the 'true' causal patterns of things. This keeps the analyses more critical and useful. Such an approach is also useful because it requires users to be in direct and constant (i.e. iterative) interaction with their respective theories of change, be they sitting implicitly in the background of their minds or formally outlined and defined. For example, as Moore et al. (2019) state, 'Of course, it is never possible to identify all potential system level mechanisms and moderators of the effects of an evaluation' (Moore et al., 2019, p. 39). 'And', they go on to state, 'no evaluation [or data mining technique] would be powered to formally model all of these. However, combining quantitative causal modelling with qualitative process data [in the form of user-engagement] can play a vital role in building and testing theories about the processes of disrupting the functioning of complex social systems to optimise their impacts on health' (Moore et al., 2019, p. 39). In other words, the goal here is not necessarily about identifying some underlying causal model, as much as it is about exploring and learning how various scenarios might play out for a given topic and the larger complex system or set of complex data in which it is situated. And such a goal, while more humble, is nonetheless very important.

Data heterogeneity and dependence

Spatial heterogeneity and dependence create context which shapes phenomena; and hence, in accordance with modern complexity theory, understanding the interactions among agents leads to explanation of emergent behaviours that cannot be understood in isolation either at the local or global vantage points. Traditional geographic research has understood the need for both nomothetic and idiographic inquiries and has for several millennia tried to reconcile one with the other. However, with emergent behaviour being fundamentally characterised as surprising, the biggest challenge is to devise approaches that deal with this aspect of big and complex data.

Data-driven knowledge discovery requires *abductive reasoning* which leads to weaker conclusions such as '*X may* be true' starting from data describing something (instead of the deductive form '*X* must be true' or the stronger inductive form '*X* is true'). Abductive reasoning requires the ability to posit new theory, a huge knowledge base to draw from, a means for searching through the knowledge base to establish connections between data patterns and explanations, and complex problem-solving strategies such as analogy, approximation and guesses. Humans have proven to be more successful than computers in performing these complex tasks. Given the size and complexity of information space covered by the deluge of data, one way is to devise a data exploration system that generates all of the interesting patterns in a database but *only* retains the interesting ones, based on *background knowledge* and *interestingness* measures. Background knowledge can be used to look for novel patterns and interestingness can be used to filter the patterns a posteriori based on dimensions such as simplicity, utility, certainty and novelty.

Data-driven modelling carries with it the challenge of (a) a lack of theoretical foundation and a proportional increase in the number of models with the increase in volume, variety and velocity leading to an enormous number of models and (b) an enormous increase in the complexity of models themselves thereby challenging the celebrated 'Ockham's razor' idea. But this is in contrast to the idea that the nature of explanation of complex phenomena is changing, and computers are able to glean out patterns (albeit without proper explanation – which is where human intervention is needed) that are beyond human comprehension. Until this gap is filled, there is a need for caution against telling stories about data instead of reality.

In sum, both approaches – that is, nomothetic and idiographic – need to be a part of the modelling and analysis of big and complex data, thereby lending itself to various levels of models starting from one model per agent or case to multiple models to clusters of similar agents or cases, all the way up to a single model for the entire data set without compromising the complexity of data.

And with this final point, we come to the end of our tour.

Chapter Summary

- The purpose of the final chapter is to not only summarise the book but, more important, to provide a final set of recommendations, guidelines and handbook-like suggestions for how to make the most of the methods and techniques outlined in this book, as well as the complex and critical framework it sought to develop.
- It also explores how academic life needs to change, particularly in terms of curriculum and training, in order to better prepare students for the digitally saturated data worlds in which they will live and work.
- Another key point is the need for users (inside and outside academia) to develop a toolbox of techniques and interdisciplinary (even transdisciplinary) teamwork.

GLOSSARY

Autonomous differential equation: An equation that does not have time as an explicit variable – that is, $c'(t) = f(c)$. The velocities in this case are independent of time.

Case c: An abstract description of the qualitative and quantitative characteristics of an object under study.

Case profile: A qualitative meaning associated with a cluster which describes the similarity of the cases in the cluster in words.

Case trajectory $c(t)$: Refers to the continuous evolution of the variables of a given case as a function of time.

Chaotic attractor: A case trajectory where small errors in the initial state $c(0)$ get amplified into large errors thereby leading to wildly divergent and unpredictable solutions. The fact that such a chaotic trajectory is a result of a deterministic differential equation is sometimes referred to as *deterministic chaos*.

Cluster: A set of cases that are closer to its centroid (the mean of the cluster) than to other centroids.

Database: A matrix with cases as row vectors, where the elements of each case form the entries of the column.

Differential equation: A model for evolution of time trajectories which takes time t and case c as input in general and gives the instantaneous velocity $c'(t)$ as the output – that is, $c'(t) = f(c,t)$, where f is the vector field of velocities. In essence, it is a model that fills in the gap in a *discrete vector field* that arises from data.

Discrete vector field: A sampling of a vector field at regularly spaced intervals of cases. In general, one can only hope to have access to a discrete vector field from data.

Diversity: Diversity of clusters of case profiles is a measure of 'richness' (or variety) and 'evenness' (ability to occur in an equally likely fashion) of occurrence.

Dynamic clustering: Refers to modelling the evolution of case profiles as a function of time.

Equilibrium point: A case trajectory that never moves – that is, $c(t) = 0$ for all time t.

Euclidean distance: The distance between cases is the square root of the sum of squares of corresponding elements between the cases.

Non-autonomous differential equation: An equation that has time as an explicit variable – that is, $c'(t) = f(x,t)$. Here, the velocities can change with time t.

Periodic orbit: A case trajectory that returns to its initial point in time T called period and cycles through the same trajectory for every time period T – that is, $c(t + T) = c(t)$.

Sink: An equilibrium point that attracts nearby case trajectories asymptotically in time.

Source: An equilibrium point that repels nearby case trajectories asymptotically in time.

State space: A k-dimensional representation where the k-coordinates of every point represent the values of the quantitative variables that constitute the case.

Static clustering: Refers to clustering case profiles for a fixed instant of time.

Vector: A mathematical object that contains a number of elements (variables) that take on quantitative values. If all the variables of a case are quantitative, then they can form a vector which will be the mathematical *state* of the case.

Vector field: A function that takes the case as input and gives the velocity vector as the output. In two dimensions, one can visualise a vector field as arrows (denoting velocities) placed at every point (denoting cases). In general, a vector field is assumed to be 'continuous' in the sense that there are no gaps in the field.

Velocity: The velocity of a case $c'(t)$ is a vector of first derivatives (instantaneous rate of change) of all the variables of a case.

REFERENCES

Abbott, A. (2001). *Chaos of disciplines*. University of Chicago Press. https://doi.org/10.7208/chicago/9780226001050.001.0001

Aggarwal, C. C. (2014). *Data classification: Algorithms and applications*. CRC Press. https://doi.org/10.1201/b17320

Aggarwal, C. C., & Wang, H. (2011). Text mining in social networks. In C. C. Aggarwal (Ed.), *Social network data analytics* (pp. 353–378). Springer. https://doi.org/10.1007/978-1-4419-8462-3_13

Aggarwal, C. C., & Zhai, C. (2012). *Mining text data*. Springer Science & Business Media. https://doi.org/10.1007/978-1-4614-3223-4

Albert, R., & Barabasi, A. L. (2002). Statistical mechanics of complex networks. *Reviews of Modern Physics, 74*(1), 47–97. https://doi.org/10.1103/RevModPhys.74.47

Allahyari, M., Pouriyeh, S., Assefi, M., Safaei, S., Trippe, E. D., Gutierrez, J. B., & Kochut, K. (2017). *A brief survey of text mining: Classification, clustering and extraction techniques*. arXiv. https://arxiv.org/pdf/1707.02919.pdf

Alp, H., Anli, E., & Özkol, İ. (2007). Neural network algorithm for workspace analysis of a parallel mechanism. *Aircraft Engineering and Aerospace Technology, 79*(1), 35–44. https://doi.org/10.1108/00022660710720476

Andersson, C., Törnberg, A., & Törnberg, P. (2014). Societal systems: Complex or worse? *Futures, 63*, 145–157. https://doi.org/10.1016/j.futures.2014.07.003

Bagler, G. (2008). Analysis of the airport network of India as a complex weighted network. *Physica A: Statistical Mechanics and its Applications, 387*(12), 2972–2980. https://doi.org/10.1016/j.physa.2008.01.077

Bailey, K. D. (1994). *Typologies and taxonomies: An introduction to classification techniques* (Vol. *102*). Sage. https://doi.org/10.4135/9781412986397

Baker, R. S., & Yacef, K. (2009). The state of educational data mining in 2009: A review and future visions. *Journal of Educational Data Mining, 1*(1), 3–17.

Bar-Yam, Y. (1997). *Dynamics of complex systems* (Vol. *213*). Addison-Wesley.

Bar-Yam, Y. (2016). From big data to important information. *Complexity, 21*(S2), 73–98. https://doi.org/10.1002/cplx.21785

Barabasi, L. (2003). *Linked*. Penguin.

Bell, D. (1976). *The coming of post-industrial society. A venture in social forecasting* (with a new Introduction by the Author). Basic Books. https://doi.org/10.1080/00131727609336501

Berkhin, P. (2006). A survey of clustering data mining techniques. In J. Kogan, C. Nicholas, & M. Teboulle (Eds.), *Grouping multidimensional data* (pp. 25–71). Springer. https://doi.org/10.1007/3-540-28349-8_2

Bernardo, J. M., & Smith, A. F. (2001). *Bayesian theory*. Wiley.

Blum, C., & Li, X. (2008). Swarm intelligence in optimisation. In C. Blum & D. Merkle (Eds.), *Swarm intelligence* (pp. 43–85). Springer. https://doi.org/10.1007/978-3-540-74089-6_2

Brown, M. L., & Kros, J. F. (2003). Data mining and the impact of missing data. *Industrial Management & Data Systems*, *103*(8), 611–621. https://doi.org/10.1108/02635570310497657

Burke, E. K., & Kendall, G. (2005). *Search methodologies: Introductory tutorials in optimisation and decision support techniques*. Springer. https://doi.org/10.1007/0-387-28356-0

Burke, E. K., & Kendall, G. (2014). *Search methodologies: Introductory tutorials in optimisation and decision support techniques* (2nd ed.). Springer. https://doi.org/10.1007/978-1-4614-6940-7

Burrows, R., & Savage, M. (2014). After the crisis? Big data and the methodological challenges of empirical sociology. *Big Data & Society*, *1*(1). https://doi.org/10.1177/2053951714540280

Byrne, D. (1998). *Complexity theory and the social sciences*. Routledge.

Byrne, D. (2012). UK sociology and quantitative methods: Are we as weak as they think? Or are they barking up the wrong tree? *Sociology*, *46*(1), 13–24. https://doi.org/10.1177/0038038511419178

Byrne, D., & Callaghan, G. (2013). *Complexity theory and the social sciences: The state of the art*. Routledge.

Byrne, D., & Ragin, C. C. (Eds.). (2013). *The SAGE handbook of case-based methods*. Sage.

Cannarella, J., & Spechler, J. A. (2014). *Epidemiological modeling of online social network dynamics*. arXiv. https://arxiv.org/abs/1401.4208

Capra, F. (1996). *The web of life: A new scientific understanding of living systems*. Anchor.

Capra, F., & Luisi, P. L. (2014). *The systems view of life: A unifying vision*. Cambridge University Press. https://doi.org/10.1017/CBO9780511895555

Carrington, P. J., Scott, J., & Wasserman, S. (2005). *Models and methods in social network analysis* (Vol. *28*). Cambridge University Press. https://doi.org/10.1017/CBO9780511811395

Castellani, B. (2014). Focus: Complexity and the failure of quantitative social science. *Discover Society.* https://discoversociety.org/2014/11/04/focus-complexity-and-the-failure-of-quantitative-social-science/

Castellani, B., Barbrook-Johnson, P., & Schimpf, C. (2019). Case-based methods and agent-based modelling: Bridging the divide to leverage their combined strengths. *International Journal of Social Research Methodology, 22*(4), 403–416. https://doi.org/10.1080/13645579.2018.1563972

Castellani, B., & Hafferty, F. (2009). *Sociology and complexity science: A new field of inquiry.* Springer. https://doi.org/10.1007/978-3-540-88462-0

Castellani, B., & Rajaram, R. (2012). Case-based modeling and the SACS toolkit: A mathematical outline. *Computational and Mathematical Organisational Theory, 18*(2), 153–174. https://doi.org/10.1007/s10588-012-9114-1

Castellani, B., & Rajaram, R. (2016). Past the power law: Complex systems and the limiting law of restricted diversity. *Complexity, 21*(S2), 99–112. https://doi.org/10.1002/cplx.21786

Castellani, B., Rajaram, R., Buckwalter, J. G., Ball, M., & Hafferty, F. W. (2015). *Place and health as complex systems.* Springer Briefs on Public Health, Germany. https://doi.org/10.1007/978-3-319-09734-3_2

Castellani, B., Rajaram, R., Gunn, J., & Griffiths, F. (2016). Cases, clusters, densities: Modeling the nonlinear dynamics of complex health trajectories. *Complexity, 21*(S1), 160–180. https://doi.org/10.1002/cplx.21728

Castells, M. (2004). Informationalism, networks, and the network society: A theoretical blueprint. In M. Castells (Ed.), *The network society: A cross-cultural perspective* (pp. 3–45). Edward Elgar. https://doi.org/10.4337/9781845421663

Castells, M. (2011). *The rise of the network society: The information age: Economy, society, and culture.* Wiley–Blackwell.

Castells, M., & Kumar, M. (2014). A conversation with Manuel Castells. *Berkeley Planning Journal, 27*(1). https://doi.org/10.5070/BP327124502

Choi, J. H., Barnett, G. A., & Chon, B.-S. (2006). Comparing world city networks: A network analysis of internet backbone and air transport intercity linkages. *Global Networks, 6*(1), 81–99. https://doi.org/10.1111/j.1471-0374.2006.00134.x

Cilliers, P. (1998). *Complexity and postmodernism: Understanding complex systems.* Routledge.

Cliff, A., & Ord, J. (1981). *Spatial processes: Models and applications.* Pion.

Cukier, K., & Mayer-Schoenberger, V. (2013). The rise of big data: How it's changing the way we think about the world. *Foreign Affairs, 92*(3), 28–40.

De Nooy, W., Mrvar, A., & Batagelj, V. (2018). *Exploratory social network analysis with Pajek.* Cambridge University Press.

Derudder, B., Devriendt, L., & Witlox, F. (2007). Flying where you don't want to go: An empirical analysis of hubs in the global airline network. *Tijdschrift voor economische en sociale geografie, 98*(3), 307–324. https://doi.org/10.1111/j.1467-9663.2007.00399.x

De Smith, M. J., Goodchild, M. F., & Longley, P. (2007). *Geospatial analysis: A comprehensive guide to principles, techniques and software tools* (2nd ed.). Troubador.

De Smith, M. J., Goodchild, M. F., & Longley, P. (2018). *Geospatial analysis: A comprehensive guide to principles, techniques and software tools* (6th ed.). Troubador.

De Smith, M. J., Goodchild, M. F., & Longley, P. (2020). *Geospatial analysis: A comprehensive guide to principles, techniques and software tools* (6th ed., Online version). Troubador. www.spatialanalysisonline.com/HTML/index.html

Dorigo, M., & Caro, G. D. (1999). The ant colony optimisation meta-heuristic. In D. Corne, M. Dorigo, & F. Glover (Eds.), *New ideas in optimisation* (pp. 11–32). McGraw-Hill. https://doi.org/10.1109/CEC.1999.782657

Fan, W., & Bifet, A. (2013). Mining big data: Current status, and forecast to the future. *ACM SIGKDD Explorations Newsletter, 14*(2), 1–5. https://doi.org/10.1145/2481244.2481246

Fayyad, U. M., Wierse, A., & Grinstein, G. G. (2002). *Information visualisation in data mining and knowledge discovery.* Morgan Kaufmann.

Feldman, R., & Sanger, J. (2007). *The text mining handbook: Advanced approaches in analyzing unstructured data.* Cambridge University Press. https://doi.org/10.1017/CBO9780511546914

Fitzmaurice, G., Davidian, M., Verbeke, G., & Molenberghs, G. (2008). *Longitudinal data analysis.* CRC Press. https://doi.org/10.1201/9781420011579

Fitzmaurice, G. M., Laird, N. M., & Ware, J. H. (2012). *Applied longitudinal analysis* (Vol. *998*). Wiley. https://doi.org/10.1002/9781119513469

Fogel, D. B. (2006). *Evolutionary computation: Toward a new philosophy of machine intelligence* (Vol. *1*). Wiley.

Fotheringham, S., & Rogerson, P. (2014). *Spatial analysis and GIS.* CRC Press. https://doi.org/10.1201/9781482272468

Gelman, A., & Shalizi, C. R. (2013). Philosophy and the practice of Bayesian statistics. *British Journal of Mathematical and Statistical Psychology, 66*(1), 8–38. https://doi.org/10.1111/j.2044-8317.2011.02037.x

Gerrits, L. (2012). *Punching clouds: An introduction to the complexity of public decision-making.* Emergent.

Gerrits, L., & Marks, P. (2017). *Understanding collective decision making: A fitness landscape model approach.* Edward Elgar. https://doi.org/10.4337/9781783473151

Giddens, A. (2001). Dimensions of globalisation. In S. Seidman & J. C. Alexander (Eds.), *The new social theory reader* (pp. 245–246). Psychology Press.

Girvan, M., & Newman, M. E. (2002). Community structure in social and biological networks. *Proceedings of the National Academy of Sciences, 99*(12), 7821–7826. https://doi.org/10.1073/pnas.122653799

Goldberg, D. E. (2002). *Design of innovation: Lessons from and for competent genetic algorithms.* Kluwer.

Gulati, R. (1995). Social structure and alliance formation patterns: A longitudinal analysis. *Administrative Science Quarterly, 40*(4), 619–652. https://doi.org/10.2307/2393756

Hammond, D. (2010). *The science of synthesis: Exploring the social implications of general systems theory.* University Press of Colorado.

Hand, D. J., & Henley, W. E. (1997). Statistical classification methods in consumer credit scoring: A review. *Journal of the Royal Statistical Society: Series A (Statistics in Society), 160*(3), 523–541. https://doi.org/10.1111/j.1467-985X.1997.00078.x

Hanneman, R. A., & Riddle, M. (2005). *Introduction to social network methods.* University of California.

Harvey, D. L., & Reed, M. (1996). Social science as the study of complex systems. In L. D. Kiel & E. Elliott (Eds.), *Chaos theory in the social sciences* (pp. 295–324). University of Michigan Press.

Haynes, P. (2017). *Social synthesis: Finding dynamic patterns in complex social systems.* Routledge. https://doi.org/10.4324/9781315458533

Held, D., & McGrew, A. (2007). *Globalisation/anti-globalisation: Beyond the great divide.* Polity Press.

Held, D., McGrew, A., Goldblatt, D., & Perraton, J. (2000). Rethinking globalisation. In D. Held & A. McGrew (Eds.), *The global transformations reader: An introduction to the globalisation debate* (pp. 67–74). Polity Press.

Hirsch, M. W., Smale, S., & Devaney, R. L. (2012). *Differential equations, dynamical systems, and an introduction to chaos.* Academic Press. https://doi.org/10.1016/B978-0-12-382010-5.00015-4

Holland, J. H. (1975). *Adaptation in natural and artificial systems.* University of Michigan Press.

Huang, G., Huang, G.-B., Song, S., & You, K. (2015). Trends in extreme learning machines: A review. *Neural Networks, 61*, 32–48. https://doi.org/10.1016/j.neunet.2014.10.001

Huisman, M., & Snijders, T. A. B. (2003). Statistical analysis of longitudinal network data with changing composition. *Sociological Methods and Research, 32*(2), 253–287. https://doi.org/10.1177/0049124103256096

Jackson, M. O. (2008). *Social and economic networks*. Princeton University Press. https://doi.org/10.1515/9781400833993

Jain, A. K. (2010). Data clustering: 50 years beyond k-means. *Pattern Recognition Letters, 31*(8), 651–666. https://doi.org/10.1016/j.patrec.2009.09.011

Jang, J.-S. R., Sun, C.-T., & Mizutani, E. (1997). *Neuro-fuzzy and soft computing: A computational approach to learning and machine intelligence*. Prentice Hall. https://doi.org/10.1109/TAC.1997.633847

Jung, T., & Wickrama, K. (2008). An introduction to latent class growth analysis and growth mixture modeling. *Social and Personality Psychology Compass, 2*(1), 302–317. https://doi.org/10.1111/j.1751-9004.2007.00054.x

Kanevsky, D., Maes, S. H., & Sorensen, J. S. (2003). *Conversational data mining*. US Patent 6,665,644.

Keim, D. A. (2002). Information visualisation and visual data mining. *IEEE transactions on Visualisation and Computer Graphics, 8*(1), 1–8. https://doi.org/10.1109/2945.981847

Keller, R. M. (2016). Ontologies for aviation data management. In *Digital Avionics Systems Conference (DASC), 2016 IEEE/AIAA 35th* (pp. 1–9). IEEE. https://doi.org/10.1109/DASC.2016.7777971

Kennedy, J. (2006). Swarm intelligence. In A. Y. Zomaya (Ed.), *Handbook of nature-inspired and innovative computing* (pp. 187–219). Springer. https://doi.org/10.1007/0-387-27705-6_6

Kennedy, J., & Eberhart, R. C. (1999). The particle swarm: Social adaption in information processing systems. In D. Corne, M. Dorigo, & F. Glover (Eds.), *New ideas in optimisation* (pp. 370–387). McGraw-Hill.

Kitchin, R. (2014). *The data revolution: Big data, open data, data infrastructures and their consequences*. Sage. https://doi.org/10.4135/9781473909472

Kitchin, R., & McArdle, G. (2016). What makes big data, big data? Exploring the ontological characteristics of 26 datasets. *Big Data & Society, 3*(1). https://doi.org/10.1177/2053951716631130

Knoke, D., & Yang, S. (2008). *Social network analysis* (Vol. *154*). Sage. https://doi.org/10.4135/9781412985864

Kohonen, T. (1990). The self-organising map. *Proceedings of the IEEE, 78*(9), 1464–1480. https://doi.org/10.1109/5.58325

Kohonen, T. (2013). Essentials of the self organising map. *Neural Networks, 37*, 52–65. https://doi.org/10.1016/j.neunet.2012.09.018

Konys, A. (2016). Ontology-based approaches to big data analytics. In *International multi-conference on advanced computer systems* (pp. 355–365). Springer. https://doi.org/10.1007/978-3-319-48429-7_32

Kosko, B. (1992). *Neural networks and fuzzy systems: A dynamical systems approach to machine intelligence/book and disk* (Vol. 1). Prentice Hall.

Kotsiantis, S. B., Zaharakis, I., & Pintelas, P. (2007). Supervised machine learning: A review of classification techniques. *Frontiers in Artificial Intelligence and Applications, 160*, 3–24. https://doi.org/10.1007/s10462-007-9052-3

Kuang, C. (2017, November 26). Can A.I. be taught to explain itself? *The New York Times*, p. 46. www.nytimes.com/2017/11/21/magazine/can-ai-be-taught-to-explain-itself.html

Kuo, R. J., Ho, L. M., & Hu, C. M. (2002). Cluster analysis in industrial market segmentation through artificial neural network. *Computers and Industrial Engineering, 42*(2–4), 391–399. https://doi.org/10.1016/S0360-8352(02)00048-7

Lee, P. M. (2012). *Bayesian statistics: An introduction.* Wiley.

Liu, B. (2015). *Sentiment analysis: Mining opinions, sentiments, and emotions.* Cambridge University Press. https://doi.org/10.1017/CBO9781139084789

Lu, D., & Weng, Q. (2007). A survey of image classification methods and techniques for improving classification performance. *International Journal of Remote Sensing, 28*(5), 823–870. https://doi.org/10.1080/01431160600746456

Lupton, D. (2014). *Digital sociology.* Routledge. https://doi.org/10.4324/9781315776880

Mackenzie, A. (2017). *Machine learners: Archaeology of a data practice.* MIT Press. https://doi.org/10.7551/mitpress/10302.001.0001

Maguire, D. J., Batty, M., & Goodchild, M. F. (2005). *GIS, spatial analysis, and modeling.* Esri Press.

Mahnke, M., & Uprichard, E. (2014). Algorithming the algorithm. In R. König & M. Rasch (Eds.), *Society of the query reader: Reflections on Web search* (pp. 256–271). Institute of Network Cultures.

Maire, S., & Spafford, C. (2017, June 16). The data science revolution that's transforming aviation. *Forbes.* www.forbes.com/sites/oliverwyman/2017/06/16/the-data-science-revolution-transforming-aviation/#16ac32237f6c

Marres, N. (2012). On some uses and abuses of topology in the social analysis of technology (or the problem with smart meters). *Theory, Culture & Society, 29*(4–5), 288–310. https://doi.org/10.1177/0263276412454460

Marres, N. (2015). Why map issues? On controversy analysis as a digital method. *Science, Technology, & Human Values, 40*(5), 655–686. https://doi.org/10.1177/0162243915574602

Marres, N. (2017). *Digital sociology: The reinvention of social research.* Wiley.

Marres, N., & Moats, D. (2015). Mapping controversies with social media: The case for symmetry. *Social Media + Society, 1*(2). https://doi.org/10.1177/2056305115604176

Marres, N., & Weltevrede, E. (2013). Scraping the social? Issues in live social research. *Journal of Cultural Economy*, 6(3), 313–335. https://doi.org/10.1080/1753 0350.2013.772070

McCulloch, W. S., & Pitts, W. (1943). A logical calculus of the ideas immanent in nervous activity. *Bulletin of Mathematical Biophysics*, 5, 115–137. https://doi.org/10.1007/BF02478259

Medhat, W., Hassan, A., & Korashy, H. (2014). Sentiment analysis algorithms and applications: A survey. *Ain Shams Engineering Journal*, 5(4), 1093–1113. https://doi.org/10.1016/j.asej.2014.04.011

Merkle, D., & Middendorf, M. (2014). Swarm intelligence. In E. K. Burke & G. Kendall (Eds.), *Search methodologies: Introductory tutorials in optimisation and decision support techniques* (2nd ed., pp. 213–242). Springer. https://doi.org/10.1007/978-1-4614-6940-7_8

Milgram, S. (1967). The small world problem. *Psychology Today*, 1, 61–67. https://doi.org/10.1037/e400002009-005

Miller, H. J., & Goodchild, M. F. (2015). Data-driven geography. *GeoJournal*, 80(4), 449–461. https://doi.org/10.1007/s10708-014-9602-6

Miller, H. J., & Han, J. (2001). *Geographic data mining and knowledge discovery*. Taylor & Francis. https://doi.org/10.4324/9780203468029

Miner, G., Elder, J., IV, & Hill, T. (2012). *Practical text mining and statistical analysis for non-structured text data applications*. Academic Press.

Mitchell, M. (2009). *Complexity: A guided tour*. Oxford University Press.

Moore, G. F., Evans, R. E., Hawkins, J., Littlecott, H., Melendez-Torres, G., Bonell, C., & Murphy, S. (2019). From complex social interventions to interventions in complex social systems: Future directions and unresolved questions for intervention development and evaluation. *Evaluation*, 25(1), 23–45. https://doi.org/10.1177/1356389018803219

Morin, E. (2007). Restricted complexity, general complexity. In C. Gershenson, D. Aerts, & B. Edmonds (Eds.), *Worldviews, science and us: Philosophy and complexity* (pp. 5–29). World Scientific. https://doi.org/10.1142/9789812707420_0002

Muthén, B., & Muthén, L. K. (2000). Integrating person-centered and variable-centered analyses: Growth mixture modeling with latent trajectory classes. *Alcoholism: Clinical and Experimental Research*, 24(6), 882–891. https://doi.org/10.1111/j.1530-0277.2000.tb02070.x

Newman, M. E. (2002). Assortative mixing in networks. *Physical Review Letters*, 89(20), Article 208701. https://doi.org/10.1103/PhysRevLett.89.208701

Newman, M. E. (2003). The structure and function of complex networks. *SIAM Review*, 45(2), 167–256. https://doi.org/10.1137/S003614450342480

Newman, M. E. (2004). Fast algorithm for detecting community structure in networks. *Physical Review E, 69*(6), Article 066133. https://doi.org/10.1103/PhysRevE.69.066133

Newman, M. E. (2006). Modularity and community structure in networks. *Proceedings of the National Academy of Sciences, 103*(23), 8577–8582. https://doi.org/10.1073/pnas.0601602103

Newman, M. E. (2010). *Networks: An introduction.* Oxford University Press.

Nylund, K. L., Asparouhov, T., & Muthén, B. O. (2007). Deciding on the number of classes in latent class analysis and growth mixture modeling: A Monte Carlo simulation study. *Structural Equation Modeling, 14*(4), 535–569. https://doi.org/10.1080/10705510701575396

Olson, D. L., & Wu, D. (2016). *Predictive data mining models.* Springer. https://doi.org/10.1007/978-981-10-2543-3

Pang, B., & Lee, L. (2008). Opinion mining and sentiment analysis. *Foundations and Trends in Information Retrieval, 2*(1–2), 1–135. https://doi.org/10.1561/9781601981516

Phyu, T. N. (2009). Survey of classification techniques in data mining. In S. I. Ao, O. Castillo, C. Douglas, D. D. Feng, & J.-A. Lee (Eds.), Proceedings of the International MultiConference of Engineers and Computer Scientists (Vol. *1*, pp. 18–20). Newswood.

Quinlan, J. R. (1986). Induction of decision trees. *Machine Learning, 1*(1), 81–106. https://doi.org/10.1007/BF00116251

Quinlan, J. R. (1987). Simplifying decision trees. *International Journal of Man-Machine Studies, 27*(3), 221–234. https://doi.org/10.1016/S0020-7373(87)80053-6

Raghavan, P. (2014). It's time to scale the science in the social sciences. *Big Data & Society, 1*(1). https://doi.org/10.1177/2053951714532240https://doi.org/10.1177/2053951714532240

Ragin, C. (2008). *Redesigning social inquiry: Fuzzy sets and beyond.* University of Chicago Press. https://doi.org/10.7208/chicago/9780226702797.001.0001

Rajaram, R., & Castellani, B. (2012). Modeling complex systems macroscopically: Case/agent-based modeling, synergetics and the continuity equation. *Complexity, 18*(2), 8–17. https://doi.org/10.1002/cplx.21412

Rajaram, R., & Castellani, B. (2014). The utility of non-equilibrium statistical mechanics, specifically transport theory, for modeling cohort data. *Complexity, 20*(4), 45–57. https://doi.org/10.1002/cplx.21512

Ram, N., & Grimm, K. J. (2009). Growth mixture modeling: A method for identifying differences in longitudinal change among unobserved groups.

International Journal of Behavioral Development, 33(6), 565–576. https://doi. org/10.1177/0165025409343765

Rihoux, B., & Ragin, C. (2009). *Configurational comparative methods: Qualitative comparative analysis (QCA) and related techniques: Vol. 51. Applied social research methods series.* Sage. https://doi.org/10.4135/9781452226569

Ritzer, G., & Dean, P. (2015). *Globalisation: A basic text.* Wiley.

Rogers, R. (2013). *Digital methods.* MIT Press. https://doi.org/10.7551/ mitpress/8718.001.0001

Rogers, R., & Marres, N. (2016). Landscaping climate change: A mapping technique for understanding science and technology debates on the World Wide Web. *Public Understanding of Science, 9*(2), 141–163. https://doi.org/10.1088/0963-6625/9/2/304

Rumelhart, D. E., Hinton, G. E., & Williams, R. J. (2017). *Learning internal representations by error propagation.* In D. E. Rumelhart & J. L. McClelland (Eds.), *Parallel distributed processing: Explorations in the microstructures of cognition: Vol. 1. Foundations* (pp. 318–362). MIT Press.

Sastry, K., Goldberg, D. E., & Kendall, G. (2014). Genetic algorithms. In E. K. Burke & G. Kendall (Eds.), *Search methodologies: Introductory tutorials in optimisation and decision support techniques* (2nd ed., pp. 93–118). Springer. https://doi. org/10.1007/978-1-4614-6940-7_4

Savage, M., & Burrows, R. (2007). The coming crisis of empirical sociology. *Sociology, 41*(5), 885–899. https://doi.org/10.1177/0038038507080443

Scott, J. (2017). *Social network analysis.* Sage.

Scott, J., & Carrington, P. J. (2011). *The SAGE handbook of social network analysis.* Sage. https://doi.org/10.4135/9781529716597

Sharma, V., Rai, S., & Dev, A. (2012). A comprehensive study of artificial neural networks. *International Journal of Advanced Research in Computer Science and Software Engineering, 2*(10), 278–284.

Snijders, T. A. B. (2001). The statistical evaluation of social network dynamics. *Sociological Methodology, 31*(1), 361–395. https://doi.org/10.1111/0081-1750.00099

Song, M. G., & Yeo, G. T. (2017). Analysis of the air transport network characteristics of major airports. *Asian Journal of Shipping and Logistics, 33*(3), 117–125. https:// doi.org/10.1016/j.ajsl.2017.09.002

Soukup, T., & Davidson, I. (2002). *Visual data mining: Techniques and tools for data visualisation and mining.* Wiley.

Srivastava, A. N., & Sahami, M. (2009). *Text mining: Classification, clustering, and applications.* Chapman & Hall/CRC Press. https://doi. org/10.1201/9781420059458

Taylor, P. J., & Derudder, B. (2015). *World city network: A global urban analysis.* Routledge. https://doi.org/10.4324/9781315730950

Teisman, G., Gerrits, L., & van Buuren, A. (2009). An introduction to understanding and managing complex process systems. In *Managing complex governance systems dynamics, self-organisation and coevolution in public investments* (pp. 1–16). Routledge.

Tirenni, G., Kaiser, C., & Herrmann, A. (2007). Applying decision trees for value-based customer relations management: Predicting airline customers' future values. *Journal of Database Marketing & Customer Strategy Management, 14*(2), 130–142. https://doi.org/10.1057/palgrave.dbm.3250044

Uprichard, E. (2009). Introducing cluster analysis: What it can teach us about the case. In D. Byrne & C. Ragin (Eds.), *The SAGE handbook of case based methods* (pp. 132–147). Sage. https://doi.org/10.4135/9781446249413.n8

Uprichard, E. (2013). Focus: Big data, little questions? *Discover Society.* https://discoversociety.org/2013/10/01/focus-big-data-little-questions/

Urry, J. (2005). The complexity turn. *Theory, Culture & Society, 22*(5), 1–14. https://doi.org/10.1177/0263276405057188

Van Dijk, J. (2012). *The network society.* Sage.

Veltri, G. A. (2017). Big data is not only about data: The two cultures of modelling. *Big Data & Society, 4*(1). https://doi.org/10.1177/2053951717703997

Wagenmakers, E. J. (2007). A practical solution to the pervasive problems of p-values. *Psychonomic Bulletin and Review, 14*(5), 779–804. https://doi.org/10.3758/BF03194105

Wagenmakers, E. J., Lodewyckx, T., Kuriyal, H., & Grasman, R. (2010). Bayesian hypothesis testing for psychologists: A tutorial on the Savage-Dickey method. *Cognitive Psychology, 60*(3), 158–189. https://doi.org/10.1016/j.cogpsych.2009.12.001

Walby, S. (2009). *Globalisation and inequalities: Complexity and contested modernities.* Sage.

Waller, M. A., & Fawcett, S. E. (2013). Data science, predictive analytics, and big data: A revolution that will transform supply chain design and management. *Journal of Business Logistics, 34*(2), 77–84. https://doi.org/10.1111/jbl.12010

Wallerstein, I. (2000). Globalisation or the age of transition? A long-term view of the trajectory of the world-system. *International Sociology, 15*(2), 249–265. https://doi.org/10.1177/0268580900015002007

Wallerstein, I., Juma, C., Keller, E. F., Kocka, J., Lecourt, D., Mudkimbe, V. Y., Miushakoji, K., Prigogine, I., Taylor, P. J., & Trouillot, M.-R. (1996). *Open the social sciences: Report of the Gulbenkian Commission on the restructuring of the social sciences.* Stanford University Press. https://doi.org/10.5860/crl.58.4.392

Wang, J. T., Zaki, M. J., Toivonen, H. T., & Shasha, D. (2005). Introduction to data mining in bioinformatics. In *Data mining in bioinformatics* (pp. 3–8). Springer. https://doi.org/10.1007/1-84628-059-1_1

Wasserman, S., & Faust, K. (1994). *Social network analysis: Methods and applications* (Vol. 8). Cambridge University Press. https://doi.org/10.1017/CBO9780511815478

Watts, D. J. (2004). The "new" science of networks. *Annual Review of Sociology, 30*, 243–270. https://doi.org/10.1146/annurev.soc.30.020404.104342

Watts, D. J., & Strogatz, S. (1998). Collective dynamics of small world networks. *Nature, 393*, 440–442. https://doi.org/10.1038/30918

Weaver, W. (1948). Science and complexity. *American Scientist, 36*, 536–544.

Wei, W. W. (2013). Time series analysis. In T. D. Little (Ed.), *The Oxford handbook of quantitative methods in psychology: Vol. 2. Statistical analysis* (pp. 458–485). Oxford University Press.

Williams, M., & Dyer, W. (2017). Complex realism in social research. *Methodological Innovations, 10*(2). https://doi.org/10.1177/2059799116683564

Wolfram, S. (2002). *A new kind of science* (Vol. 5). Wolfram Media.

Yao, X., & Liu, Y. (2014). Machine learning. In E. K. Burke & G. Kendall (Eds.), *Search methodologies: Introductory tutorials in optimisation and decision support techniques* (2nd ed., pp. 477–518). Springer. https://doi.org/10.1007/978-1-4614-6940-7_17

Yuan, Y., & Shaw, M. J. (1995). Induction of fuzzy decision trees. *Fuzzy sets and systems, 69*(2), 125–139. https://doi.org/10.1016/0165-0114(94)00229-Z

INDEX

time, 69–71, 74, *74*
  see also longitudinal analysis
time domain plots, 71–2
Tobler's law, 136, 137
tokenisation, 175
toolkits of methods, 188–91
  see also SACS Toolkit
topographical neural nets, 83,
  84, 97–9, *97*, *99*
transitivity of networks, 154
transportation problem, 141
travelling salesperson problem
  (TSP), 82, 93, 100, 102, 140, 141
triangulated irregular networks, 139
triples, 60–1, *61*
Turing, Alan, 174

U-matrix, 98–9
uniformly random growth network model,
  164–5, 166–7
unsupervised learning, self-organising maps,
  97–9, *97*, *99*
unsupervised learning methods, 37, 94
Uprichard, Emma, 4, 25–6
Urry, John, 48

validity, 38–40
Van Dijk, Jan, 28
vector fields, 71–6, *73*, *74*, 139
vector representation of spatial data, 139
vectors, defined, 64–5, *65*
velocity of big data, 29
velocity vectors, 72–5, *73*
visual data mining *see* textual and
  visual data mining
visualisation, 180
volunteered geographic information (VGI), 138
Von-Neumann neighbourhoods, 139

Wagenmakers, Eric-Jan, 108, 110, 111, 112
Wallerstein, Immanuel, 20, 47
Watts, Duncan, 21, 156–7
wavelet compression, 175
wavelet transformation, 175
wayfinding, 133–4
Weaver, Warren, 15–16, 18–19, 46, 49
web mining, 174, 177–8
Welsh Index of Multiple Deprivation, 133, *133*
Weltevrede, Esther, 178

Zika virus, *132*

CPSIA information can be obtained
at www.ICGtesting.com
Printed in the USA
JSHW042206230522
26107JS00003B/76